The Union Preserved

A Joint Publication by

Fordham University Press

and the

New York State

Archives Partnership Trust

New York

1999

The Union Preserved

A Guide to Civil War Records in the New York State Archives

Edited by Harold Holzer   Compiled by Daniel Lorello

Introduction by Harold Holzer & Hans L. Trefousse

Foreword by James M. McPherson

Copyright © 1999 by
The New York State Archives Partnership Trust

LC 98-47258

ISBN 0-8232-1900-3

Library of Congress Cataloging-in-Publication Data
The Union preserved : a guide to Civil War records
in the New York State Archives / edited by Harold
Holzer : compiled by Daniel Lorello : introduction by
Harold Holzer and Hans L. Trefousse : foreword by
James M. McPherson.
p. cm.
Includes bibliographical references (p.   ) and index.
ISBN 0-8232-1900-3 (alk. paper)
1. United States—History—Civil War, 1861–1865—
Sources—Bibliography—Catalogs. 2. New York
(State)—History—Civil War, 1861–1865—Sources—
Bibliography—Catalogs. 3. New York State Archives
and Records Administration—Catalogs. I. Holzer,
Harold.
CD3047.U55 1999
016.9737—dc21   98-47258
                 CIP

Printed in the United States of America

Contents

Letter From the Governor

It is a pleasure to offer greetings and to have this opportunity to express my shared pride with regard to the significant and unique place that New York State holds in United States history.

Among the ways to fully appreciate New York's role in shaping our Nation is to examine the written material, artifacts, and vast reserve of information from the Civil War period. One of the most important and extensive collections of Civil War records in the Nation is under the care and protection of the New York State Archives in Albany. These records are now described and detailed in the pages of *The Union Preserved*, a publication that also gives background and references to Civil War materials held by the New York State Museum, State Library, and the Division of Military and Naval Affairs. This book is a valuable learning tool and source of enrichment for all students of Civil War history, and a permanent record for all posterity.

I commend the Archives Partnership Trust for its work to preserve our State's heritage with the publication of this text highlighting New York's pivotal role during this important period in American history.

September 1998

George E. Pataki
Governor

Acknowledgments

This publication is the product of a unique collaboration between the public and private sectors to make accessible one of New York's most valuable treasures, the Civil War collections of the New York State Archives. The New York State Archives is a public cultural institution under the stewardship of the Board of Regents in the New York State Education Department. Although it is the last state archives to be created in the nation and has been open to the public for only twenty years, ours is now a leading state archives, with hundreds of thousands of records documenting New York's pivotal role in the Civil War. The records in this collection were acquired since 1978 through the cooperation of many state government agencies that transferred records to the Archives' custody. The records catalogued in *The Union Preserved* reflects more than fifteen years of work by State Archives staff to identify, arrange, and describe this tremendous store of documents, which were largely disorganized and lacked a comprehensive inventory.

The Union Preserved is the first publication project undertaken by the Archives Partnership Trust, a 501(c)3, public benefit corporation created to sustain the excellence of the New York State Archives and to make its collections more widely accessible to the public. The project is also the first nationally focused outreach by the Trust board, a group of leading citizens appointed by New York's governor, legislature, and Board of Regents. The Trust obtained private foundation support from the H. W. Wilson Foundation for the preparation and publication of the book and from the Henry Luce Foundation for the scholarly interpretation of New York's role in the Civil War and the significance of New York's holdings. The Trust is most grateful for the leadership support of the H. W. Wilson and Henry Luce Foundations. It also extends its thanks to Board of Regents Chancellor Carl T. Hayden, whose introduction to the H. W. Wilson Foundation made their grant possible.

The road from conception to the publication of this book is marked by the contributions of numerous individuals and institutions. Without the lead efforts and enthusiastic support of Harold Holzer, renowned Civil

War author and board member of the Archives Partnership Trust, the publication in its present form would not be possible. Mr. Holzer recognized the State Archives' exceptional collections management work, as well as the importance of the Archives' Civil War holdings, and became an early champion for the publication of this work, as well as its editor and a contributor. We are also deeply indebted to Mr. Holzer for bringing New York's Civil War holdings and collections management work to the attention of James M. McPherson and Hans L. Trefousse, whose contributions to this publication enhance the presentation of the records catalogue and supplemental materials. We deeply appreciate this endorsement by Professors McPherson and Trefousse.

The expert collections management work by the State Archives staff produced detailed records descriptions, administrative histories, and comprehensive appendices that laid the groundwork for this publication. A team of talented archivists, led by Associate Archivist Daniel Lorello, performed this exceptional archival work, exemplary of the State Education Department's commitment to make New York's cultural resources available and accessible. This team, supported by Kelly Gicobbi and Ellen Szmyr, included Dr. James D. Folts, William A. Evans, and Christine Karpiak. Mr. Lorello is an extremely talented archivist, with a deep personal passion for both archival work and the Civil War. Without his leadership, the State Archives would not have completed the collections management work on its Civil War holdings. Additionally, for this publication Mr. Lorello made a tremendous personal commitment of hundreds of hours over the last two years, refining the Archives' staff groundwork into the records catalogue and appendices that appear in this publication and conducting important primary research on Lockwood Doty.

The photographic materials in this publication would not have been possible without the cooperation and assistance of Maggie Sebastian, Greg Troup, Dr. Joseph Meany, and Craig Williams of the New York State Museum; Edward McGuire, Paul Mercer, Fred Bassett, and James Corsaro of the New York State Library; Tom Duclos, William Julien, Eric Stott, and Chris Morton of the New York State Division of Military & Naval Affairs; Kenneth Bartowski of the State Archives; and the retired Military Curator from the State Museum, Robert Mulligan. The staffs of the State Library, State Museum, and Division of Military & Naval Affairs provided many useful suggestions as to which collections might hold relevant objects and documents for use as illustrations and made the necessary arrangements for the photography. The final photographs were taken by Kenneth Bartowski and Greg Troup. Dean Thomas, of Thomas Publications, provided valuable technical information concerning Civil War small arms and ammunition.

We also extend a special thanks to artist Don Troiani for his generosity in permitting the use of his extraordinary painting of the 140th New York Volunteers, "Excelsior," which adorns the dust jacket of this publication, and we are grateful to Saverio Procario and Loomis Mayer at Fordham University Press for their care in bringing the project to publication.

Finally, the hundreds of details required to bring this project from concept to a manuscript and then to publication were handled expertly by Judy Hohmann, Public Programs and Outreach Manager. Ms. Hohmann's oversight of the details included coordination of the publication's content, developing content to extend the book's usefulness to primary and secondary educators, and management of the relationship with Fordham University Press. The final product reflects Ms. Hohmann's constant striving for excellence.

V. Chapman-Smith
New York State Archivist;
Executive Officer, Archives Partnership Trust

Foreword

James M. McPherson

More than 130 years after Appomattox, the Civil War remains the most written-about event in American history. Hundreds of titles pour from presses every year to join more than fifty thousand already in existence. Several million tourists and students visit Civil War battlefields annually. Thousands of monuments to Union and Confederate soldiers stand proudly in town squares or parks. Some forty thousand re-enactors don replica wool uniforms and take up replica Springfield rifled muskets several times a year to re-fight Antietam, Shiloh, Gettysburg, and dozens of other battles. Hollywood and the television industry have gotten into the Civil War in a big way since the extraordinary success of Ken Burns's video documentary in 1990.

What explains this phenomenon, which has no parallel in the history of this or any other country? There is no single or simple answer to the question. Part of the answer stems from the enormous loss of life and destruction of resources wrought by the war. More than 620,000 soldiers died in the Civil War, 2 percent of the American population. If the same percentage of the population were to die in a war fought at the end of the twentieth century, the number of American war dead would total more than five million. The Civil War killed one quarter of the white men of military age in the Confederate states and destroyed two-thirds of Southern wealth. The impact of this trauma has reverberated through generations, especially in the South, which has tried to compensate for its enormous physical loss and psychological shock by romanticizing the courage of Confederate soldiers in their heroic battle for a noble but lost Cause.

Yet that Cause was the dissolution of the *United* States and the preservation of slavery. Northern victory in the Civil War resolved two fundamental questions that had been left unresolved by the Revolution and Constitution that had created the nation. Would this fragile republic survive as one nation indivisible in a world of monarchies and empires, a world in which republics routinely succumbed to tyranny or fragmentation? And would this brave new republic, founded on a charter of liberty that declared all men created equal, continue to court the charge of hypocrisy by maintaining its status as the largest slaveholding society in the world? These issues plagued the republic and threatened its survival through four score and seven stormy years. They were finally resolved by the nation's new birth of freedom that Abraham Lincoln heralded at Gettysburg in 1863. Since 1865 slavery has no longer existed in the United States and no state or section has seriously threatened secession. Those questions were settled by a war that forever changed the face and fate of this nation.

Lincoln's martyrdom in the moment of victory has also given the Civil War a tragic and poignant place in the American consciousness. Indeed, the towering qualities of so many famous personalities associated with the war—Lincoln, Robert E. Lee, Ulysses S. Grant, William T. Sherman, Thomas J. "Stonewall" Jackson, Clara Barton, Frederick Douglass, and many others—have infused the war with a special power over our imaginations. And this power extends downward from famous leaders to all levels of society North and South, especially to the three million soldiers in blue and gray who fought it out during four years of ferocity unmatched in the Western world between the Napoleonic Wars and World War I.

We know more about those soldiers than about any others in our history. Their literacy rate was higher than that of an previous army anywhere. Many thousands of them kept diaries and most of them wrote frequent letters home—letters that were not subject to censorship, as have been the letters of soldiers in twentieth-century wars. For much of the past ten years my wife and I have been reading hundreds of their diaries and thousands of their letters in an attempt to understand what made them tick and why they fought—mostly as volunteers. We have come to know these men better than we know most of our living acquaintances, for in their personal letters written in a time of crisis that might end their lives at any moment they revealed more of their inner selves than we do in our normal everyday lives.

Our ability to share the fears and triumphs of these soldiers and of their families is another reason for our fascination with the Civil War. We are able to reach out across the generations to identify with ordinary people who lived in an extraordinary time and who rose to meet the crisis of their time—the greatest crisis in our history. That is the great reward of research in the abundant records of the Civil War.

And that also is the great value of this guide to the rich resources of the New York State Archives and Records Administration for the study of all aspects of the Empire State's role in the Civil War. This reference work is a gold mine for historians. Because it is logically organized with cross references and a detailed index, researchers can find almost anything they want to know about New York in the war, from Artillery Batteries to Zouaves. The largest state in the nation, it contributed more soldiers and sailors to the Union armed forces (16 percent of the total) than any other state. But New York also suffered more internal division and dissent over war aims and means than any other state, climaxed by the terrible Draft Riots in New York City in July 1863. Historians who want to understand the Northern war effort must understand New York, and to do that there is no better place to start than with this guide.

Preface

Daniel Lorello

This comprehensive guide makes available to a wide public for the first time one of the most important and extensive Civil War resources in the nation: the collections of the New York State Archives and Records Administration. Fully documenting the Empire State's crucial wartime role, from the outbreak of the Rebellion in 1861 through post-war efforts by the state to memorialize the deeds of New Yorkers who fought and died in battle, the records total more than 184 cubic feet of unbound paper and fill an additional 2,155 bound volumes.

Collectively, these records offer one of the most complete and detailed pictures available to scholars and general readers alike of a state at war in nineteenth-century America. They are invaluable to the study of the Civil War from a Union perspective and are particularly important in the areas of military and family history. The records shed much light on New York State's role in preserving the Union. And they document many of the individual contributions of the more than 448,000 enlistments that New York State furnished to the Union armed forces during the war.*

The primary objective of this guide is to describe and make available the Civil War-related records that are held by the New York State Archives. At the same time, the guide also seeks to make readers aware of the vast collections of wartime manuscripts, newspapers, maps, rare books, ephemera, and artifacts held by the New York State Museum, the

---

*This figure comes from William F. Fox's *Regimental Losses in the American Civil War, 1861–1865* (1898; reprint, Dayton, Oh.: Morningside Bookshop, 1985), p. 533. However, Frederick Phisterer in his *New York in the War of the Rebellion* 6 vols. 3rd ed. (Albany: J. B. Lyon, 1912) places the total number of enlistments from New York State at 503,765 (1:65). For a full discussion of how Fox arrived at his numbers see pp. 525–37. For Phisterer's explanation of how he arrived at a figure more than 50,000 higher than Fox's, see 1:65. Readers should also note that the number of troops (i.e., enlistments) furnished by any given state is not the same as the number of men who actually served because many men enlisted more than once during the war. Fox (p. 535) places the actual number of white men that New York State provided during the war at 369,948.

New York State Library, and the Division of Military and Naval Affairs, all of which, like the State Archives, are located in the Albany area. Throughout the guide, readers will find numerous references to these institutions and their unique Civil War holdings. In addition, all of the illustrations featured in the guide (with one exception) depict items from these repositories.

The Manuscripts and Special Collections Unit of the New York State Library, for example, contains a diverse collection of materials concerning New York State and the Civil War. These range from single items, such as letters from individual soldiers, to the voluminous papers of Major Generals John E. Wool and Gouverneur Kemble Warren, both of whom played prominent roles in the war. The unit also maintains thousands of prints, engravings, lithographs, broadsides, and photographs depicting the war and its participants. In addition to its manuscript material, the State Library holds scores of newspapers published throughout the state between 1860 and 1865, containing an incredible wealth of information on New York's role during the Civil War.

The Civil War holdings of the New York State Museum, while not as extensive as those of the New York State Library, also contain many rare and historically significant items. These include an exquisite sword presented to General Warren from the citizens of Cold Spring in recognition of his faithful service during the war; an extremely rare Gibbs carbine used by New York City authorities while repressing the New York City draft riots; and a complete Zouave uniform worn by Sergeant Henry Vredenburg of the 5th New York Volunteers. In addition, the State Museum holds many unique broadsides, engravings, and other printed matter pertaining to the war.

Finally, the Division of Military and Naval Affairs maintains one of the largest Civil War-related collections in the Northeast United States. Among the most cherished items in this priceless collection are over 900 flags carried by New York State troops during the Civil War. The division also holds thousands of photographs of New Yorkers who fought during the war; hundreds of military artifacts, including many Confederate items, brought home after the war by New York soldiers who in turn donated them to the state for safekeeping; newspaper clippings; broadsides, engravings; approximately 10,000 cards that record the burial locations of New York State residents who fought in the Civil War; and administrative records pertaining to the Bureau of Military Statistics.

When the records held by the State Archives are also taken into consideration, it is no understatement to say that the holdings of these four institutions together constitute one of the largest and most significant collections of Civil War materials available to the public. New York State is proud to maintain and make available these resources to its citizens—and now, through this guide, to the growing number of Americans throughout the country who share a passionate interest in the Civil War.

One caution must be offered to those preparing to deal with the data in this book. Throughout the guide, readers will encounter statistics concerning New Yorkers who served in the Civil War. But while scholars have never doubted the massive commitment that the state's citizens made to the Union cause, they have sometimes disagreed about precise numbers.

Although record-keeping during the war proved more reliable than in previous American conflicts, statistical data on casualties, numbers who actually served, etc., are notoriously inconsistent. Much of the statistical information provided throughout this guide comes from Fox's *Regimental Losses*, which many historians consider to be the standard statistical reference because its author based much of his data on United States War Department records and publications. However, Fox's work does have its limitations, and in those instances where statistical data are unavailable, incomplete, or misleading, the guide relies upon Phisterer's *New York in the War of the Rebellion*. Readers should also be aware that additional information (with different figures) is available from both Thomas L. Livermore's *Numbers and Losses in the Civil War in America* (Boston: Houghton, Mifflin, 1901) and an earlier work by Phisterer entitled *Statistical Record of the Armies of the United States* (New York: Charles Scribner's Sons, 1886). The latter two volumes, along with Fox's work, have been reprinted and are widely available.

Introduction: "A State of War"

Harold Holzer & Hans L. Trefousse

In a way, New York State's Civil War began more than five months before the first guns were fired at Fort Sumter—on November 8, 1860, to be precise. On that presidential election day, the state gave Abraham Lincoln its 35 electoral votes and a strong 50,000-vote popular plurality over Democrat Stephen A. Douglas.

But Lincoln's seemingly decisive victory in New York masked a deep north-south schism in the state that mirrored the sectional strife then threatening to divide the country as a whole. Lincoln triumphed handily upstate, winning substantial popular majorities in the counties embracing such northern cities as Syracuse, Rochester, and Buffalo. But downstate, in the southern portions of the state, the story was altogether different. In the bustling commercial center of Manhattan, it was Douglas who triumphed, beating Lincoln by more than 24,000 votes and earning 62 percent of the ballots cast. Across the East River in Brooklyn, 57 percent voted for Douglas, a 5,000-vote plurality. And in nearby West Chester (later, Westchester) County, the result was much the same: 57 percent for Douglas, with a 2,500-vote cushion. Here was a tale of two New Yorks, split across geographic lines, one section at political war against the other.

Making matters even more ominous was the vote on a proposed Constitutional Amendment to grant suffrage to free African Americans. It went down to a resounding defeat statewide. In Manhattan alone, the initiative failed by more than 55,000 votes, with fewer than 14 percent voting yes. Bigotry was not the exclusive province of states or citizens located below the Mason-Dixon Line.[1]

Ironically, it was in Manhattan that the newly elected Lincoln had enjoyed his first important East Coast exposure back in February. His speech at the Cooper Union was ecstatically received by local Republicans and helped make Lincoln a contender for national office. To the *New York Tribune* the address was "one of the happiest and most convincing political arguments ever made in this city." Earlier that same day, Lincoln visited the galleries of the city's best-known photographer, Mathew B.

Brady, sitting for a handsome portrait destined to ease potential supporters' worries about the rising politician's unconventional appearance. The photograph went on to inspire countless flattering newspaper woodcuts and popular prints. Brady himself believed it "the means of his election" that fall.[2]

So strong was the impression Lincoln made in New York that when he next set foot in the state, en route to his inauguration in 1861, newly bearded (thanks in part to the suggestion of an 11-year-old New Yorker from upstate Westfield), he seemed a different man. Slowly, the official train took him through Buffalo, Batavia, Rochester, Clyde, Syracuse, Utica, Little Falls, Fonda, and Schenectady. Arriving in the state capital, Albany, "President-elect Lincoln was barely recognized by the crowd," a journalist reported, adding that he "looked so unlike the hale, smooth-shaven, red-cheeked individual who is represented upon the popular prints . . . that it is no wonder the people do not recognize him."[3]

Nor was the novelty of newly sprouted whiskers sufficient to warm Lincoln's reception when he reached New York City. The *New York Herald* conceded that his welcome there lacked "human roar and magnetism." It was small wonder. Six Southern states had already seceded from the Union, and when news of their departure first reached New York, its mayor, Fernando Wood, had proposed that the city secede as well and become a free commercial port—"entirely independent," according to a contemporary. "I reckon," Lincoln is said to have responded, "that it will be some time before the front door sets up housekeeping on its own account." To a crowd gathered at City Hall, the President-elect declared: "There is nothing that can ever bring me willingly to consent to the destruction of this Union, under which not only the great commercial city of New York, but the whole country has acquired its greatness."[4]

But Lincoln was fully aware that New Yorkers "do not by a majority agree with me in political sentiments." He looked to history, admitting on his inaugural journey that he was inspired by "this great State, the renown of those great men who have stood here, and spoke here, and been heard here."[5]

But nostalgia proved insufficient to calm the storm. In December 1860, a group of New York City business leaders held the notorious, so-called "Pine Street" meeting, producing a manifesto assuring Southerners of their full sympathy. "We are neither a Northern nor a Southern City," one Hiram Ketchum declared at that meeting. Then, voicing the fear that Lincoln's pledges to resist secession were designed to promote abolitionism, not save the Union, Ketchum bluntly warned: "If ever a conflict arises between races, the people of the city of New York will stand by their brethren, the white race. We will never suffer you to be trampled upon by those of another blood." His remarks would prove portentous indeed.[6]

New York diarist George Templeton Strong, for one, was aghast at the stirrings of disloyalty in the city and the nation:

> This is a time of humiliation for the country. . . . We are a weak, divided, disgraced people, unable to maintain our national existence. We are impotent even to assert our national life. . . . I'm tempted to emigrate, to become a neutralized British subject.[7]

Strong had ample reason to be alarmed. By March 1861, the determined new Confederate nation was printing its first currency—$1 million worth—not in the South, but at the National Bank Note Company, in New York City![8]

Ultimately, Strong remained loyal to the Union. And when it came time to respond to actual rebellion, so did New York State. When Lincoln called for 75,000 troops to respond to the attack on Fort Sumter in distant Charleston, South Carolina, New York responded with an outpouring of volunteers, along with tens of thousands of well-wishers to cheer the troops as they departed for the front.

Four days after Sumter's surrender, the elite Seventh New York Regiment marched down Broadway en route to the defense of Washington to a thunderous send-off. New York artist Thomas Nast, later to gain fame as a crusading cartoonist, was on the scene to sketch the soldiers as they paraded by, later expanding his observations into a famous painting. Watching the parade, too, was none other than Major Robert Anderson, commander of abandoned Sumter, now receiving a hero's welcome in New York City. The next day, Anderson was a special guest at a huge Union Square rally called to reaffirm local support for the preservation of the country, by war if necessary. Tens of thousands attended, turning Manhattan into a sea of red, white, and blue.[9]

Governor Edwin D. Morgan, who had been one of the founders of New York's Republican party in the 1850s, now worked quickly to meet the state's early quota of seventeen volunteer regiments. Through Morgan's efforts, the state recruited and armed 223,000 men for the Union army. Lincoln rewarded him by naming him a major general of volunteers in September 1861, with command of the entire Department of New York.

War fever notwithstanding, the political situation in New York would remain unstable for the first few years of fighting, what with a Republican in the White House, a Republican governor sitting in Albany, but Democratic Mayor Wood presiding at City Hall downstate. Lincoln had appointed as Secretary of State the former New York governor and United States Senator William H. Seward of Auburn, who had been the early favorite to win the 1860 Republican nomination ultimately captured by Lincoln. Seward would spend considerable time during the first year of the Administration concentrating not only on foreign affairs, but on New York politics as well. As Lincoln made clear as late as 1864: "New York should be on our side by honest possession. . . . I am anxious for New York."[10]

Lincoln had ample reason for that anxiety, especially after the loyal Governor Morgan bowed to the no-third-term tradition, along with opposition from the Radical faction within his own party, and declined to seek re-election in 1862. But by the time the war was over in 1865, no state had committed more men to the fight, or appropriated more money to win it. The state boasted 3.8 million residents at the outbreak of the rebellion, some 17 percent of the total population of the Union. New York would send more than 448,850 enlistees between 1861 and 1865, some 16 percent of the total men in arms throughout the loyal states.[11]

New York could claim, too, the first officer to die for the Union cause. Ephraim Elmer Ellsworth, born in Malta, New York, had earlier organized a unit of Zouave Cadets in Chicago which became famous for its colorful uniforms and precision drill demonstrations. When war broke out, he returned east to organize a new unit, the New York Fire Zouaves, and then marched them off to Washington. On May 24, 1861, Colonel Ellsworth led his troops across the Potomac River into Alexandria, Virginia, where he tore down a Confederate flag waving from a local hotel. As he marched down the hotel stairway carrying the banner in his arms, the furious innkeeper shot him to death. He was only 23 years old. A grieving Abraham Lincoln, in whose Illinois law office Ellsworth had once clerked, gave the young hero a White House funeral. The North mourned its youthful martyr deeply.[12]

Throughout the first year of the war, New York contributed men and matériel in abundance, fueling the Union war effort. And then there was the indomitable United States Military Academy at West Point, which had trained dozens of generals now fighting on both sides of the bitter conflict (including Robert E. Lee, once its superintendent, who had refused to draw his sword against his native Virginia and now led Confederate armies). West Point continued to churn out officers of the future. At the Parrott Gun Foundry in the nearby town of Cold Spring, new weapons were continually tested and perfected, and munitions manufactured in huge quantities. And at the Brooklyn Navy Yard, shipbuilders assembled the most revolutionary vessel in recent maritime history: the all-ironclad *U.S.S. Monitor*. It was commissioned in February 1862, and a few months later engaged the fearful Confederate ironclad, the *Merrimack*, in one of the most famous sea battles in American naval history.

President Lincoln returned to New York on June 24, 1862, to visit West Point, at a time when many New Yorkers—along with Union men throughout the North—were growing weary of the long, bloody, inconclusive months of fighting. At the Military Academy, Lincoln held a strategy session with the distinguished ex-general-in-chief, Winfield Scott, and was serenaded by the West Point band. But his trip was about far more than pomp and tradition. It was about modern, high-technology warfare as well, and at Parrott's foundry, Lincoln watched with enthusiasm as newly developed rifled cannon were fired across the Hudson River with deadly precision, hitting distant targets with routine accuracy. Lincoln then toured the foundry itself, personally inspecting the huge "pouring pit," hellishly aglow with molten metal, getting a first-hand look at New York's industrial might in action. That might would serve the Union cause well.[13]

Another strong Lincoln ally in New York was the elderly Catholic Archbishop, John Joseph Hughes. A longtime Seward confidante, he now undertook an arduous tour of Europe, preaching the cause of Union—and non-intervention—to dubious leaders in the Catholic countries of France, Spain, Italy, and Ireland. His mission took him from the court of Napoleon III to the halls of the Vatican. And when he returned to New York City in August 1862, he used his first Mass at St. Patrick's to warn worshipers that continued Democratic opposition to the Lincoln Administration would certainly encourage Europe to enter the war on the side of the Confederacy. Ultimately, city voters would replace Democratic Mayor Wood with moderate Republican reformer George Opdyke.[14]

But the underlying, simmering threat of dissension—destined in 1863 to erupt into the infamous New York City Draft Riots—continued to percolate in the nation's most populous state. Sometimes it erupted. Claiming unprecedented constitutional authority because of the rebellion, federal authorities closed critical New York newspapers on several occasions, charging them with crossing the line of dissent into disloyalty.

And if there was pressure from the anti-war front, there was no less criticism from the opposite side of the political spectrum. The influential editor Horace Greeley regularly used the pages of his *New York Tribune* to denounce the Lincoln Administration for moving too slowly on expanding the war to include the destruction of slavery. Greeley's stinging editorial, "The Prayer of Twenty Millions," published on August 20, 1862, denounced the President for being "strangely and disastrously remiss" on emancipation. Little did Greeley know that Lincoln had already drafted a Proclamation freeing the slaves held in rebel states. He was merely waiting for a Union victory to announce it with confidence. He would soon do so.[15]

By 1862, New Yorkers had already lost sons at Bull Run, Antietam, Fredericksburg, and other battles, and casualties were mounting. The losses were deeply felt—in individual homes and in the collective spirit as well. The young hero Theodore Winthrop, killed at Big Bethel in June 1861, became a literary sensation with a series of posthumously published novels.

Ultimately, of the nearly 360,000 men who died from wounds or disease during the Civil War, some 53,000 were from New York.[16] No American war before or since—not even all the wars combined—ever exacted such a toll on human life. The depth of that sacrifice was vividly revealed when photographer Mathew Brady placed on public display in New York, for the first time anywhere, the horrific images of dead and wounded soldiers piled on the distant fields of action. The human cost of the war had finally come home to haunt New York, and the exhibition caused a sensation. Wrote the *New York Times* of Brady:

> If he has not brought home bodies and laid them along the streets, he has done something very much like it. . . . It seems somewhat singular that the same sun that looked down on the faces of the slain, blistering them, blotting out from their bodies all semblance of humanity, and hastening their corruption, should have thus caught their features.[17]

Yet when the public announcement of Emancipation finally came that autumn, re-defining and ennobling the war effort for which so much had already been sacrificed by so many, it was not greeted with universal approbation. White Americans remained deeply divided on the issues of war, race, and politics, no less so in New York than throughout the nation whose very survival was still hanging in the balance.

The fall of 1862 proved a difficult period for the national administration. In September, Abraham Lincoln issued his Preliminary Emancipation Proclamation, providing for the freedom of all slaves in states or parts of states still in rebellion on January 1, 1863. Conservatives, particularly Democrats opposed to abolition, were dismayed that he was moving closer to the radical wing of his party. Then, elections in Ohio and Pennsylvania registered severe Republican losses, and in November, New York followed suit. As soon as the elections were over, Lincoln dismissed General George B. McClellan, a conservative Democrat, as commander of the Army of the Potomac and replaced him with the apolitical Ambrose E. Burnside, again angering the conservatives. And in December, after the disastrous battle of Fredericksburg, a delegation of Congressmen demanded that he dismiss Secretary of State Seward, who promptly handed in his resignation. Lincoln parried this thrust by so embarrassing Salmon P. Chase, the Secretary of the Treasury, who had spread stories of the malfunctioning of the cabinet, that Chase, too, offered his resignation. The President was thus able to reject both resignations. But his critics' dissatisfaction merely increased. Then, on January 1, he published his final Emancipation Proclamation, a move that further disturbed the conservatives.[18]

These events greatly complicated matters in New York, where the Democrats had succeeded in electing the opposition leader Horatio Seymour governor and in capturing half the seats in the state assembly. This created the anomalous situation of partially turning over the state that furnished the greatest number of troops and supplied the principal financial backing to the Union to active opponents of the administration. These Democrats, though not necessarily disloyal, nevertheless resisted emancipation; they demanded strict adherence to the Constitution so that the Union could be restored "as it was" and, as they said, the Constitution could be maintained "as it is." At a time when Lincoln had already moved toward the radicals by issuing his Emancipation Proclamation—and he would continue to uphold their ideas by refusing to alter or repeal it—it would require all of his skill to maintain a working relationship with the new governor of the Empire State.

Horatio Seymour's inaugural address immediately highlighted this difficulty. Pleading for a speedy restoration of the Union and strict adherence to the Constitution, and denouncing arbitrary arrests, the governor set the tone for his administration. He went on to veto a bill granting absentee voting rights to soldiers. In May he condemned the arrest of Clement C. Vallandigham, the Copperhead Ohio congressman incarcerated by General Burnside for delivering an anti-war speech. The President sought to bridge the gap by pleading with the governor to cooperate. While there could be differences between them, he wrote, these were differences of means and not of purpose. Seymour answered several weeks later in a non-committal letter asserting that no political resentments would turn him aside from the pathway he had marked for himself. Although he insisted that he was firmly committed to the preservation of the Union, in another fervent plea on July 4, at the New York Academy of Music, he strongly reiterated his well-known views and placed himself in total opposition to the Lincoln administration.[19]

This situation was soon to have serious consequences. In March of 1863 Congress passed a conscription act; the draft, denounced by the governor, caused deep resentment in the state. Many New Yorkers, particularly workingmen, felt that the state did not receive sufficient credit for the troops already furnished; that its quota, determined by a percentage of those liable to be drafted while subtracting those who had enrolled earlier, was too high; and that the exemption clauses of the legislation, enabling persons of means to hire substitutes, constituted a serious discrimination against the poor.

These feelings were especially bitter in New York City, which, unlike many upstate counties, tended to be Democratic, and where racial feelings were embittered by fears of black competition. Particularly pronounced among the Irish immigrants, these resentments led to a serious riot. When drafting began on July 13, a group of discontented laborers and firemen attacked the district office of the Provost Marshal at 47th Street and Third Avenue. They wrecked the building, stopped the selection, and nearly beat Superintendent of Police John A. Kennedy to death. Three days of uncontrolled rioting followed. Trolley tracks and telegraph wires were torn up, shops and the homes of the rich were plundered, Colonel Henry O'Brien of the 11th New York was murdered, and

African-Americans were brutally hunted down, lynched, and driven from their homes. The "Colored Orphan Asylum" at Fifth Avenue between 43rd and 44th Street was burned to the ground. Mobs threatened publisher Horace Greeley, attacked police stations, the state armory, and the Brooks Brothers clothing store as well as hotels, bars, and brothels. Business came to a standstill.

On the second day the governor returned from the New Jersey shore and attempted to assuage the crowd by addressing it with the words "My friends," a speech that was ever after held against him. It was only with the help of troops recalled from Pennsylvania that the police and the Republican mayor, George Opdyke, were able, after three days, to bring the riot under control. By Friday, July 16, when Archbishop John Hughes joined the authorities in attempts to calm the crowds, the disorders were finally over.[20]

It was estimated that the riots cost some $1,000,000 of property and resulted in the deaths of some 119 and the wounding of over 300 persons. The draft was temporarily suspended, but Lincoln refused to declare martial law. To guard against further outbreaks, the common council, overriding the mayor's veto, voted a fund to recompense draftees for their exemption fees. When drafting was resumed, the results were meager, a much greater number succeeding in obtaining exemptions than those actually inducted.[21]

In the elections of 1863, following Union victories at Gettysburg and Vicksburg, the Republicans, now called Unionists, managed to regain full control of the legislature, which attempted to strip the governor of the power to appoint army officers, permitted state banks to nationalize, and allowed payment of public and private creditors in greenbacks, a measure Seymour had steadily opposed.[22]

In spite of these victories, the Union party remained in a state of disarray. Radical elements opposed the state convention's endorsement of the renomination of Abraham Lincoln. Although the separate radical ticket of John C. Frémont and John Cochrane in May did not receive wide backing, during the summer of 1864, following Lincoln's renomination, the President's opponents launched a movement to replace him. The journalists Parke Godwin, the close collaborator with William Cullen Bryant on the *New York Evening Post*, and Horace Greeley, the editor of the *New York Tribune*, among others, supported this effort, which failed after William T. Sherman captured Atlanta and other Union victories improved Lincoln's chances of victory. At the same time, Greeley, always ready for peace, attempted to negotiate a settlement at Niagara Falls, but the Confederates were unwilling to accept Lincoln's conditions of re-union and emancipation. The publisher's efforts, like similar ones by others, failed.[23]

In the meantime, the Democrats, though also split into a peace faction and a war contingent, had every hope of success. Governor Seymour was one of the principal candidates for the presidential nomination, and when he withdrew, he was elected permanent chairman of the national convention in Chicago. There, in a forceful speech, he declared that the administration had no faith in the people of the states that had placed it in power and was prolonging the war for unattainable goals. The Democrats nominated General McClellan on a peace platform which he promptly repudiated; he obtained considerable support in New York, but in the end he was unable to prevail. Confederate agents had hoped to disrupt the elections by burning down various buildings in New York City on election day, but the authorities had been alerted and the Confederates, foiled, did not attempt to start several fires in the metropolis until November 25, after the voting was over. The government had sent a number of federal troops under General Benjamin F. Butler to the city to keep order, and on election day the state endorsed the President and elected the Republican Reuben Fenton governor—by a larger margin, in fact, than that given to Lincoln. At the same time, the Unionists elected 20 of 31 members of the House of Representatives.[24]

Following the election, Lincoln used all the powers of his office to obtain the necessary two-thirds vote in the House of Representatives to pass the Thirteenth Amendment abolishing slavery, and the state was among the first four to ratify it.[25]

When, in April 1865, Robert E. Lee surrendered at Appomattox, New Yorkers widely celebrated the victory, but their joy was quickly turned to mourning when news of the assassination of the President reached the state. The arrival of the funeral train on its way to Springfield was marked by universal displays of respect as the sad journey progressed from New York City by way of Albany to the western border of the state.[26]

New York's contribution to the war effort had been considerable. Enlisting some 448,000 men during the four years of the conflict, the state never hesitated to comply with requests for troops, Governor Seymour sending 19 regiments to Pennsylvania alone when that state was invaded in 1863. New York was especially proud of the general officers it furnished to the Union army; among them were Gouverneur Kemble Warren, Fitz John Porter, Henry A. Barnum, John A. Dix, James Wadsworth, John M. Schofield, Philip Kearny, George Stoneman, Henry W. Slocum, Darius N. Couch, Francis C. Barlow, Emory Upton, and Abner Doubleday. Winfield Scott, too, lived in the state during much of the conflict, and Philip Sheridan was born in Albany.[27]

The aftermath of the war did not usher in a period of reform. In fact, it was at this time that the city of New York was captured by Tammany Hall and its leader, William M. Tweed, who, together with his henchmen, Richard B. Connolly and Peter B. Sweeney, succeeded in defrauding the city of between $30,000,000 and $200,000,000. These defalcations were revealed in 1871; Tweed was jailed and finally died a prisoner. But the corruption which had beset the city was to be a permanent legacy.

Nor did the end of the war bring about immediate justice for African Americans. The New York constitution allowed them to vote only if they owned $240 worth of property, a requirement not imposed upon whites. The constitutional convention of 1867 attempted to right the injustice, but in an election in 1869, the change was rejected by the voters. Only the ratification of the Fifteenth Amendment in 1870 finally righted this ancient wrong.[28]

In spite of these problems, the war had initiated a period of tremendous economic growth, which rebounded to the benefit of the state. Manufacturing increased, wages went up, and the position of the city of New York as a financial leader of the country was strengthened by the introduction of the national banking system. The casualties incurred during the conflict were a high price to pay, but the industrial upswing of the state as a result of the war was undeniable.

NOTES

1. *The Tribune Almanac for the Years 1838 to 1864, Inclusive . . .* (New York: The New York Tribune, 1868), p. 41.

2. *New York Tribune*, February 28, 1860; Mathew Brady quoted in Francis B. Carpenter, *Six Months at the White House with Abraham Lincoln: The Story of a Picture* (New York: Hurd & Houghton, 1867), p. 47.

3. Roy P. Basler, et al., eds., *The Collected Works of Abraham Lincoln*, 9 vols., hereafter

cited as *Coll. Works* (New Brunswick, N.J.: Rutgers University Press, 1953–55), IV:219; Harold G. and Oswald Garrison Villard, *Lincoln on the Eve of '61: A Journalist's Story by Henry Villard* (New York: Alfred A. Knopf, 1941), p. 93.

4. Iver Bernstein, *The New York City Draft Riots: Their Significance for American Society and Politics in the Age of the Civil War* (New York: Oxford University Press, 1990), p. 143; *Coll. Works* IV:233.

5. *Coll. Works* IV:225, 232.

6. Bernstein, *The New York City Draft Riots*, pp. 142–43.

7. Andrew A. Freeman, *Abraham Lincoln Goes to New York* (New York: Coward-McCann, 1960), pp. 106–109.

8. Gordon Bleuler, "Southern Currency," in Richard N. Current, editor-in-chief, *Encyclopedia of the Confederacy*, 4 vols. (New York: Simon & Schuster, 1993), I:434.

9. *New York Evening Express*, April 22, 1861.

10. John M. Taylor, *William Henry Seward: Lincoln's Right Hand Man* (New York: HarperCollins, 1991), p. 147; Allen Thorndike Rice, ed., *Reminiscences of Abraham Lincoln by Distinguished Men of His Time* (New York: North American Publishing, 1886), pp. 68–69.

11. E. B. Long, ed., *The Civil War Day by Day: An Almanac, 1861–1865* (New York: Doubleday, 1971), pp. 701, 705; William F. Fox, *Regimental Losses in the American Civil War, 1861–1865* (1898, reprint, Dayton, Oh.: Morningside Bookshop, 1985), p. 533.

12. For examples of nationally distributed pictorial tributes to the New York hero, see Winfred Porter Truesdell, *Catalogue Raisonné of the Portraits of Colonel Elmer E. Ellsworth* [*sic*] (Champlain: The Print Connoisseur, 1927), listing following p. 26.

13. Earl Schenck Miers, editor-in-chief, *Lincoln Day by Day: A Chronology, 1809–1865*, 3 vols. (Washington, D.C.: Lincoln Sesquicentennial Commission, 1961), III:123.

14. Jay Monaghan, *Diplomat in Carpet Slippers: Abraham Lincoln Deals with Foreign Affairs* (Indianapolis: Bobbs-Merrill, 1945), pp. 156, 246; the authoritative biography is John R. G. Hassard, *Life of the Most Reverend John Hughes, D.D. . . .* (New York: D. Appleton, 1866).

15. *Coll. Works*, V:389.

16. The figure of 53,114 is derived from Frederick Phisterer, *New York in the War of the Rebellion*, 6 vols. 3rd edition (Albany: J. B. Lyon, 1912), 1:285. This figure differs from William F. Fox's total of 46,534 New York deaths because Fox based his figure "upon the statistics prepared in the War Department at Washington" and "embraces . . . the Regular Army" and "the volunteers." Phisterer, on the other hand, arrived at his figure of 53,114 by adding to Fox's number the number of men "who served . . . in other divisions of the Army of the United States and in the Navy and Marine Corps." See Fox, *Regimental Losses in the American Civil War, 1861–1865*, p. 525 and Phisterer, *New York in the War of the Rebellion*, 1:284–85. Phisterer's higher figure was selected because it includes men who served and died in all branches of the armed services during the war.

17. *The New York Times*, October 20, 1862.

18. *Coll. Works*, V:433–36, VI:28–31; Allan Nevins, *The War for the Union*, 2 vols. (New York: Scribners, 1960), pp. 218–22; David Herbert Donald, *Lincoln* (New York: Simon & Schuster, 1995), pp. 282–87, 390, 400–408.

19. Alexander C. Flick, ed., *History of the State of New York*, 10 vols. (New York:

Lockwood Lyon Doty, Chief, Bureau of Military Statistics

Many of the Civil War records held by the New York State Archives were gathered or created by the Bureau of Military Statistics, which Doty headed from its creation in 1862 until he resigned in 1866. This engraving is the only known likeness of Doty; it appeared in his History of Livingston County, *which was published in 1876, three years after his death.*

Courtesy of the New York State Library.

commanded them on former occasions. They came to me at the right time, and well did they perform their duty.

Captain J. G. Smith, commanding the Fourth New York Independent Battery, says:

We had been swept from the crest of the hill (Devil's Den), leaving three of our guns behind, and had opened with the remaining three from a position seventy-five yards nearer Little Round Top. Our fire was directed at the enemy stationed at or near Plum Run gorge. We were trying to keep up the character of a fight, hoping for help, and fearing that the enemy were about to charge, in which event our weakness would be discovered, and then our bold front would avail us nothing. All that men could do the artillerists of the battery were doing. If the enemy would stand off and fight us, the battle would last as long as therw was a man left to load a gun, but, when it came to a change, we must either fall back or yield. During this critical moment the fate of Round Tops hung in the balance. Five minutes more, and the battery must retire or fall into the hands of the enemy. The Round Tops were still defenseless. General Warren, who had gone in search of troops for the purpose of defending this important position, had not yet returned. Time was precious. The Nation was greatly in need of men at this point of the Federal line. Brave men had fought over this ground but a few minutes before, and left many of their comrades to tell the tale of this unequal contest. Still the harvest was incomplete; more human grain must be garnered before the destruction could be appeased. It was coming. The Fortieth New York Regiment, led by the indomitable Thos. W. Egan, had heard the roar of cannon, and, without waiting for orders, following the true instincts of a band of heroes, moved at a double quick, and were soon charging through the battery.

A new lease of life was given us. In fact, this timely assistance enabled the battery to renew the contest, and, with the aid of the Fortieth, impose a longer delay of half an hour upon the troops of General Hood, there giving the needed succor, under the command of Vincent, O'Rourke and others, just time, sufficient time to scale the summit of Little Round Top, together with Hazlett's battery, and after a short, sharp struggle repulse the foe.

opposite

The Round Tops Still "Defenseless"

In the late 1890s, New York State Historian Hugh Hastings asked veterans who belonged to Grand Army of the Republic posts throughout the state to provide him written accounts of their Civil War experiences. Hastings received an astonishing array of responses, ranging from completed printed forms that he had forwarded to the G.A.R. posts to, as in this case, an original typescript of a complete history of the 40th New York Volunteers. It was prepared by the regiment's historian, Joseph Murphy. This section of Murphy's manuscript recounts the 40th's role during the second day's action at the Battle of Gettysburg, when the men of the "Mozart Regiment" helped to repulse the onslaught of General John B. Hood's men against Little Round Top.

Courtesy Manuscripts and Special Collections Unit, New York State Library

An Eyewitness Recalls Antietam

The Battle of Antietam proved to be the single bloodiest day of the Civil War, with some 23,000 casualties on both sides. In this account, also forwarded to State Historian Hastings, F. N. Bell, President of the 104th New York Regimental Association, vividly describes the action near the East Woods in which Captain William Duryea, who had served on General Joseph K. F. Mansfield's staff until the latter was mortally wounded, led a charge that included men of the 104th New York against General John Bell Hood's Texans. Shouting "Boys, will you follow me?" Duryea led the men of the 104th until he too fell seriously wounded.

Courtesy Manuscripts and Special Collections Unit, New York State Library

The Preliminary Emancipation Proclamation

One of the nation's great documentary treasures, the Preliminary Emancipation Proclamation was written and issued by President Abraham Lincoln on September 22, 1862, five days after the federal victory at the Battle of Antietam. It gave states in rebellion 100 days' notice to return to the Union and cease hostilities, or face the permanent loss of all slaves. After opposing slavery all his life, Lincoln had finally found a way to cripple the institution. On January 1, 1863, as promised, the President issued a final proclamation that declared all the slaves in the rebellious states "thenceforward, and forever free." But that prized document was later destroyed in the great Chicago Fire of 1871. Lincoln himself donated this preliminary proclamation to be sold at New York State's Army Relief Bazaar in 1864. It was won in a charity lottery by the famous abolitionist Geritt Smith, who in turn donated it back to the U.S. Sanitary Commission to raise more funds for soldier relief. Shortly after Lincoln's assassination, the State Legislature voted to purchase the document for $1,000—and it has remained in the possession of the New York State Library ever since.

Courtesy Manuscripts and Special Collections Unit, New York State Library

qualified voters of such state shall have participated, shall, in the absence of strong countervailing testimony, be deemed conclusive evidence that such state and the people thereof, are not then in rebellion against the United States.

That attention is hereby, called to an Act of Congress entitled "An Act to make an additional Article of War," approved March 13. 1862, and which act is in the words and figure following:

Also to the ninth and tenth sections of an act entitled "An Act to suppress Insurrection; to punish Treason and Rebellion, to seize and confiscate property of rebels, and for other purposes," approved July 17. 1862, and which sections are in the words and figure following:

And I do hereby enjoin upon and order all persons engaged in the military and naval service of the United States to observe, obey, and enforce, within their respective spheres of service, the act and sections above recited.

In due time ~~and the next session of Congress~~ And the executive will, recommend that all citizens of the United States who shall have remained loyal thereto throughout the rebellion shall (upon the restoration of the constitutional relation between the United States, and their respective states, and people, if that relation shall have been suspended or disturbed) be compensated for all losses by acts of the United States, including the loss of slaves.

In witness Whereof, I have hereunto set my hand, and caused the seal of the United States to be affixed.

L. S.

Done at the City of Washington, this twenty second day of September, in the year of our Lord, one thousand eight hundred and sixty two, and sixty two, and of the Independence of the United States, the eighty seventh. Abraham Lincoln.

By the President:
William H. Seward,
Secretary of State.

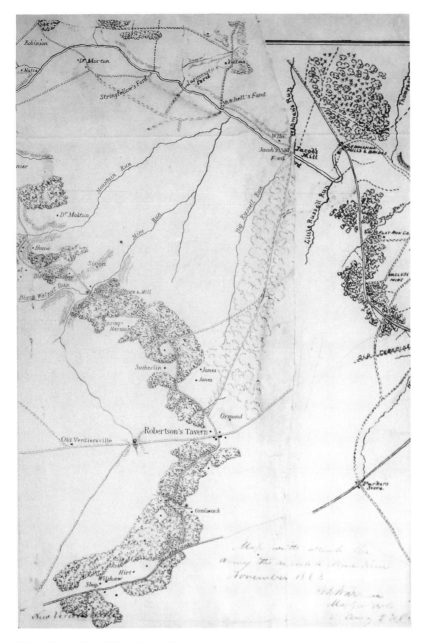

Map From the Mine Run Campaign

Following General Lee's unsuccessful Bristoe Campaign in October and early November 1863, General George G. Meade, Commander of the Army of the Potomac, attempted to maneuver Lee out of his position on the Rapidan River. After some auspicious Union thrusts, Confederate cavalry detected Meade's intentions, allowing Lee time to fortify strongly along Mine Run. Finding no assailable point, Meade reluctantly withdrew and went into winter quarters around Culpeper, Virginia, thus ending major operations in the Eastern Theater until General Grant launched his Wilderness Campaign the following May. At the time Major General Gouverneur K. Warren used this map, he commanded the Second Corps during the Mine Run Campaign in the absence of Major General Winfield Scott Hancock, who had been wounded at Gettysburg.

Letter to the Secretary of War

Writing two days after the New York City Draft Riots had finally been suppressed, 79-year-old Major General John E. Wool, a veteran of both the War of 1812 and the Mexican War, informs Secretary of War Edwin M. Stanton that the rioters "have generally returned to their occupations" and "quiet and peace" prevail throughout the Union's largest city. Wool, who commanded the Department of the East at the time the riots erupted on July 13, 1863, also acknowledges that he has received Stanton's order relieving him of command. Less than two weeks later, the Newburgh-born Wool was retired from the United States Army after more than half a century of distinguished service.

Courtesy Manuscripts and Special Collections Unit, New York State Library

Requiem for a Union Hero

Almost immediately after Colonel Ephraim Elmer Ellsworth was gunned down in Alexandria, Virginia, on May 24, 1861, becoming the first Union officer killed in the war, Northern publishers issued a deluge of material commemorating the dashing martyr who had been honored with a White House funeral. George William Warren composed this requiem, the title page to which is adorned with various scenes depicting the brief career of the young Zouave officer who had first attracted attention by leading a crack cadet drill team before the war.

Courtesy Manuscripts and Special Collections Unit, New York State Library

Pass Authorizing Transportation of Colonel Ellsworth's Body

On May 25, 1861 Brigadier General Joseph K. F. Mansfield issued this pass to Lieutenant Stephen W. Stryker authorizing him to bring Colonel Ephraim Elmer Ellsworth's body through Union lines to Ellsworth's home town of Mechanicville, New York, for burial. Ellsworth, a personal friend of President Lincoln, was shot on May 24, 1861, by an Alexandria, Virginia, hotel keeper after he tore down a Confederate flag flying from the hotel's rooftop. Ellsworth's death was mourned throughout the Union. Mansfield was subsequently mortally wounded during the Battle of Antietam in 1862.

Series A4111 Administrative Correspondence Files [of the Bureau of Military Statistics], 1859–1875.

Color Sergeant James Simpson(?), 44th New York Volunteers

The back of this carte-de-visite *identifies the man holding one of the two national flags issued to the 44th New York Volunteers as Color Sergeant James Simpson. However, records show that no man by this name served with the 44th during the war. The subject may be Sergeant James Strong, who did in fact serve as a color bearer for the regiment. Also known as "Ellsworth's Avengers," the 44th was organized in the fall of 1861 and was filled by men from different towns, villages, and cities throughout the state. The regiment was mustered into service on September 24 and fought in many of the Army of the Potomac's great battles, including Antietam, Chancellorsville, Gettysburg, and the Wilderness, until it was mustered out in 1864. Both of the regiment's national flags were deposited with the Bureau of Military Statistics and are now part of a collection, containing more than 900 Civil War flags, that is maintained by the New York State Division of Military & Naval Affairs.*
Courtesy New York State Division of Military & Naval Affairs

The Seventy-Ninth Highlanders

As bagpipes play "Blue Bonnets Over the Border," the thousand men of the distinctively uniformed 79th New York Cameron Highlanders march through the streets of New York City to join the war in 1861. Their departure is illustrated in the May 25 issue of Harper's Weekly. *The regiment's full dress uniforms, which included Glengarries, kilts, sporrans, and kilt hose, were modeled after those worn by the British Queen's Own 79th Cameron Highlanders. Ultimately, as the war progressed, the men exchanged kilts and sporrans for more practical tartan trousers known as "trews," or wore regulation U.S. Army pants and Glengarries or kepis. The 79th played a major role at Bull Run in July, where it suffered nearly 200 casualties, most of them on Henry House Hill. Among the dead left on the battlefield was Colonel James Cameron, the 79th's commander and brother of Union Secretary of War Simon Cameron.*

Courtesy Manuscripts and Special Collections Unit, New York State Library

SOLDIERS' HEALTH.

1. In any ordinary campaign sickness disables or destroys three times as many as the sword.

2. On a march, from April to November, the entire clothing should be a colored flannel shirt, with a loosely-buttoned collar, cotton drawers, woolen pantaloons, shoes and stockings, and a light colored felt hat, with broad brim to protect the eyes and face from the glare of the sun and from the rain, and a substantial but not heavy coat when off duty.

3. Sun stroke is most effectually prevented by wearing a silk handkerchief in the crown of the hat.

4. Colored blankets are best, and if lined with brown drilling the warmth and durability are doubled, while protection against dampness from lying on the ground is almost complete; but to have complete protection while lying on the ground, or during storms, an India rubber blanket is necessary.

5. Never lie or sit down on the grass or bare earth for a moment; rather use your hat; a handkerchief even is a great protection. The warmer you are, the greater need for this precaution, as a damp vapor is immediately generated, to be absorbed by the clothing, and to cool you off too rapidly.

6. While marching, or on other active duty, the more thirsty you are, the more essential it is to safety of life itself to rinse out the mouth two or three times, and *then* take a swallow of water at a time, with short intervals. A brave French general, on a forced march, fell dead on the instant, by drinking largely of cold water, when snow was on the ground.

7. Abundant sleep is essential to bodily efficiency, and that alertness of mind which is all-important in an engagement; and few things more certainly and more effectually prevent sound sleep than eating heartily after sundown, especially after a heavy march or desperate battle.

8. Nothing is more certain to secure endurance and capability of long continued effort and a rapid recovery from wounds, which would prove fatal to intemperate men, than the avoidance of everything as a drink, except cold water, not excluding coffee at breakfast. Drink as little as possible of even cold water.

9. After any sort of exhausting effort, a cup of coffee, hot or cold, is an admirable sustainer of the strength, until nature begins to recover herself.

10. Never eat heartily just before a great undertaking; because the nervous power is irresistibly drawn to the stomach to manage the food eaten, thus drawing off that supply which the brain and muscles so much need. And during hot weather eat little if any oily meats.

11. If persons will drink brandy, it is incomparably safer to do so after an effort than before; for it can give only a transient strength, lasting but a few minutes; but it can never be known how long any given effort is to be kept in continuance, and if longer than the few minutes, the body becomes more feeble than it would have been without the stimulus, it is clear that its use before an effort is always hazardous and is always unwise.

12. Never go to sleep, especially after a great effort, even in hot weather, without some covering over you.

13. Under all circumstances, rather than lie down on the bare ground, lie in the hollow of two logs placed together; or across several smaller pieces of wood, laid side by side; or sit on your hat, leaning against a tree. A nap of ten or fifteen minutes in that position will refresh you more than an hour on the bare earth, with the additional advantage of perfect safety.

14. If from any wound the blood spirts out in jets instead of a steady stream, you will die in a few minutes unless it is remedied; because an artery has been divided, and that takes the blood direct from the fountain of life. To stop this instantly, take a handkerchief or other cloth, fold it like a neck-handkerchief, make a knot in the centre of it; and if the foot, leg, or thigh be wounded, tie the handkerchief loosely around the thigh *close* to the *groin*, the knot in the centre of the handkerchief should be placed on the *front* of the thigh; if the hand or arm be wounded tie near the shoulder, the knot should be on the inside of the arm, put a stick, bayonet or ramrod between the skin and the handkerchief, and twist it around until the bleeding ceases, and keep it thus until the surgeon arrives. A *cut* is less dangerous than a bullet-wound, and heals more rapidly.

15. Wash the feet every night, and the whole body once a day if possible.

Health Advice for Soldiers

An example of the kind of printed materials acquired by the Bureau of Military Statistics, this small broadside presents 15 suggestions for raw recruits, taking to the field for the first time, on how to safeguard their health on campaign. The origin of the broadside is unknown, but it may have been printed by the state, or perhaps by a private organization such as the United States Sanitary Commission, whose primary mission was the care and comfort of soldiers.

Series A4129 Assorted Printed Material, 1861–1864.

Letter from a Colonel to a Future President

Writing in 1861 on the distinctive letterhead of the 6th New York Volunteers (Governor's Guard), Colonel James C. Pinckney asks Quartermaster General Chester Alan Arthur (a future President of the United States) to forward to him "one hundred gray uniforms" for his regiment. During the early months of the war, both sides wore a variety of uniforms: some Confederates actually wore blue, and some Union soldiers gray. Not surprisingly, this resulted in considerable confusion during the war's first major battle at Bull Run in July 1861.

Series A4106 Administrative Correspondence Files and Related Records [of the Quartermaster General's Office], 1861–1868.

Gov. E.D. Morgan
Albany N.Y.

New York May 17/61

I cannot stand a day longer the pressure upon me for Shirts, Drawers &c. for six thousand men, mustered into the U.S. service. I am blamed here for the want of them. If they are not not sent from Albany to night, can they not be bought here at once. They should be supplied without another day's delay.

C.A. Arthur

From Quartermaster General to Governor

Writing barely a month after the bombardment of Fort Sumter, Quartermaster General Chester Alan Arthur complains to Governor Edwin D. Morgan about "the pressure upon me for shirts, drawers, etc." and asks him for his help in getting 6,000 uniforms shipped from Albany to New York City "without another day's delay." This letter clearly reveals the strain facing state officials as they struggled to equip the thousands of men who responded to President Lincoln's initial call for 75,000 men to put down the Rebellion. Lethargic and sluggish prior to the Civil War, New York's military bureaucracy would soon grow into a large and active operation, moving efficiently to get men into the field as rapidly as possible.

Series A4106 Administrative Correspondence and Related Records [of the Quartermaster General's Office], 1861–1868.

Men of the 12th New York State Militia at Camp Anderson

Taken in the summer of 1861, this remarkable image shows a number of men from the 12th New York State Militia (Independence Guard) at Camp Anderson, which was located in Franklin Square in the heart of Washington, D.C. The photograph clearly reveals the unique uniform of the regiment, patterned upon those of the French chasseurs a pied, *and adopted by the regiment on the night of the bombardment of Fort Sumter. Many of the men visible in this albumen print belong to the regiment's "Sappers and Miners" company, a unit that had been added to many infantry regiments a few years before the Civil War to perform pioneering and similar duties. Seated just to the left of the soldier in full uniform—to whose musket is affixed a saber bayonet—is Lieutenant Francis C. Barlow. Barlow was left for dead on the field at Gettysburg but survived dreadful wounds and eventually rose to become a major general. Known as the "boy general," Barlow later served as the model for Winslow Homer's famous painting* Prisoners From the Front. *A variation of this image appears in Francis T. Miller's* Photographic History of the Civil War *(Volume VIII, p. 89).*

Courtesy New York State Division of Military & Naval Affairs

Invoice of ORDNANCE AND ORDNANCE STORES *issued by* BENJAMIN WELCH, JR., *Commissary General of the State of New-York, to the* 134th *Regiment New-York State Volunteers.*

1862

Geo. E. Danforth Col. Com'g

Aug. 13	50	Altered Muskets.
	3	Arm Chests
Sept 28	825	Vincennes Rifles. Cal 69.
	825	Cartridge Boxes and Plates.
	825	Cartridge Box Belts and Plates.
	825	Privates Waist Belts and Plates.
	825	Cap Pouches and Picks
	825	Gun Slings
	825	Frogs for Sword Bay't Scabbards
	825	Sword Bayonet Scabbards
	15,000	Exp'dg Ball Cartridges. Cal. 69.
	20,000	Percussion Caps.
	300	Cones Spare.
	120	Cone Wrenches and Screw Drivers
	46	Arm Chests.
	15	Cases for packing Ammunition
	20	" " " Equipments.

Ordnance Invoice

As the 134th New York Volunteers prepared to leave for active campaigning in the fall of 1862, the state's commissary general, Benjamin Welch, Jr., issued the regiment its arms. This invoice reveals that instead of receiving model 1861 Springfield rifle-muskets, the standard Civil War infantry arm, the regiment was issued 50 altered muskets, 825 .69 caliber "Vincennes Rifles," and 15,000 rounds of "Exp'dg Ball Cartridges," of the same caliber. Although not as effective from long distances, this ammunition could prove extremely lethal at close ranges, a common result during Civil War battles.

Series A4105 Administrative Files [of the Commissary General's Office], 1861–1866.

Columbia University Press, 1935), VII:113–15; *Coll. Works*, V:433–36; *The New York Times*, January 8, July 6, 1863.

20. *New York Herald*, July 3–18, 1863; James McCague, *The Second Rebellion: The New York City Draft Riots of 1863* (New York: Dial, 1968), esp. 116 ff.; Adrian Cook, *The Armies of the Streets: The New York City Draft Riots of 1863* (Lexington, Ky.: The University Press of Kentucky, 1974).

21. Earnest A. McKay, *The Civil War in New York City* (Syracuse: Syracuse University Press, 1990), pp. 209, 212–15; Bernstein, *The New York City Draft Riots*, pp. 60–65.

22. Flick, *History of the State of New York*, VII:117.

23. J. G. Randall and Richard N. Current, *Lincoln the President: Last Full Measure* (New York: Dodd, Mead, 1955), p. 125; David E. Long, *The Jewel of Liberty* (Mechanicsburg, Pa.: Stackpole, 1994), pp. 180–82, 193–94, 115ff.; *Coll. Works*, VII:435–36, 459–601.

24. *The New York Times*, August 31, November 25–29, 1864; McKay, *The Civil War and New York City*, pp. 279–84, 287–89; *Tribune Almanac*, 1865, p. 48; William Frank Zornow, *Lincoln and the Party Divided* (Norman: University of Oklahoma Press, 1954), pp. 129–31; David Stanwood Alexander, *A Political History of the State of New York*, 4 vols. (Port Washington: Ira J. Friedman, 1969), IV:125.

25. Randall and Current, *Lincoln*, pp. 309–10, 313; *The New York Times*, February 4, 1865.

26. *New York Herald*, April 10, 15, 16–21, 1865.

27. Fox, *Regimental Losses in the American Civil War, 1861–1865*, p. 533; Flick, *History of the State of New York*, VII:165; Mark Mayo Boatner III, *The Civil War Dictionary* (New York: David McKay, 1959), pp. 891, 661, 46, 241–42, 882–83, 726–27, 449, 801, 765, 204–205, 747–48; *Dictionary of American Biography*, VIII:510.

28. Flick, *History of the State of New York*, VII:139ff., 205, 203.

Documenting New York's Role in the Civil War

Daniel Lorello

Overview

At the start of the Civil War in 1861, New York was the largest and wealthiest state in the nation. By the time the last guns were fired in 1865, New York had provided more soldiers, supplies, and money to the war effort than any other state. Throughout the war years New Yorkers paid more taxes than citizens of other states; they gave the most to charity and relief organizations (e.g., the United States Sanitary Commission); and they purchased the most war bonds. But the highest price for New York, as for the nation, was in human suffering and loss of life. Records show that as many as 53,114 men from New York State (soldiers, seamen, and marines) died while serving in the war. Of these, 14,227 were killed in action, 7,599 died of wounds received in action, and a colossal 31,288 died of disease and accidents while in service.[1]

Approximately 30 percent of the New Yorkers who served were foreign-born. These included 42,095 Irish, 41,179 Germans, 12,756 English, 11,525 British-Americans (mostly Canadians), 3,693 French, 3,333 Scots, 2,014 Welsh, 2,015 Swiss, and 2,350 of other nationalities. The foreign nativity of so many New York participants is reflected by the many "ethnic" units, such as the Irish Brigade, the Garibaldi Guard, and the Turner Rifles. New York also sent 4,125 African Americans to serve in the regiments of "United States Colored Troops," as well as an unknown number of Native Americans who served in various regiments and some special units.[2]

In terms of military organization, the state contributed:

15 regiments and 37 companies of artillery
27 regiments and 10 companies of cavalry
186 regiments of infantry*

*This figure is derived from Fox's *Regimental Losses in the American Civil War, 1861–1865*, pp. 476–81. However, researchers should also note that Phisterer's *New York in the War of the Rebellion* (Vol. 1, pp. 78–80) provides a figure of 248 regiments and 10 companies. The major reason for this discrepancy is the fact that Phisterer included in

8 companies of sharpshooters

3 regiments of engineers

New Yorkers also formed a significant segment of the Union military leadership. Twenty major generals and 98 brigadier generals came from the state. New Yorkers served with distinction at all military levels: over 15,000 were "mentioned in dispatches," that is, individuals and their actions were singled out by name in after-battle reports. The Medal of Honor, the nation's highest military award, was bestowed on 132 New York soldiers and seamen.[3]

A glance at New York's role in the pivotal battle of Gettysburg illustrates the importance of the state's contribution to the war. Of the 345 Union units that fought at the battle, 90 were from New York. Six of the 19 infantry divisions deployed in the battle were commanded by New Yorkers, while 21 of the 72 brigades that saw action were led by officers from the Empire State. Of the 23,000 Union casualties at Gettysburg, 6,800 (nearly one-third), by some estimates, were from New York.[4]

The Bureau of Military Statistics

Many of the Civil War-related records and artifacts presently residing in the custody of various New York State agencies—including the New York State Archives, the New York State Library, and the Division of Military and Naval Affairs—were collected and compiled by a little known agency created during the Civil War: the Bureau of Military of Statistics.

All but forgotten today except by a small number of curators and archivists responsible for maintaining its invaluable legacy, the Bureau of Military Statistics was one of the most important state agencies operating during the Civil War. Thanks to the foresight, dedication, and perseverance of its first chief, Lockwood Lyon Doty, modern researchers interested in New York State's role during the Civil War have a wealth of records and artifacts that they may consult to learn about the Empire State's contribution during this titanic struggle.

---

his figure those New York Militia units that were temporarily mustered into federal service for anywhere from 30 days to 100 days. Although most of these units were never formally incorporated into the federal army, they were nonetheless mustered into federal service and subsequently mustered out of federal service. Thus, a strong case could be made for citing either set of numbers over the other.

Although some of the information appearing below is summarized in the administrative history pertaining to the Bureau of Military Statistics, this brief history of the bureau explains why and how its records were created and what happened to them.[5]

Realizing the magnitude of his state's efforts and seeing that nothing was being done to document its contribution toward the prosecution of the war, Governor Edwin D. Morgan decided to rectify the situation. In December 1862, the lame-duck Morgan, through the state's adjutant general, Thomas Hillhouse, issued Special Orders No. 866, establishing a Bureau of Military Statistics, and appointed Lockwood L. Doty as the bureau's chief. Doty was to receive an annual salary of $2,000.[6]

The state legislature and newly elected Governor Horatio Seymour apparently agreed with Morgan's idea, because on April 8, 1863, the legislature passed and Seymour signed a bill appropriating $6,000 to the bureau. In addition, the statute required that Doty "collect and preserve an authentic sketch of every person from this state who has volunteered into the service of the general government since April 15, 1861 and likewise a record of the service of the several regiments, which shall include an account of their organization and subsequent history and generations, together with an account of the aid afforded by the several towns and counties of this State." Doty, however, had a much broader vision of what he expected the bureau to accomplish. After only eight months in his new office, he confidently explained in his first annual report that it was his intention to have the bureau collect not only what was mandated, but also "every fact relating to the rebellion, and especially to the part which New York has taken in the war, whether now recorded or printed, or still existing in memory. . . ." Doty proved as good as his word.[7]

Although Doty was interested in any aspect of New York State's participation in the war, his principal goal was to capture the experiences of the common soldier. To achieve this, Doty devised a one-page form that enabled him to collect an amazing amount of data on each individual. The form (printed on both sides) inquired not only about the soldier's (or seaman's) military history, but his civilian history as well. Questions were asked about the individual's date and place of enlistment; regiment, company (or ship) and rank; promotions or transfers; previous military history in the militia or U.S. Regular Army, Navy, or European military organizations; battles or skirmishes participated in during the Civil War;

descriptions of wounds received or illnesses contracted while in the service; date of discharge or death; date and place of birth; parents' names and nationalities; level of education; if married, wife's name and number of children; residence at date of enlistment; profession prior to enlistment; military experiences of relatives in either the Revolutionary War, War of 1812, or European wars; relatives presently in service, including regiment and rank; and if the individual was deceased and the form completed by an acquaintance, remarks concerning the individual's general character. Finally, and almost as an afterthought, Doty asked that, if possible, "a photographic or other likeness" be included with the form. According to his first annual report, which covered the period from April through December 1863, Doty distributed over 125,000 biographical forms to soldiers' relatives throughout the state and among New York regiments in the field. Unfortunately, Doty failed to comment upon how many forms had been returned for this period.[8]

In addition to amassing statistical and biographical data, Doty began actively to collect, mostly through donations, newspapers, sheet music, books, pamphlets, photographs, maps, biblical tracts, military reports, federal and state published reports, scrapbooks, and recruiting posters. Doty also began to collect artifacts. In 1863 alone, Doty managed to procure over fifty regimental flags carried by New York State units. In addition, military items such as rifles, muskets, bayonets, swords, carbines, ammunition, knives, and uniforms were acquired. Many of these items were captured from Southerners or picked up on battlefields and forwarded to Doty from soldiers serving with New York State units. As a result, the bureau began to take on the appearance of a museum.[9]

Some of Doty's more spectacular acquisitions included the gun that killed Colonel Ephraim Elmer Ellsworth, which was donated by Lieutenant Frank Brownell, the man who shot and killed Ellsworth's slayer; and a collection of Parrott shells which was donated by Robert Parrott himself. Doty was pleased with the bureau's accomplishments and he hoped that the "objects and plan of the Bureau will commend themselves to the continued favor of the Legislature."[10]

The state legislature recognized the value of Doty's work by more than doubling the bureau's annual budget for 1864 (to $16,300). In addition, the legislature repealed the original enabling statute and separated the bureau from the Adjutant General's Office. The law also mandated the bureau to procure a seal and empowered it to issue copies of any record in its possession. Apart from these administrative changes, the bureau's duties remained the same as prescribed in the 1863 statute.[11]

Throughout 1864, Doty displayed his customary relentlessness in striving to achieve the bureau's goals. Although over two-fifths of the state's towns and counties were visited by agents of the bureau, Doty found these visits too costly and time-consuming. Seeking a means by which to increase the bureau's information-gathering capacity, he requested the state legislature to require local officials to supply him with the information he needed to document their ongoing contribution to the state's effort.[12]

Once again the state legislature agreed with Doty, for in May 1865 it significantly increased the bureau's functions. The bureau's name was changed to the Bureau of Military Record in order to more accurately reflect the fact that the bureau was not exclusively a statistics-gathering mechanism. The legislature also required that, along with the records described in earlier statutes, various local officials were to file specific records with the Bureau of Military Record. As a result of these increased powers and duties, Doty was able to acquire systematically even more information about New York's experiences during the war.[13]

By the end of 1865, the collections of the Bureau of Military Record had become so extensive that Doty actively lobbied for a separate facility in which to store the 750 battle flags, thousands of artifacts, newspapers, scrapbooks, individual soldiers' histories, photographs, local government accounts, and other records he had amassed in less than three years. At the same time, however, Doty found himself involved in a bureaucratic dogfight with the state's adjutant general, William Irvine, the outcome of which would determine the future of the bureau. Irvine, in his annual report for 1865 to Governor Reuben Fenton, argued that under federal law the Adjutant General's Office was the only office authorized to maintain official military records and the state legislature could not alter this fact. Irvine opined that without federal approval all state legislation conferring record-keeping responsibilities upon the Bureau of Military Record was unconstitutional. According to Irvine, the bureau "can not have . . . custody of a single official roster, muster roll, enlistment paper or other document which belongs to the official military records of this State."[14]

Doty replied that he "in nowise" was seeking "to interfere or embarrass any other department. . . ." Rather, the bureau was simply carrying out its duties prescribed by statute and "its own obligations to fulfill the declared will of the people in relation to those records and memories of the war. . . ."[15]

The state legislature and Governor Fenton apparently agreed with Irvine; a new law was passed in April 1866 that redesignated the Bureau of Military Record as the Bureau of Military Statistics and organized it as an "additional Military Staff Department." The statute also reduced the bureau's budget from $23,000 to just $9,500. Seeing the handwriting on the wall, Doty tendered his resignation, which Governor Fenton reluctantly accepted. In Doty's stead, Colonel A. J. H. Duganne was appointed.[16]

Colonel Duganne strove to maintain the high standards that characterized the bureau under Doty's leadership. Initially, Duganne was successful; his annual reports for the years 1866 and 1867 indicate that the bureau was still actively seeking and acquiring the same types of material elicited by Doty. However, this abruptly changed in 1868 when the state legislature enacted a statute that specifically ordered the Bureau of Military Statistics to be "transferred and constituted a bureau in the department of the Adjutant General."[17]

For the next eighteen years the bureau's duties consisted mainly of displaying the various Civil War flags, artifacts, and books it had acquired. The bureau continued for a few years to collect photographs and individual histories of soldiers who had fought in the war, but on a much smaller scale. Basically, the bureau had been transformed from a vibrant information-collecting agency into a moribund museum relegated to counting the number of its visitors each year. Finally, the state legislature abolished the bureau in 1887, when it required the adjutant general "to establish as part of his office a bureau of the records of the war of the rebellion, in which all records in his office relating to said war, and the records and relics of the bureau of military statistics shall be united and kept."[18]

Although the state legislature ordered the adjutant general to unite and keep the bureau's "records and relics" with the records maintained in his office, the mandate was not fulfilled. Today, very little remains of the extensive collection that Doty labored so intensively to amass in order to document the state's participation in the country's most important experience up to that time. The bulk of what remains of the collection is administered by the New York State Division of Military and Naval Affairs.

Most of the regimental flags that were deposited with the Bureau of Military Statistics do still exist. Many of them are on display (furled in glass cases) in the State Capitol in Albany, while others are stored separately in another facility that is largely inaccessible to the public. The flags, however, are in dire need of conservation and preservation treatment in order to prevent further deterioration.

The rest of the vast collection of military artifacts that Doty managed to obtain was scattered throughout the state over the years. The bulk of what is left of the collection is also administered by the Division of Military and Naval Affairs. Other parts of the collection are stored in National Guard armories across the state.

According to the bureau's annual reports, Doty and his successor, Duganne, collected more than 10,000 photographic images. Most of these were small *cartes-de-visite*, popular during the war years. However, the annual reports also indicate that the bureau acquired tintypes, ambrotypes, daguerreotypes, and larger albumen prints, including imperial-sized images. Today, the Division of Military and Naval Affairs retains custody of only about 2,500 of the *cartes* and a much smaller number of the rarer types of images.

Tragic as the loss of these approximately 7,500 images is, it almost pales in comparison with the virtually total loss of the questionnaires described earlier. Although a precise figure of how many questionnaires the bureau acquired cannot be determined, its annual reports suggest a number of at least 25,000. Today, literally only a handful of these questionnaires survive.[19]

Not all of Doty's collections became the victims of neglect. The New York State Archives contains almost a complete set of registers compiled by the state's town clerks, providing the names of soldiers and seamen comprising each town's quota of troops during the war. The State Archives also contains the accounts submitted by local officials describing their war-related financial transactions, such as the issuance of bounty bonds during the war. In addition, the Manuscripts and Special Collections Unit of the New York State Library contains many of the broadsides, handbills, posters, and other printed matter and ephemera collected by Doty. Finally, the Division of Military and Naval Affairs holds a sizeable number of military artifacts that were donated to the bureau for safekeeping by soldiers returning home from the war.

The story of the Bureau of Military Statistics is somewhat ironic. New

York State had the foresight to create the bureau and place such a man as Doty at its head. But it also eventually allowed Doty's legacy to disappear, bit by bit, artifact by artifact, photograph by photograph, until just a fraction of its original holdings remains today.

The Guide and How to Use It

This guide provides an overview of the organization of New York's military forces during the Civil War and identifies record series useful for genealogical research (see Appendix A). It also contains brief administrative histories of the major offices and agencies responsible for organizing and administering the state's military efforts during the war, and of other agencies that produced Civil War-related records as a result of various mandated functions. The bulk of the guide consists of narrative descriptions of the records series pertaining to the Civil War held by the State Archives. Finally, the guide contains several appendices and a bibliography identifying significant published sources relating to New York State in the Civil War. These appendices are intended to help researchers use this guide more efficiently (see, for example, Appendices C and D) as well as to facilitate research on specific individuals and units and on the state's military organization. The detail of descriptive information for each record series varies, based on the level of arrangement and description accomplished. This guide should therefore be considered a first attempt to gather these sources until full descriptive work can be completed for all series. When available, information on the arrangement of records, existence of indices or other finding aids, and availability of microfilm is also provided. For some series, more extensive descriptions and container lists are available at the State Archives.

Prior to the Civil War, primary responsibility for military organization and the supply of men and matériel resided with the individual states. This meant that the federal government was compelled to call on state militias to wage war. The result, for reasons ranging from politics to philosophy to pusillanimity, was that some states did nothing, some made only token efforts, and others bore almost the entire initial brunt of the war effort. This system changed radically during the Civil War.[20]

As war became imminent, traditional systems of state mobilization began to operate. Early battles were fought by troops brought to the battlefield through that traditional system. But beginning in 1862 and culminating in the late summer and fall of 1863, all war-making activities, from recruiting to supply, were assumed by the federal government. Thus, the records of New York State's involvement in the Civil War begin to "thin out" in both quality and quantity as the war progresses. In many respects, the Civil War was the last military conflict in which records generated by state governments comprised such a significant source of primary material for understanding the organization of the military effort.

Most of the records listed in this guide were originally created by the State's Adjutant General's Office and transferred to the State Archives from the Division of Military and Naval Affairs, which was established in 1926 in a constitutional reorganization of New York State government. The division assumed responsibility for all of the records, including those pertaining to the Civil War, created by and filed with the Adjutant General's Office up to that time.

The guide is organized into sections reflecting the organization of the Adjutant General's Office as it operated during the Civil War, its subsequent reorganization after the war, and other New York State agencies responsible for creating Civil War-related records.[21] Although the guide is organized according to the various "creating agencies," researchers should be aware that interrelationships among many record series cross agency lines. Consequently, functionally related series might be located under several different creating agencies.

Understanding the historical context and organizational terminology (which may vary significantly from contemporary understanding) that apply to the Civil War records in the New York State Archives can make research in them more meaningful and fruitful. The organization of the state's military departments during the Civil War is explained in the administrative histories preceding each section of the guide. Within these histories and the descriptions of the record series certain military organizational terms appear regularly. A soldier's placement in the military system is one of assignment to a pyramidal organizational structure beginning with the "squad" and expanding to an army. In order of ascending size these units are: squad, company, regiment, brigade, division, corps, and army. Definitions of these terms as they apply to the Civil War are set forth below.[22]

- Squad: Comprised of 15 to 20 men and commanded by a sergeant or corporal. The individual soldier's squad is almost never indicated in military service records.
- Company: Comprised of 50 to 100 men (or four squads) and commanded by a captain. Normally, ten companies comprised a regiment. However, cavalry and artillery regiments frequently contained more than ten companies. A company is designated by a letter (usually A through M, omitting the letter J) and is generally listed in a soldier's military service record (e.g., Co. B, 79th New York Volunteers).
- Regiment: Comprised generally of 1,000 men and officers (ten companies). A regiment was designated by a number (e.g., 95th New York Volunteers) and was commanded by a colonel. During the Civil War a regiment was normally composed of men from the same geographic area. Consequently, a soldier's strongest sense of affection and attachment was for his regiment. Cavalry and artillery regiments were generally larger than infantry regiments and typically consisted of twelve companies. It is significant that because of absences due to other assignments, death, desertion, or illness, the average Union regiment normally went into battle at about 50 percent of its authorized strength. By mid-point in the war, many regiments were no larger than companies. Grossly under-strength regiments were primarily the result of another peculiar aspect of Civil War military organizational procedures. As attrition occurred within the regiment, there were very few replacements with new recruits. Normal procedure was to let a regiment serve until either all enlistments expired or the regiment totally lost its ability to function as a fighting body due to casualties, whereupon it was disbanded or "mustered out" or occasionally incorporated into other regiments. In other words, new recruits were formed into new regiments rather than fed into existing regiments as replacements. There were exceptions to this procedure, as in the case of a few regiments that were designated as "veteran" regiments.[23]
- Brigade: Normally comprised of between four to six regiments in the infantry and cavalry, the brigade was usually commanded by a brigadier general. The brigade was the basic tactical unit on

the Civil War battlefield. A few renowned brigades enjoyed the prestige and loyalty typically reserved by men for their regiment. On the Union side, two of the most famous were the "Iron Brigade," composed of men primarily from Michigan, Indiana, and Minnesota, and the predominantly New York "Irish Brigade."

- Division: Comprised normally of three brigades or about 12,000 men, a division was commanded by either a brigadier or a major general. Drawn up in a line of battle, an infantry division covered about one mile of front.

- Corps: Comprised of two or more divisions, or in the case of cavalry, all units of that arm, serving in the same army. The term "corps" is derived from the French phrase *corps d'armée*. The corps was usually commanded by a major general. Union army corps were designated by roman numerals (e.g., II Corps or III Corps).

- Army: Comprised of three or more corps, the army was the largest operational military organization in a geographic area or "department." On the Union side, armies were designated by the names of rivers, such as the "Army of the Potomac" and the "Army of the Cumberland." Armies were normally commanded by a major general.

The original records described in this guide are available to researchers at the State Archives' research facility in the Cultural Education Center located in Albany. Researchers may also find information on these and other records in the collection electronically, through "Excelsior," the Archives' online catalog, which is constantly updated. The catalog supports searches by author, title, or subject keyword or by series number as given in this guide. Access to Excelsior can be gained through the Internet via the New York State Archives and Records Administration World-Wide Web site (www.sara.nysed.gov).

The State Archives, part of the Office of Cultural Education in the State Education Department, is mandated to identify, acquire, preserve, and make available for research state government records of enduring value. Since the opening of the State Archives' storage and research facility in 1978, approximately 65,000 cubic feet of records have been transferred to the Archives from all branches of state government, and additional records are continuously acquired. Further information about the content of or access to the Civil War-related records or other State Archives holdings is available from:

New York State Archives

Cultural Education Center, Room 11D40

Albany, NY 12230

Telephone: (518) 474–8955

Email: archref@mail.nysed.gov

NOTES

1. Frederick Phisterer, *New York in the War of the Rebellion* 6 vols. 3rd ed. (Albany: J. B. Lyon, 1912), 1:285.

2. Phisterer, *New York in the War of the Rebellion*, 1:70, 305. See also Laurence M. Hauptman, *The Iroquois in the Civil War: From Battlefield to Reservation* (Syracuse: Syracuse University Press, 1993), pp. 3–5.

3. Phisterer, *New York in the War of the Rebellion*, p. 78; Daniel E. Sickles, "Military Affairs in New York: 1861–65," in *The Union Army: A History of Military Affairs in the Loyal States 1861–1865—Records of the Regiments in the Union Army—Cyclopedia of Battles—Memories of Comrades and Soldiers*. 8 vols. (Madison, Wis.: Federal Publishing Co., 1908), 2:44.

4. The figure concerning the total number of Union and New York State units at the battle of Gettysburg was obtained from Edmund J. Raus, Jr., *A Generation on the March: The Union Army at Gettysburg* (Gettysburg, Pa.: Thomas Publications, 1996), pp. 1, 60–97. The figures concerning the number of divisions and brigades and New Yorkers who commanded them were obtained from Edwin B. Coddington, *The Gettysburg Campaign: A Study in Command* (New York: Charles Scribner's Sons, 1968), pp. 575–87; Ezra J. Warner, *Generals in Blue: Lives of Union Commanders* (Baton Rouge, La.: Louisiana State University Press, 1964); Roger D. Hunt and Jack R. Brown, *Brevet Brigadier Generals in Blue* (Gaithersburg, Md.: Olde Soldiers Books, 1990); and George W. Cullum, *Biographical Register of the Officers and Graduates of the U.S. Military Academy, From 1802 to 1867*. 3 vols. (New York: James Miller, 1879). The figure regarding the number of New Yorkers who died at Gettysburg is from Phisterer, *New York in the War of the Rebellion*, 1:199–201.

5. For those interested in more detail concerning the bureau's accomplishments, trials, tribulations, and eventual demise (and consequences for future generations), the reader is strongly recommended to refer to the various reference notes cited within.

6. Special Order No. 866 dated December 20, 1862. Series 14405 Special Orders, 1855–1975. New York State Archives.

7. New York State Legislature, *Laws of the State of New York*, 86th sess., chapter 113 (April 8, 1863) (Albany: Weed, Parsons, 1863), pp. 171–72; *First Annual Report of the Chief of the Bureau of Military Statistics* (Albany: Comstock & Cassidy, 1864), p. 4.

8. Ibid., pp. 6, 21.

9. Ibid., p. 12. Pages 181–212 of this report contain an itemized description of every item donated to the bureau through 1863.

10. Ibid., pp. 13, 14, 18.

11. New York State Legislature, *Laws of the State of New York*, 87th sess., chapter 51 (March 21, 1864) (Albany: Banks & Brothers, 1864), pp. 80–82.

12. *Second Annual Report of the Chief of the Bureau of Military Statistics of the State of New York* (Albany: C. Wendell, 1865), p. 6.

13. New York State Legislature, *Laws of the State of New York*, 88th sess., chapter 690 (May 11, 1865) (Albany: Van Benthuysen's Steam Printing House, 1865), pp. 1399–1406.

14. *Third Annual Report of the Bureau of Military Record of the State of New York* (Albany: C. Wendell, 1866), pp. 12, 14; *Annual Report of the Adjutant General of the State of New York* 2 vols. (Albany: C. Wendell, 1866), 1:21.

15. *Third Annual Report of the Bureau of Military Record of the State of New York*, p. 5.

16. New York State Legislature, *Laws of the State of New York*, 91st sess., chapter 665 (April 18, 1866) 2 vols. (Albany: Lewis & Goodwin, 1866), 2:1603; Lockwood L. Doty, *A History of Livingston County, New York: From its Earliest Traditions to its Part in the War for Our Union: With an Account of the Seneca Nations of Indians, and Biographical Sketches of Earliest Settlers and Prominent Public Men* (Geneseo: Edward E. Doty, 1876), p. xviii.

17. See generally *Fourth Annual Report of the Bureau of Military Statistics* (Albany: C. Van Benthuysen & Sons, 1867) and *Fifth Annual Report of the Chief of the Bureau of Military Statistics with Appendices* (Albany: C. Van Benthuysen & Sons, 1868). Also, New York State Legislature, *Laws of the State of New York*, 91st sess., chapter 717 (May 8, 1868), 2 vols. (Albany: Van Benthuysen's Steam Printing House, 1868), p. 1603.

18. New York State Legislature, *Laws of the State of New York*, 110th sess., chapter 247 (April 30, 1887) (Albany: Banks & Brothers, 1887), pp. 310–11. This legislation established the Bureau of Records of the War of the Rebellion and it was this bureau that was responsible for the compilation of series 13775, Civil War Muster Roll Abstracts of New York State Volunteers, United States Sharpshooters, and United States Colored Troops (see description on pp. 65–66).

19. The New York State Archives and the Manuscripts and Special Collections Unit of the New York State Library hold a few of these questionnaires. In addition, individual questionnaires periodically appear on the manuscript market for sale. However, it is believed that the vast majority of the questionnaires were destroyed, along with other valuable Civil War-related records maintained by the Adjutant General's Office, during the well-known paper drives held during World War II.

20. For an excellent discussion of the militia system and its relationship to the federal government see John K. Mahon, *History of the Militia and the National Guard* (New York: Macmillan, 1983). For an account of the New York State Militia before the Civil War, see Gustav Person, "The Role of the New York State Militia in the Civil War" (unpublished M.A. thesis, Queens College of the City University of New York, 1992), pp. 1–69.

21. It should be noted that administrative histories are provided only for those offices for which the New York State Archives holds records and which are described in this guide. For example, the Office of the Engineer-in-Chief, which was an administrative component of the state's military bureaucracy prior to and during the Civil War, is not described because the State Archives holds no records pertaining to this office. However, most of the state's military administrative bodies are represented in this guide.

22. Much of this information is taken from Patricia L. Faust, ed., *Historical Times Illustrated Encyclopedia of the Civil War* (New York: Harper & Row, 1986). Additional information on Civil War units and ninteenth-century military terminology is also contained in Mark Boatner, *The Civil War Dictionary* (New York: David McKay, 1959) and Phillip Katcher, *The Civil War Source Book* (New York: Facts on File, 1992).

23. An example of this is the case of the 7th New York Volunteers and the 7th New York Veteran Volunteers. The latter designation came about when the original 7th's enlistments expired and the surviving members re-enlisted and were augmented by new recruits, to bring the regiment to strength. The regiment then returned to war as the 7th Veteran Infantry. See Phisterer, *New York in the War of the Rebellion*, 2:1788, 1805−1806.

Administrative Histories and
Record Series Descriptions

New York State Adjutant General's Office

By an act of Congress passed May 8, 1792, entitled "An act more effectively to provide for the national defense by establishing a uniform militia throughout the United States," each state was required to appoint an adjutant general. New York State, however, had made provisions for such an office since its organization as a state, and on April 13, 1786, the Council of Appointment named Nicholas Fish as the state's first adjutant general. Prior to 1786 no formal appointment had been made to the position. The governor, who was also the commander in chief of the militia, acted as the adjutant general.[1]

The legislature re-enacted and put into force the federal statute of 1792 with the passage of Chapter 45 of the Laws of 1793. For years afterward, all subsequent state militia legislation was based upon the 1792 federal act. Two amendatory acts, passed by Congress on March 2, 1803, and May 12, 1820, further defined the duties and functions of the Adjutant General's Office.[2]

By 1858 federal and state legislation required the adjutant general to distribute all orders of the commander in chief to the militia; obey all orders relative to executing and perfecting military discipline as stipulated by law; furnish blank forms of different returns that might be required and to explain the principles on which they should be made; receive and preserve, from the officers of the different corps throughout the state, returns reporting the actual condition of arms "and everything which relates to the advancement of good order and discipline"; compile abstracts from the returns and present them annually to the commander in chief; and to compile and file an annual return, complete with descriptions of arms and accoutrements, to the president of the United States.

On an everyday basis, the duties of the Adjutant General's Office consisted of publishing orders in writing; compiling and transmitting written instructions; receiving and filing reports and returns; compiling tables showing the condition and composition of the state's militia; regulating details of service; corresponding with the heads of administrative departments, such as the quartermaster general or commissary general, relative to the needs of troops; and corresponding with the corps, detachments, or individual officers of the militia.[3]

Up to the outbreak of the Civil War on April 14, 1861, the Adjutant General's Office, for the most part, concerned itself with the duties outlined above. However, with the issuance of President Lincoln's proclamation on April 15, 1861, calling for 75,000 men, new duties devolved upon the office. Under Lincoln's first call, New York State was assigned a quota of seventeen regiments to consist of not less than 13,280 men. By the end of the war, the state furnished over 448,000 troops, more than any other state in the Union, to the federal government.[4]

As the principal liaison between the state's Executive Department and the federal government, specifically the U.S. War Department, the adjutant general was responsible for establishing procedures governing the recruiting, organizing, quartering, provisioning, uniforming, transporting, and, for a short period, paying of troops raised by the state. As the war progressed, the adjutant general became involved with the enrolling and drafting of men as well as the paying of bounty monies.

The Adjutant General's Office also established institutions to provide for sick and wounded troops in the field as well as for men en route to or from their homes. In short, during the Civil War the Adjutant General's Office was the scene of intense activity, as evidenced by the thousands of documents generated and filed by the office. Although there are a significant number of records series which are known to have been generated and filed with the Adjutant General's Office but which are not now extant, the State Archives contains many series that document the activities of the office during the Civil War.

In addition to his regular duties, during the war the adjutant general was a member of the Board of Managers of the New York State Soldiers' Depot.[5]

B0462 Correspondence and Petitions, 1821–1896. 61.5 c.f.

Arrangement: Chronologically by year and therein numerically by a number assigned by the Adjutant General's Office. This is essentially a chronological arrangement by date of receipt.

These files consist of correspondence, memoranda, petitions, orders, and letters of transmittal. Most of the records were generated by New York State military personnel, but there is a significant amount of material from private citizens; federal officials; adjutant generals from other states; New York State senators and assemblymen; representatives of firms manufacturing military arms, equipment, and accoutrements; and various state officials. Much of the material is of a routine, administrative nature but there is a significant number of items of noteworthy historical interest. Subjects include the New York City Draft Riots, payment of bounties, courts martial, regimental strengths, reports concerning past activities of regiments, promotions, and transfers.

Finding aids: Container listing available.

Indexes: See description for Series 13722 below.

13722 Register of Letters Received, 1862–1866. 14 volumes.

Arrangement: Chronologically by year.

These volumes serve as the name index to a portion of the correspondence and petitions files described above. For each letter received the register provides: date of receipt; sender's name; file number assigned; addressee's name, place and date of writing; disposition; and a one line summary of the contents. Each register contains its own alphabetical index to names of senders and persons mentioned in the summaries of each letter's contents.

Finding aids: Volume listing.

14403 General Orders, 1802–1975. 83 volumes.

Arrangement: Chronologically by year and therein numerically by order number.

The orders concerning the Civil War are contained in a single volume. On the whole, the general orders pertain to the overall administration and organization of the state's militia and volunteer forces raised during the war. Specific subjects include the appointment of officers to the state's military department; the raising, organizing, and equipping of volunteer regiments; promotions, appointments, and resignations of officers in volunteer regiments; procedures for implementing the draft; and the establishment and payment of bounties.

Finding aids: Volume listing.

Indexes: Most (but not all) volumes contain alphabetical name and subject indexes.

14405 Special Orders, 1855–1975.

343 volumes.

Arrangement: Chronologically by year and therein by order number.

These orders were issued by the adjutant general and commanding officers of specific military units. The orders pertaining to the Civil War deal with numerous topics, including the re-assignment of regiments to brigades and divisions; formation and assignment of companies to regiments; revocation of previously issued orders; promotions and demotions; issuance of arms, uniforms, equipment, and accoutrements to units and training institutions; courts martial and appeals; details for special occasions (e.g., the arrival of Lincoln's funeral train or the capture of Richmond); areas from which volunteer regiments were recruited; troop inspections; discharges; training exercises; transfer of personnel; issuance of regulations; and grants or suspensions of leaves of absence.

Contained within the series is a subseries of sixteen volumes of orders produced during the Civil War. The New York State Adjutant General's Office issued these orders to implement various general orders promulgated by the United States War Department. The War Department general orders deal mainly with the recruitment and enrollment of men into the U.S. Volunteer Army and were issued in response to President Lincoln's first and second calls for volunteers. Other general orders pertain to the authorization of qualified individuals to enroll new volunteers and to the enrollment of volunteers already in federal service. This set of special orders is arranged according to the U.S. general order to which they pertain and therein chronologically by year. The orders are then consecutively numbered within each year.

Finding aids: Volume listing.

Indexes: Each volume, including the subseries of sixteen volumes described above, contains an alphabetical name index.

13728 Abstracts of Military Commissions, 1823–1909. 15 volumes.

Arrangement: The entries in Volume Twelve are arranged by descending rank and therein alphabetically by first letter of last name. Those in Volume Thirteen are in chronological order by date of commission.

Volumes Twelve and Thirteen contain the abstracts of commissions issued to officers who served in New York State Militia regiments during the Civil War (the two volumes actually span from 1851 through 1875). They provide the officer's name; office; regiment, brigade or division number; residence; date of commission; and date of rank.

Finding aids: Volume listing.

13729 Organization Rosters of Military Officers, 1800–1899. 14 volumes.

Arrangement: Chronologically by date of commission.

Volumes Seven, Eight, Nine-A, and Nine-B contain the names of officers who served in New York State Militia regiments during the Civil War. In addition to name, the volumes provide rank, date of commission, date of rank, post office address, county of residence, in whose place appointed, and remarks concerning promotions and resignations. General staff officers are listed first, followed by brigade and regimental officers for infantry, cavalry, and artillery units. This series does not contain any data pertaining to officers who served in New York State Volunteer units mustered into federal service during the war.

Finding aids: Volume listing.

Indexes: Each volume contains an index to the

organizations, but there are no personal name indexes.

13727 Register of Supernumerary Officers, 1848–1883. 1 volume.

Arrangement: Alphabetically by last name and therein chronologically by date of discharge.

This volume is an alphabetical register of officers in the New York State Militia and National Guard who were retired or discharged. Each entry provides the name of officer; office held; regiment number; brigade, division, or corps; residence; date of certificate of discharge; and remarks.

B0463 Resignations of New York State Militia and National Guard Officers, 1811–1895. 5 c.f.

Arrangement: Alphabetically by last name of resigner and therein chronologically by date of acceptance.

These files are fairly routine and will typically provide the resigning officer's name, rank, unit to which presently attached, reason(s) for resignation, statement of unindebtedness, date, and signature. The disposition of the request is usually noted on either the bottom of the form or its reverse.

Finding aids: Container listing.

A4109 Militia Enrollment Returns Filed by County Boards of Supervisors, 1858. 0.5 c.f.

Arrangement: Alphabetically by name of county.

This series consists of printed forms submitted by the clerks of county boards of supervisors to the Adjutant General's Office detailing the number of men liable to perform military duty. County assessment rolls were used to produce returns, which contain name of town or number of ward, number of persons enrolled belonging to fire companies, number of persons liable to perform military duty not belonging to military or fire companies, total number enrolled, and remarks. Each return is signed and dated by the clerk of the board.

A4155 Registers Recording Enrollment of Persons Liable to Military Duty (1st Ward Buffalo, and Tonawanda), 1862. 2 volumes.

Arrangement: The names in the registers are grouped alphabetically.

These two volumes record the names, ages, and occupations of men liable to military duty who lived in Tonawanda and in Buffalo's First Ward. Although they may occasionally be found at the local level, the location of the bulk of the enrollment registers for the remainder of the state is unknown. In addition to the information listed above, the registers also denote those individuals who were exempt from the enrollment due to occupation, age, mental capacity, physical fitness, or current military status.[6]

Finding aids: Volume listing.

A4156 Statistical Register Pertaining to the 1864 Enrollment of Men Liable To Duty In the National Guard, 1864. 1 volume.

Arrangement: Alphabetically by county.

This volume contains the statistical results of the 1864 enrollment as mandated by Chapter 477 of the Laws of 1862. The 1864 enrollment pertains to men eligible for service in the state's National Guard, as opposed to the enrollment of 1862, which dealt with men eligible to be drafted into federal service (see below). Data provided include district number; and for each town, the total number of men enrolled, exempt, and liable to duty. These figures are totaled on a county-wide level.

B1382 Statistical Register of State Draft Quotas and Volunteers, 1862. 1 volume.

Arrangement: Entries are arranged alphabetically by county.

This series consists of statistical data compiled by the Adjutant General's Office in preparation for a draft contemplated by state authorities after President Lincoln's call on August 4, 1862, for 300,000 men to be mustered into federal service for nine months. The draft, however, was not carried out.[7] For each county, statistics are provided for population and "quota for 120,000," 5 percent, and total number of men to be furnished by the draft. In tabular form, the following statistics are provided for each town: population, "quota for 120,000," 5 percent, total, number of volunteers raised, surplus, and deficit.[8]

A4110 Rough Abstracts of Expenditures for Salaries and Ordnance, 1863–1866. 0.5 c.f.

Arrangement: Roughly chronological by year and therein by office.

This series consists of handwritten abstracts of expenditures which, for the most part, detail the names, grades, positions, and salaries of employees of the various offices of the state's Military Department. There are abstracts from the Offices of the Surgeon General, Inspector General, Commissary General, Judge Advocate General, Paymaster General, and Quartermaster General. Other abstracts provide information on ordnance distributed to various units, but they are few in number and differ greatly in content.

A4130 Duplicate Correspondence Directed to and Received from Military Officers, 1861–1866. 0.5 c.f.

This series consists almost entirely of duplicate correspondence and special orders dating between May and August 1861. There are also a few items dating from 1862 and one document dating from 1866. These are mainly copies of bills, vouchers, and ordnance inventories. As a whole, the correspondence deals almost exclusively with the organization and supply of volunteer units raised by the state in response to President Lincoln's call for men in 1861. To a lesser extent, the documents also deal with state militia units.

A4148 Telegrams Received and Sent, 1862. 2 volumes.

Arrangement: Chronologically by date.

These telegrams pertain mainly to the state's effort to raise and equip the volunteer forces mustered into federal service during the early years of the Civil War. Specific subjects include the appointment of officers, mustering in of regiments, assignment of companies to regiments, promotions, arrangement of transportation for regiments leaving the state, recruitment of new regiments, procurement of arms from the Commissary General's Office, mustering out of three-month regiments, and the payment of troops.

Finding aids: Volume listing.

Indexes: Volume One contains an alphabetical name index; Volume Two does not.

A4153 Registers Recording the Transmission of Documents to Militia Officers, 1858–1863. 2 volumes.

Arrangement: Chronologically by date of transmission.

These registers record the names of militia officers to whom various types of forms and other printed material were sent by the Adjutant General's Office. Each entry typically provides the name of the officer to whom the material was mailed; regiment, brigade, or division number; number of copies mailed; date; and type of record. Types of records sent include regulations, enlisting orders, adjutant general's reports, manuals of arms, inspection returns, laws pertaining to the militia, and certificates of membership.

Finding aids: Volume listing.

A4152 Roster of Officers of New York State Volunteer Regiments, 1861–1862.
1 volume.

Arrangement: Numerically by regiment number and therein alphabetically by company letter.

This volume contains the names of officers of the First through Thirteenth Regiments of New York State Volunteers. In addition to the officer's name, the date of his commission and previous rank are usually, but not always, recorded. Occasionally, a note states that an officer was killed in action, resigned, promoted, or wounded. Ranks recorded include not only colonel through second lieutenant, but also the regiment's surgeon, assistant surgeon, chaplain, adjutant, and quartermaster. The location of volumes dealing with other volunteer regiments is unknown.

A4160 Register of United States Colored Troops Who Filed Claims Against the Federal Government, 1866–1869. 1 volume.

Arrangement: Alphabetically by first letter of last name.

This volume records the names of United States Colored Troops who filed claims against the United States for back pay and bounties for service during the Civil War.[9] Data include claim number, name, rank, company, regiment, date of enlistment, date dis-

charged, and the date when the claim was filed. Some entries provide the authorization by which the claimant was discharged and a notation whether the claim was settled or rejected. If the claim was settled, the amount is usually stated.

13725 Descriptive Roll of the Howitzer Battery of the Eleventh Brigade, National Guard, 1864–1884. 1 volume.

Arrangement: Entries are arranged by rank and therein chronologically by year.

This volume contains a listing of officers and privates in the Howitzer Battery of the Eleventh Brigade, New York National Guard. The first part of the volume deals with commissioned and non-commissioned officers. Information provided includes name, date of election or appointment, and remarks on promotion, discharge, or other changes in status. Following this section is a listing of men transferred, discharged, or deceased. The remainder of the volume consists of an alphabetical register of privates. Each entry provides name; age at enlistment; when, where, and by whom enlisted; when, where, and by whom mustered; term of enlistment; birthplace; occupation; and remarks on change in status.

B0633 Descriptive Book of the 193rd New York Volunteer Infantry Regiment, 1865. 1 volume.

Arrangement: Alphabetically by company and therein alphabetically by last name of volunteer.

This volume provides physical descriptions and enlistment information on the majority of men who served in the 193rd New York Volunteer Infantry Regiment during the closing months of the Civil War. The first part of the volume contains a listing of the regiment's officers. Each entry provides name, rank, date of appointment, date mustered, and remarks (usually about change in status). The middle portion of the volume contains data on enlisted men. Information provided includes age; height; complexion; eye and hair color; place of birth; occupation; date, place, and by whom enlisted; term of enlistment; and remarks. The remarks usually refer to desertions, promotions, transfers, or discharges. The last section of the volume contains, somewhat curiously, a lengthy discourse on the qualifications and characteristics that generals should possess.

A0227 Regimental Records Pertaining to the First Regiment of Artillery, New York State Volunteers, 1863–1865. 2 volumes.

Arrangement: Chronologically by date of report.

These two volumes were apparently compiled by Sergeant David Cole, who was a member of Battery C of the First Regiment of New York Artillery. Volume One contains a list of all members of Battery C of the unit and a monthly attendance record of the company between 1864 and 1865. Volume Two consists of printed morning reports for Battery C dating between January 1863 through May 1865. The reports provide totals of men who were present for duty; on special, extra, and daily duty; sick; in arrest or confinement; horses serviceable or unserviceable; and details of absences (on detached service, with leave, without leave, sick, or retained by civil authorities); and alterations since last report (new enlistments, killed, discharged, wounded, etc.). Most of these categories are subdivided by rank. Each report is signed by the first sergeant and the company commander.

Finding aids: Volume listing.

A4166 Regimental Records Pertaining to the Twenty Second Regiment of New York State Volunteers, 1861–1865. 4 volumes.

Arrangement: The orders in volumes three and four are arranged chronologically.

These volumes contain descriptive lists, names and addresses of ex-members of the regiment, and general and special orders. The descriptive lists (contained in volume one) provide company, rank, name, age, height, complexion, eye and hair color, birthplace, occupation, date and place of enlistment, by whom enlisted, length of enlistment, and remarks. The remarks usually provide information on wounds received, transfers, discharges, deaths, promotions, muster-out dates, and resignations. A second list provides the name, rank, date of appointment, and changes in status of each of the regiment's commissioned officers. The second volume appears to be an address book of ex-members of the regiment and provides name, address, county, and state. Occasionally, references to deaths are recorded. The remaining two volumes consist of copies of general and special orders, instructions, and circulars concerning the regiment issued by brigade, division, and army commanders. The orders usually deal with routine administrative procedures such as the issuance of rations; resignations; promotions; details for courts martial, inspections, and picket duty; and furloughs.

Finding aids: Volume listing.

A4124 Correspondence Pertaining to Enrollment Procedures, 1864. 0.5 c.f.

This series consists mainly of incoming correspondence directed to Adjutant General John T. Sprague and Brigadier General Issac Vanderpoel. In addition to his duties as Engineer-in-Chief, Vanderpoel was also the Acting Assisting Adjutant General during 1864. The bulk of the correspondence deals with the enrollment of men into the state's National Guard. Specific subjects relate mostly to routine administrative matters such as requests for enrollment books by enrolling officers, appointments of enrolling officers, transmission of enrollment records and lists of enrolling officers for regimental districts, requests for certificates, and questions concerning enrollment procedures. A large part of this correspondence was at one time probably filed with the Correspondence and Petitions since the letters are recorded in the Register of Letters Received (see series B0462 and series 13722 respectively, both of which are described above). For some reason the letters were separated and filed as a distinct series by parties unknown.

A0087 Records of the 51st Regiment, New York State Volunteers, 1861–1864. 1.5 c.f.

Arrangement: By type of document and therein chronologically by date.

This series consists of correspondence, general and special orders, medical discharges, furloughs and leaves of absence, quarterly returns, requisitions for and inventories of military stores, receipts, invoices, muster rolls, and payrolls pertaining to the 51st New York State Volunteers. In addition, the series also contains one microfilm reel of correspondence dating from 1861 through 1864 from Captain Henry W. Francis to his wife.

Finding aid: Folder listing.

A0563 National Guard Records, 1861–1917. 20 c.f.

This series consists of a variety of records that appear to relate mainly to the 14th New York State Militia, the 23rd New York National Guard, and the 12th New York National Guard. Records contained in this series include correspondence, general and special orders, printed orders relating to the Army of the Potomac, payrolls, invoices, morning reports, muster rolls, transcripts and other records relating to courts martial, circulars, printed materials (e.g., manual of arms, invitations and programs relating to various celebratory events concerning the regiments, proceedings of meetings, etc.), descriptive books, letterpress books, scrapbooks containing newspaper articles and other memorabilia, treasurer's records, and photographs of various regimental events. The bulk of the records post-date the Civil War, but a significant portion, especially those pertaining to the 14th New York State Militia, document Civil War-related activities. These records were probably deposited with the Adjutant General's Office by the regimental historians sometime during the first quarter of the twentieth century.

Finding aid: Rough container listing.

A0172 Correspondence, Certificates of Appointment, and General and Special Orders, 1823–1864. 0.5 c.f.

This series consists of printed copies of general and special orders issued by the Adjutant General's Office between 1861 and 1862. The original manuscript orders are contained in series 14403, General Orders (1802–1975) and series 14405, Special Orders (1855–1975) described above. The series also contains a small quantity of certificates of enrollment issued to state militia officers in 1864 and a small quantity of correspondence of Adjutant General William Fuller dating between 1823 and 1824.

Restricted: Fragile condition due to burn damage.

A4123 Records Pertaining to Various Monuments and Dedication Ceremonies, 1893. 0.5 c.f.

Arrangement: By dedicatory event and therein chronologically.

This series consists of correspondence, reports, copies of financial statements, and other records concerning the celebration of New York Day at the Chicago World's Fair; the dedication of the Trenton, New Jersey Battle Monument at Van Cortlandt Park; and the dedication of the New York State Monument at Gettysburg. The bulk of the series deals with the latter event and consists mainly of materials prepared by A. J. Zabriskie, the Engineer and Secretary of the New York Monuments Commission.[10]

A4125 Records Pertaining to Resignations and Claims, 1861–1890. 0.5 c.f.

This series consists of a small quantity of resignations submitted by officers resigning their commissions, and forwarded to the Adjutant General's Office. The resignation will typically provide the name of the individual resigning and rank, regiment, date, and reason for resignation. The provenance of these resignations is unclear, but they may be alienated items from series B0463 Resignations of New York State Militia and National Guard Officers, 1811–1895. The remainder of the series consists of a varied collection of vouchers and receipts that pertain mainly to expenditures incurred by National Guard units after the Civil War.

A0107 Records of the Independent Corps, New York Light Infantry, 1862–1864. 0.5 c.f.

This series consists of a small quantity of correspondence, reports, rosters of commissioned officers, provision returns, special and general orders, reports, morning reports and related records concerning the Independent Corps, Light Infantry. The regiment, which was also known as the *Enfants Perdus*, or Lost Children, was initially mustered into federal service in 1862. The unit was disbanded in 1864 when the enlisted men were transferred to several regiments.

A0195 Records of the 2nd New York State Volunteers, 1856–1863. 0.5 c.f.

This series consists of descriptive lists, correspondence, extracts of courts martial, discharges, furloughs, special orders, general orders, receipts, invoices, quarterly returns of ordnance stores, and muster-out rolls. The bulk of these documents deal with Company B of the regiment. Contained within the series is one pre-war letter (1856) written from Joseph B. Hazen, who later served as a captain with Company B, to his father.

A0189 Quartermaster's Special Requisitions and Abstracts for Articles Received and Expended for the 77th Battalion, New York State Volunteers. 0.5 c.f.

Arrangement: Roughly chronological.

This series consists of imprints completed by the quartermaster for the 77th Battalion, New York State Volunteers from March through June 1865. The forms consist mainly of special requisitions listing materials which need to be replaced because of excessive use, damage, or loss; monthly abstracts detailing expended stores; and monthly abstracts listing items received.[11]

A3283 National Guard Regimental and Brigade Files of Brigadier General James Gibson, 1862–1871. 1 c.f.

This series consists of correspondence, special and general orders, morning reports, descriptive lists, and ordnance returns pertaining to commands held by Brigadier General James Gibson in the New York State National Guard. The bulk of the series post-dates the Civil War and concerns Gibson's command of the 12th Brigade of the Third Division. The series also contains a small amount of material concerning Gibson's command of the 30th New York State National Guard between 1862 and 1865. These records are of an administrative nature and pertain mostly to the appointment of officers and enrollment procedures.

A0154 Records of the 1st New York Light Artillery, 1862–1865. 1.5 c.f.

This series consists of correspondence; proceedings relating to courts-martial, descriptive lists, inspection reports, ordnance returns, muster rolls, morning reports, and general and special orders pertaining to the 1st New York Light Artillery. As a whole, the series pertains to the administration of the unit rather than its role in combat. Consequently, most of the records concern subjects such as battery inspections, the replacement of lost or unserviceable equipment, the appointment of officers, the granting or denial of leaves of absence, and various courts-martial on which the unit's officers served.

Inspector General's Office

Chapter 180 of the Laws of 1851 authorized the commander in chief of New York's militia (i.e., the governor) "to appoint an inspector general, with the rank of brigadier-general, whose duty it shall be to attend to the organization of the militia. . . ." The adjutant general specified further duties in General Order No. 368, which required the inspector general to "inform himself of the actual condition of the several corps . . . and render all proper aid in improving their organization, discipline and efficiency;" inspect every branch connected with the militia, including armories, arsenals, and all military property; and to report his proceedings to the commander in chief.[12]

The *General Regulations for the Military Forces of the State of New York*, published in 1858, specified the following additional duties of the Inspector General's Office: inspect, at least once every two years, each regimental district in the state; report to general headquarters on the improvement in discipline and tactical instruction of the uniformed forces; report to the commander in chief on missing, injured, unfit, or deficient property stored, or which should be stored at any armory, arsenal, or military storehouse; inspect, after the first of November each year, the tents and camp equipage belonging to the state; report on which general field officers commanded parades or encampments and what changes of officers occurred; report upon the qualifications of persons recommended to the commander in chief for appointment to military office, as well as applicants wishing to organize companies; receive reports from division and brigade inspectors describing the condition of their respective organizations; ascertain whether the troops were properly in-structed "in the exercises and evolutions of the field" by having them perform drills prescribed by regulations; and examine, at least once every two years, each regiment's Board of Auditors' proceedings along with the accounts filed with the boards' secretaries, to determine their accuracy.[13]

With the start of the Civil War, the Inspector General's Office was assigned extra duties. Special Order No. 317, dated July 30, 1861, required the inspector general to supervise and control "the expenditures of money at the military depots and for other incidental purposes connected with the organization" of the troops called by President Lincoln after the Union disaster at Bull Run earlier that month. As a result, the office became, to a considerable extent, "an office of accounts, audit and control, and reference and instruction." All money and property accounts were placed under the supervision of the inspector general until the disbursements were placed under the direct control of United States officers in September and October of 1861.[14]

In 1862, General Order No. 52 required the inspector general to establish rules and regulations governing regimental camps "as he shall think best calculated to promote discipline." These rules and regulations were put into effect with the issuance of General Order No. 59, and the inspector general was to enforce them through personal inspections "as often as may be required."[15]

In addition to inspecting regimental camps and the troops quartered therein, the inspector general was required to inspect each volunteer regiment upon its arrival in New York City en route to the seat of war, approve the requisitions of the unit's commanding officers for arms and accoutrements, and to inspect incomplete organizations preparatory to consolidation.

In January 1863, by order of the commander in chief, the Inspector General's Office began the compilation of an inventory to determine the amount and condition of military property in possession of and belonging to the state. During the fall of that year, a more detailed inspection was begun concerning the number and kind of arms, equipment, and military property of the state, including tents and camp equipage issued to or in possession of the respective regiments within each brigade and division district, as well as all property which ought to have been in such district, but which was missing, injured, unfit for use, or deficient in any respect. Inspections were also undertaken of every arsenal, armory, and military storehouse. These inspections resulted in a special report in which the inspector general recommended sweeping changes in the state's system of purchasing and distributing military property.[16]

On June 19, 1863, General Order No. 24 enacted the provisions contained in Chapter 477 of the Laws of 1862. This statute, commonly referred to as "the Militia Law of 1862," drastically changed the state's militia system. The law also enlarged the duties of the Inspector General's Office in relation to organizing and equipping the National Guard. Furthermore, several statutes and orders enacted and issued in 1862 and 1863 appointed the inspector general to various boards required to perform the following duties: audit all claims incurred in the organization, equipment, and subsistence of troops while in the service of the United States; receive proof and ascertain the sums due to regiments or members of the militia for clothing and equipment lost or destroyed while in the service of the United States (Chapter 421, Laws of 1862); examine

persons seeking authority from the state to recruit for the United States (Special Order No. 190, April 21, 1863); select and adopt a suitable uniform for the National Guard (General Order No. 18, May 4, 1863); and initiate and put into effect such measures as would "most effectively contribute to the relief and comfort of the soldiers of this State" (Special Order No. 151, March 31, 1863).[17]

For the remainder of the war, the Inspector General's Office basically concerned itself with the duties assigned it by the Militia Law, other statutes, and general and special orders previously described. With the end of the war in the spring of 1865 and the gradual return of the volunteer troops, the Inspector General's Office became increasingly involved with the settlement of claims submitted by soldiers for such things as back pay or bounty monies due, or clothing and equipment lost or destroyed while in the service of the United States. In addition, the inspector general played an active role during the transition period in which the New York State National Guard was transformed from an instrument to wage war to one that would maintain peace.

A4100 Administrative Correspondence Files, 1859–1875. 0.5 c.f.

Arrangement: Bulk arranged chronologically by year and therein alphabetically by first letter of last name.

This series consists mainly of incoming correspondence directed or forwarded to the Inspector General's Office. The bulk of the documents date between 1858 and 1862 and concern mainly routine administrative matters such as the construction and repair of state armories, inspection of troops at depots and recruiting stations, and review of various claims. The files also contain a number of replies to a circular issued by the inspector general in 1867 requesting county clerks and newspaper editors to submit the names and addresses of all general officers appointed from their county during the Civil War. The correspondence dating from 1875 consists of acknowledgments for receipt of general and special orders issued by the Adjutant General's Office. It is obvious these files are only a small part of this office's correspondence files, since there are many gaps. The location of additional records, however, is unknown.

Finding aids: Folder listing.

A4103 Copies of Correspondence Forwarded from the Governor's Office, 1861–1862. 0.5 c.f.

Arrangement: Chronologically by date of correspondence.

The correspondence in this series was originally directed to Governor Edwin D. Morgan, who most likely had copies of the letters forwarded to the inspector general in order to keep him informed of current events or because they pertained to matters requiring his attention. The correspondence dates between April 15, 1861, and March 1, 1862, and was originally filed among the Administrative Correspondence Files described above. A large portion of the series dates from April 1861, the first month of the Civil War, and concerns mainly the organization, supply, and disposition of state militia and volunteer units.

This correspondence reflects the urgency of the period through several letters expressing concern that Washington and Baltimore will be captured shortly by Confederate forces. The remainder of the series is somewhat more routine and administrative in nature. Subjects include the supply of ammunition to troops, courts martial, pardons, and the granting of commissions.

Finding aids: Folder listing.

A4133 Letter Book, 1863–1868. 1 volume.

Arrangement: Chronologically by date of correspondence.

This oversized volume contains mainly copies of outgoing correspondence generated by the Inspector General's Office. There are also copies of special and general orders, some incoming correspondence, and reports directed to or issued by the inspector general. Topics include the inspection of various armories, arsenals, and military storehouses; the inspection of military property issued to National Guard units; and the auditing of accounts. On the whole, this letter book pertains to matters relating to the New York National Guard, and not with volunteer units raised during the Civil War.

Indexes: Alphabetical name index at fore of volume.

Commissary General's Office

The Office of Commissary General dates from the Revolutionary War, when Congress appointed Peter Curtenius as the Commissary of Military Stores in New York on June 2, 1775. The first state appointee was Andrew Moodie, who was named to the position on April 13, 1784, by the Council of Appointment. Chapter 253 of the Laws of 1815 changed the name of the office from Commissary of Military Stores to Commissary General, and for the first time explicitly stated the duties of the commissary general. According to the statute, the commissary general "shall direct which of the arsenals shall be under the care of respective assistant commissaries" as well as compile and distribute to concerned parties "all needful rules and regulations for the collection and preservation of the military stores and munitions belonging to this state."[18]

The State Constitution of 1821 abolished the Council of Appointment and stipulated that the commissary general be nominated and appointed by the legislature. The commissary general's term of office was set at three years. The constitution made no other provisions for the office. However, Chapter 244 of the Laws of 1823 imposed the following additional duties on the commissary general: maintain in good repair the state's arsenals and magazines; preserve, clean, and repair the state's supply of ordnance, arms, accoutrements, ammunition, munitions, and "implements of every description"; sell at cost to any citizen belonging to the militia certain arms and accoutrements from the state's arsenals; dispose of all damaged military property deemed unsuitable for use; provide the governor with an account of all sales made by him; furnish, upon approval of the commander in

chief, colors, drums, fifes, and bugles to battalions requiring these articles; issue powder and balls to artillery companies for practice; transmit annually to the commander in chief "a true and particular statement, showing the actual situation and disposition of all the ordnance, arms, ammunition, and other munitions of war, property, and things, which in any wise appertain to . . . the department confided in his keeping"; and to deliver to the comptroller, at least semi-annually, an account of all expenses incurred.[19]

With the adoption of the state's third constitution in 1846, the governor, with the senate's consent, appointed the commissary general. In addition, the constitution reduced the term of office from three to two years. The constitution made no other changes and the duties of the commissary general remained essentially the same between 1823 through 1857. The *General Regulations for the Military Forces of the State of New York*, published in 1858, required the commissary general, in addition to the duties set forth in the state's Militia Law, to preserve, issue, and transport the arms, equipment, camp equipage, and ammunition from the state's arsenals and armories and make monthly reports of all issues to general headquarters; take receipts for all items issued; file statements of audited accounts with the commander in chief along with statements for the sale of old arms and equipment; recover possession of improperly issued arms and equipment; and maintain a roster of all militia officers down to company level, noting the quantity and kind of arms and equipment issued to each officer, date issued, and where stored.[20]

During the Civil War the commissary gen-

Confederate General Turner Ashby's Saber

Previously published photographs of this Model 1840 cavalry saber have identified it as the one that General Turner Ashby was carrying when he was killed during a skirmish outside Harrisonburg, Virginia, on June 16, 1862. The tip of the blade was supposedly broken off by the volley that killed the flamboyant cavalryman. Subsequent research, however, has revealed that it was in fact captured from then-Lt. Colonel Ashby during a skirmish with the 3rd New York Cavalry near Winchester on March 10, 1862. Shortly thereafter, the regiment's colonel, Simon H. Mix, placed the sword with the Bureau of Military Statistics. Colonel Mix was himself later mortally wounded before Petersburg.

Courtesy New York State Division of Military & Naval Affairs

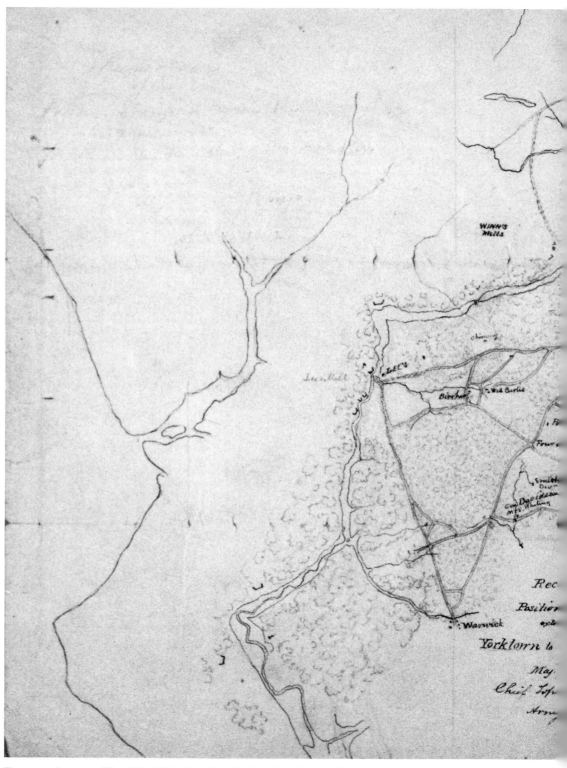

Reconnaissance Map Used During the Peninsular Campaign

As Major General George B. McClellan began his advance up the Yorktown Peninsula toward Richmond in early April 1862, he unexpectedly encountered a defensive position held by Confederate General John B. Magruder along the Warwick River. Prepared by Major Andrew A. Humphreys, who at this time was the Army of the Potomac's chief topographical engineer, this map depicts the

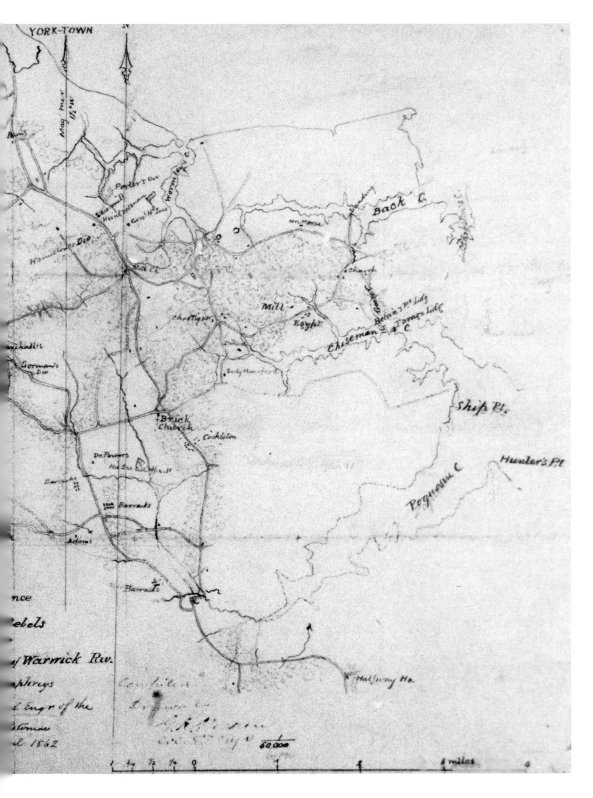

"Position of the Rebels" confronting McClellan from Yorktown to the mouth of the Warwick River. Humphreys eventually rose to become a major general and assumed command of the Army of the Potomac's Second Corps in November 1864.

Courtesy Manuscripts and Special Collections Unit, New York State Library

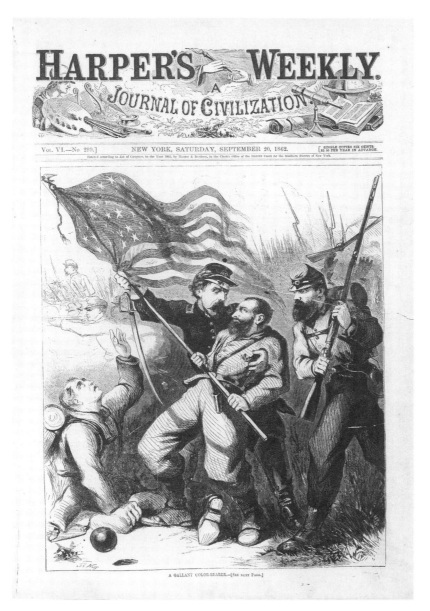

HARPER'S WEEKLY.

JOURNAL OF CIVILIZATION.

Vol. VI.—No 299.] NEW YORK, SATURDAY, SEPTEMBER 20, 1862. [SINGLE COPIES SIX CENTS. $2.50 PER YEAR IN ADVANCE.

Entered according to Act of Congress, in the Year 1862, by Harper & Brothers, in the Clerk's Office of the District Court for the Southern District of New York.

A GALLANT COLOR-BEARER.—[SEE NEXT PAGE.]

"A Gallant Color Bearer"

This wood engraving, which adorned the cover of the popular newspaper Harper's Weekly *on September 20, 1862, supposedly depicts the wounding of Color Sergeant H. Alexander of the 10th New York Volunteers. As the accompanying article recounts, despite receiving three terrible wounds at "a recent engagement," Alexander ". . . clung to his colors with a tenacious grasp." Later, "while being taken to the hospital he became insensible . . . an attempt was made to take the flag away, but his unconscious hand held it more powerfully; even then his ruling passion was strong." In fact, the soldier depicted here is Sergeant* Albion *Alexander, who was wounded at the Second Battle of Bull Run on August 30, 1862. This Alexander was discharged from the service on January 17, 1863, because of the wounds he received at this engagement. The engraving was based on an on-the-scene sketch by* Harper's *special artist Thomas Nast.*

Courtesy Manuscripts and Special Collections Unit, New York State Library

SOLDIERS' AID SOCIETY!

Any one having YARN to donate to the Society to be knit into Soldiers' Socks, is requested to leave it at the basement of the Presbyterian Church any Thursday afternoon, and at the residence of Mrs. **J. R. PARKER** on other days.

All having pieces of thick **WOOLEN CLOTH,** (new, or partly worn,) that will answer for Mittens, will please leave them as directed above.

Fredonia, Dec. 6, 1862.

Requesting Yarn from Fredonia

At the start of the Civil War, the entire United States Regular Army numbered 17,000 men. When President Lincoln issued his first call for 75,000 volunteers after the bombardment of Fort Sumter, New York State was assigned a quota of 13,280. Unable to meet the needs and comforts of so many men, federal and state authorities looked to the private sector for help. Throughout New York, small towns sought to respond to the call. This small broadside, published by the Soldiers' Aid Society of Fredonia, New York, asks its citizens for wool which can be made into socks and mittens for the men at the front.

Courtesy New York State Museum

ARTILLERY!

CONSTITUTION & UNION.

$565 BOUNTY!

To Soldiers of the Present War who Re-enlist.

$175,00 TO NEW RECRUITS!

150 MEN WANTED FOR

A BATTERY OF ARTILLERY!

To be raised in Lewis County, and attached to the 14th New York Artillery. By special authority of Gov. Seymour.
☞ *Last chance to Volunteer and get BOUNTY. Enlist and AVOID THE DRAFT.* ☜

THE ARTILLERY IS DECIDEDLY THE BEST BRANCH OF THE SERVICE.

NO GUARD DUTY, NO MUSKET OR KNAPSACK TO CARRY.

AVOID THE NEXT DRAFT.

WHICH TAKES EFFECT IMMEDIATELY.

HEADQUARTERS AT THE BOSTWICK HOUSE, LOWVILLE

LIEUT. R. LOUD,   **CAPT. WM. A. TREADWELL.**

Recruiting Broadside

Proudly proclaiming that "the artillery is decidedly the best branch of service" because it performs no guard duty and its men do not tote muskets or knapsacks, this 1863 recruiting broadside also attempts to lure enlistees into the 14th New York Artillery by offering $565 to veterans who re-enlist, and $175 to new volunteers. The 14th New York indeed enjoyed a quiet history until it was converted to an infantry regiment in 1864 when the need for men increased during Grant's bloody campaign against Lee in Virginia. The 14th suffered extensive casualties during three days of action before Petersburg in June 1864 and the following month at the Battle of the Crater.

Wounded Veteran, Ready for Action

Despite the loss of his leg, a determined-looking James W. Singleton still chose to have himself photographed in his uniform, armed with the British-made Enfield rifle-musket, in this undated tintype.

Courtesy New York State Division of Military & Naval Affairs

Men of the 177th New York Volunteers

Although this albumen print has a distinctively post-Civil War look about it, the image actually depicts eight men from the 177th New York Volunteers during the war. The men posing here are armed with what appear to be model 1855 Springfield muskets that have been altered to accept Maynard primers. The soldiers' distinctive militia-style uniforms are attributable to the fact that the Tenth Regiment of the New York National Guard composed the nucleus of the 177th. Mustered into service on November 21, 1862, the regiment left the state on December 16 and served mainly in Louisiana until it was mustered out on September 24, 1863.

Courtesy New York State Division of Military & Naval Affairs

HANGING A NEGRO IN CLARKSON STREET.

"Hanging a Negro in Clarkson Street"

For three terrible days in July 1863, New York City was the scene of the most violent insurrection in American history except for the Civil War itself. Beginning as a demonstration against the first federal military draft, the protest soon exploded into a full-fledged assault against local institutions and the Republican Party, and culminated as a race riot. Free African Americans, whom many rioters irrationally blamed for conscription, became the particular victims of much of the violence. When it was over, the New York City Draft Riots had claimed the lives of 119 persons, the wounding of an additional 300, and the destruction of some $1,000,000 in property. This illustration from Harper's Weekly *for August 1, 1863, frankly portrayed one atrocity in Lower Manhattan.*

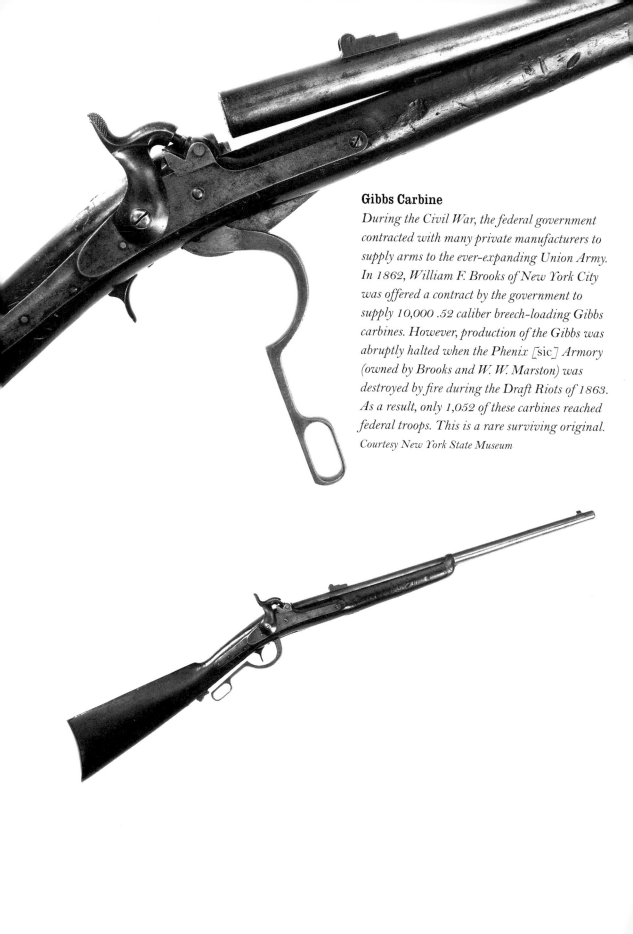

Gibbs Carbine

During the Civil War, the federal government contracted with many private manufacturers to supply arms to the ever-expanding Union Army. In 1862, William F. Brooks of New York City was offered a contract by the government to supply 10,000 .52 caliber breech-loading Gibbs carbines. However, production of the Gibbs was abruptly halted when the Phenix [sic] Armory (owned by Brooks and W. W. Marston) was destroyed by fire during the Draft Riots of 1863. As a result, only 1,052 of these carbines reached federal troops. This is a rare surviving original.
Courtesy New York State Museum

Cooperstown NY
July 27, 1863

Lockwood L. Doty Esq
Albany NY
Dear Sir
Your
favor of the 20th inst is
at hand & contents noted.
I will comply with
your request in writing a
brief personal history,
civil & military, of my
brother, Lieut. U. F. Doubleday
who was killed at the battle
of Fredericksburg, May 3, 1863.
How long should it be. — a page
or two, or only a dozen lines.
Shall I fill out the blank you
enclosed also. Please reply at
once & I will then cheerfully
perform the task   Yours &c
A. D. Doubleday

Letter from Major General Doubleday to Lockwood Doty

Writing from Cooperstown shortly before enlisting in the 2nd New York Heavy Artillery, Abner D. Doubleday (not to be confused with his more famous cousin, Major General Abner Doubleday) informs Lockwood Doty, Chief of New York's Bureau of Military Statistics, that he will forward a "personal history (civil and military)" of his brother, Lieutenant Ulysses F. Doubleday, who was killed earlier that year during the Chancellorsville Campaign. During his tenure as Chief of the Bureau of Military Statistics, Doty amassed a remarkable array of artifacts and records documenting New York State's role during the Civil War, including tens of thousands of the kind of "personal histories" referred to by Doubleday. Unfortunately, almost all these were lost sometime after the bureau was abolished in 1887. Series A4111 Administrative Correspondence Files [of the Bureau of Military Statistics], 1859–1875.

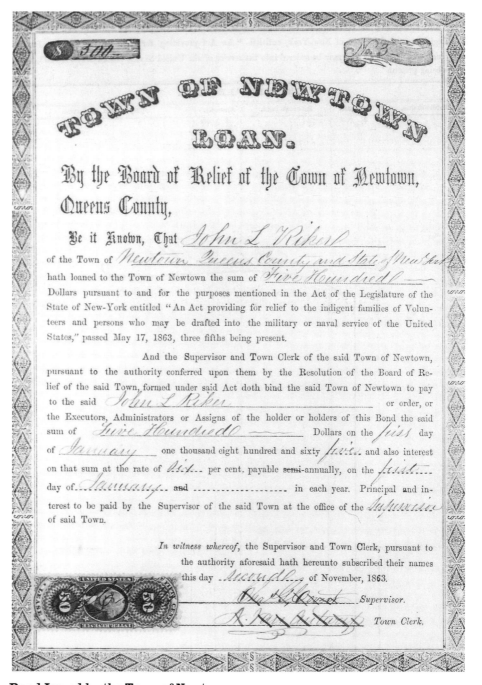

Bond Issued by the Town of Newtown

This $500 bond, purchased by one John L. Riker on November 2, 1863, was issued by the local government of Newtown, in Queens County. During the Civil War it was common for New York State's localities to issue bonds in order to finance the payment of bounties for recruits or to provide aid to the wives and children left behind by the soldiers. This particular bond was designed to raise funds for the "indigent families" of both volunteers and draftees.

Series A4114 Accounts Submitted by Local Officials Detailing Monies Raised and Expended and Men Furnished During the Civil War, 1861–1866.

NATIONAL FAST

CLOSING OF STORES

The President of the United States, having, in accordance with the recommendation of the Senate, proclaimed a National Fast, on THURSDAY, APRIL 30TH, notice is hereby given that, by general agreement, the Stores and business places of this village WILL BE CLOSED on that day.

Fredonia, April 27, 1863.

Announcing a National Fast Day

During the war, President Lincoln periodically proclaimed national fast days to invoke divine blessings on the Union cause, express gratitude for battlefield successes, and remember "widows, orphans, mourners," and others suffering from the effects of the Rebellion. These were the precursors to the later, formal national Thanksgiving holiday, also originated by Lincoln, at which feasting, not fasting, became the rule. In declaring the fast day of April 30, 1863, for which this broadside announced stores would be closed in Fredonia, New York, Lincoln warned that Americans had "forgotten the gracious hand which . . . enriched and strengthened us," and acknowledged that the war might be "a punishment, inflicted upon us, for our presumptuous sins." He asked people to reserve the day for "humiliation, fasting, and prayer," to "confess our national sins, and to pray for clemency and forgiveness."

Courtesy New York State Museum

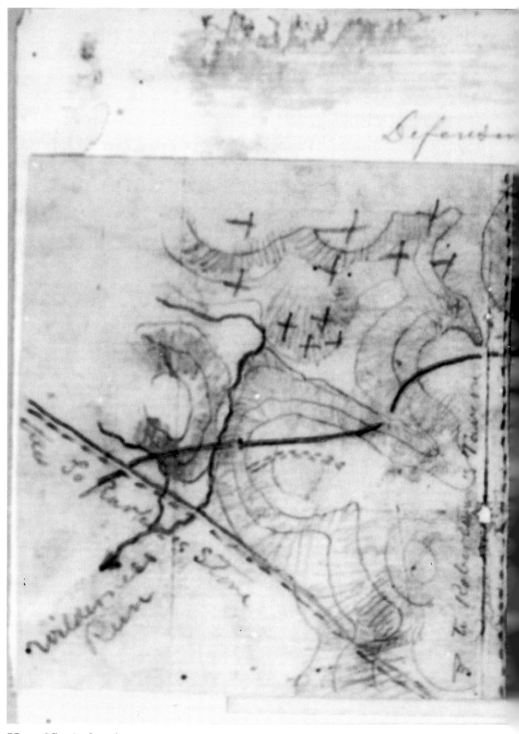

Map of Spotsylvania

After Grant failed to defeat Lee in the Wilderness on May 5-6, 1864, he issued orders early on the morning of May 7 for the Army of the Potomac to head south in an attempt to envelop Lee's flank and move toward Richmond. Thus commenced the Spotsylvania Campaign, which lasted until May 20 and saw some of the most bloody and savage fighting of the entire war. Major Gene

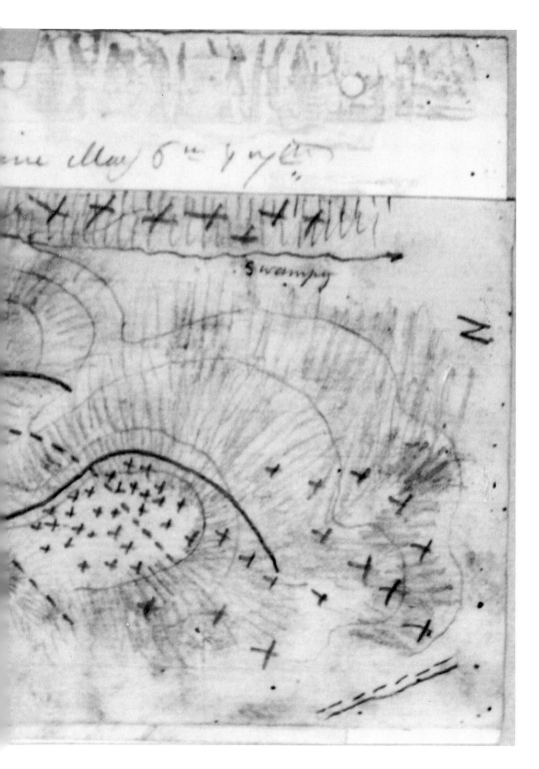

Gouverneur K. Warren, who commanded the army's Fifth Corps, prepared this rough sketch map on the spot, showing Union troop positions at the start of the crucial campaign.

General Warren's Headquarters, by Alfred R. Waud

One of the most prolific campaign artists of the Civil War, English-born Alfred R. Waud covered the war exclusively for Harper's Weekly *from February 1862 through Lee's surrender in April 1865. Waud produced this sketch of Major General G. K. Warren's headquarters at Beverly Mansion, near Spotsylvania Court House, Virginia, on May 17, 1864, during a lull in the vicious Spotsylvania Campaign. The Library of Congress contains the bulk of Waud's sketches, but this particular drawing resides among the papers of General Warren in the possession of the New York State Library.*

Courtesy Manuscripts and Special Collections Unit, New York State Library

eral performed the duties and functions mandated by the above statutes and regulations on
a much larger scale. Instead of providing
arms, equipment, and munitions for a state
militia which totaled 19,189 men in 1860,
the commissary general had to procure and
issue material for hundreds of thousands of
men.

To facilitate the arming and provisioning
of the state's militia and volunteer troops, the
legislature created the Office of Commissary
General of Subsistence (Chapter 477, Laws of
1862). The Commissary General's Office was
renamed the Commissary General of Ordnance and was required to furnish "upon the
requisition of the Commander-in-Chief such
arms, ordnance and ammunition as may be
necessary for the use of the military forces."
The commissary general of subsistence was
to provide the troops with food that was "to
conform in price and quantity to the ration
prescribed by the general regulations for the
army of the United States." This administrative arrangement continued for the remainder
of the war and for some years thereafter.[21]

A4105 Administrative Files, 1861–1866.
1.5 c.f.

*Arrangement: By subseries and therein roughly
chronological by year.*

This series consists of invoices of ordnance
and ordnance stores, receipts, monthly ordnance returns, incoming correspondence, requisitions, duplicate bills and invoices, and lists
of military expenditures directed to and generated by the Commissary General's Office.
The bulk of the records in the series were
generated during the Civil War. The invoices,
receipts, and returns of ordnance, although
incomplete, provide detailed information on
the types of arms, equipment, and accoutrements stored by state arsenals and armories
and which were issued to both Volunteer and
National Guard (Militia) units. The correspondence basically pertains to the procurement and issuance of arms by the state to its
military forces from private firms, such as
Remington and Sons.

Finding aids: Bundle listing.

Quartermaster General's Office

The Office of Quartermaster General can be traced to 1818, when the legislature made provisions for a Quartermaster General's Department within the state's militia. The department was to be headed by a quartermaster general with the rank of brigadier general. The law failed, however, to specify the functions and duties of the quartermaster general. Subsequent state legislation enacted between 1819 and 1854 also failed to describe the quartermaster general's duties.[22]

In 1858 the Adjutant General's Office issued the *General Regulations for the Military Forces of the State of New York*. The regulations, for the first time, stipulated that the quartermaster general's main duties were "to insure an efficient system of supply for the troops, and to give facility and effect to the movement and operations of a force in service." The department was also to be responsible "at encampments, in the field and on marches" for all tents, camp equipage, and baggage trains; laborers and other personnel serving in camp or with the trains; the transportation of the troops and military stores; and the providing of quarters, forage, fuel, straw and stationery.[23]

During the Civil War the Quartermaster General's Office was one of great activity. For the first three months of the war the office was responsible for the transportation, subsistence, quartering, and clothing of the 30,000 volunteer troops raised pursuant to Chapter 277 of the Laws of 1861. The quartermaster general also administered rendezvous camps established at New York, Elmira, and Albany.[24]

As the war progressed and additional men were raised, state and federal authorities worked closely to ensure that these men were adequately clothed and quartered before leaving the state for active service. The state's Quartermaster General's Office turned over to its federal counterparts all uniforms, clothing, and camp and garrison equipage required by state regiments then in the field. Conversely, federal authorities turned over for distribution by the state's quartermaster general all supplies needed by troops who had yet to leave the state.

To facilitate the organization and supply of the additional troops raised, the quartermaster general supervised the construction and administration of thirty regimental camps throughout the state. It was the quartermaster general's responsibility to ensure that recruits were transported from enlistment centers to the appropriate regimental camp, where they were then issued all necessary clothing and equipment before leaving the state.

As the war progressed the quartermaster general was assigned additional duties. Chapter 397 of the Laws of 1862 appointed the quartermaster general to a board to examine claims incurred in the organization of troops raised since April 16, 1861. Chapter 421 of the Laws of 1862 named the quartermaster general as one of the commissioners to a board mandated to examine claims for clothing or equipment lost or destroyed by militia and National Guard units while in the service of the United States. By Special Order No. 246 issued on May 27, 1863, the quartermaster general was designated as acting paymaster general in order to pay detachments of the 12th and 14th New York Volunteer Cavalry Regiments bounties to which they were entitled under Chapter 184 of the Laws of 1863.[25]

On March 31, 1864, the United States War Department issued General Order No. 131, which effectively revoked the state's rights to equip and subsist volunteer troops prior to their muster into United States service. As a result, the Quartermaster General's Office was relieved from a duty that had previously occupied the bulk of its time and efforts. Although relieved of this important function, the quartermaster general became closely associated with the New York State Soldiers' Depot and the New York Military Agency.[26]

The New York State Soldiers' Depot was established on March 31, 1863, pursuant to Special Order No. 151. The order appointed the quartermaster general, adjutant general, inspector general, and surgeon general as a board authorized to adopt rules and regulations necessary for the administration of the institution. The board was recognized and its power extended and defined by Special Order No. 204 (May 8, 1863). By the board's authority the quartermaster general was responsible for all expenditures made in connection with the administration of the depot.[27]

The Soldiers' Depot was located on Howard Street in New York City and was opened on May 18, 1863. The facility was intended to be a "place of rest and relief for the sick and wounded, furloughed, and discharged soldiers" who were in transit to or from their homes. The depot maintained a hospital to treat sick and wounded men, as well as a library. In addition, the depot aided disabled soldiers in securing their discharges, assisted soldiers with the necessary paperwork required to obtain back pay or bounty money due, and provided new clothing to men whose uniforms had worn out. With the end of the war and the return of most of the state's volunteers to civilian status, the services of the Soldiers' Depot were no longer required. The depot was closed on March 31, 1866, and its records forwarded to the Adjutant General's Office.[28]

The New York Military Agency can be traced to the organization of a private association on January 7, 1862. This association was established in Washington, D.C. and provided relief to sick, wounded, and destitute soldiers from New York who were stationed in the army or recuperating in hospitals in the Washington area. The organization was entirely privately funded, relying mostly on voluntary contributions of patriotic citizens.

On April 23, 1862, the state legislature appropriated $30,000 to purchase hospital supplies and to defray expenses incurred in the transportation and care of the state's sick and wounded soldiers for which no provision had been made by the federal government. The private association mentioned above turned over its supplies at the end of the year to S. H. Swetland, who was designated as the state's agent to supervise the disbursement of funds appropriated by the legislature.[29]

The following year the legislature appropriated an additional $200,000 for the care of wounded and disabled soldiers in the field. However, these funds were to be disbursed by the Board of Managers of the New York State Soldiers' Depot, which in turn devolved this authority upon the quartermaster general. In addition, the board appointed John F. Seymour as "General Agent of the State of New York, for the Relief of the Soldiers of this State."[30]

Under the authority conferred upon him, Seymour appointed agents to operate out of Washington, Alexandria, Fredricksburg, Norfolk, Baltimore, Harrisburg, Philadelphia, New Orleans, Buffalo, Louisville, and Nashville. Temporary agencies were also established at Belle Plain and in the Shenandoah

Valley in Virginia. Seymour required these agents to perform the following duties:

- visit all hospitals within their jurisdiction and ascertain the treatment of sick and wounded New York soldiers;
- supply clothing and other reasonable wants not supplied by hospitals;
- correspond, when requested, with the friends or relatives of soldiers;
- forward to the central office in New York the names of all New York soldiers in hospitals, along with their regiment number and a description of their wounds or sickness; and
- maintain an office where soldiers or their friends could apply for assistance in obtaining furloughs or discharges, transportation home, or back pay.[31]

In February 1865, the legislature appropriated another $200,000 for the continuance of the agencies, but after the fall of Richmond and the surrender of Lee's army in April, many of the field agencies were closed. However, with the mustering out of the federal forces, the remaining agencies (Washington, Albany, Buffalo, and New York) undertook a new responsibility. This involved assisting soldiers settling their claims for back pay or bounty money due. Between the end of the war and 1868 these agencies helped to settle the claims of thousands of soldiers and sailors. In late 1868 the quartermaster general closed the remaining two agencies in Washington and Albany because no funds were appropriated by the legislature for their continuance.[32]

In June of 1868 the Quartermaster General's Office was consolidated with the Commissary General of Ordnance's Office (General Order No. 5). Although the commissary general of ordnance assumed all of the duties of the quartermaster general, the later posi-

tion continued to exist within the militia. It was, however, nominal and without any real function.[33]

A4106 Administrative Correspondence and Related Records, 1861–1868. 1.5 c.f.

Arrangement: Roughly chronological by year.

This series consists mainly of incoming correspondence to the Quartermaster General's Office but also includes copies of special orders and resolutions of the Military Board, invoices, vouchers, receipts, canceled checks, inspection reports, and samples of cloth to be used in manufacturing uniforms. Much of the series deals with the procurement, inspection, and issuance of and payment for uniforms, rations, and tents obtained by the state during the Civil War. In addition, the series contains a large amount of correspondence directed to the "Acting Assistant Quartermaster General" and future President of the United States, Chester A. Arthur, which reflects his administrative duties during the first years of the war.

Finding aids: Bundle listing.

A4108 Proceedings and Reports of the Board of Managers of the New York State Soldiers' Depot, 1863–1864. 0.5 c.f.

Arrangement: Chronologically by month of proceeding or report.

This series consists of minutes, resolutions, reports, and a small amount of correspondence generated by or directed to the board. The bulk of the series is comprised of minutes of meetings of the board and monthly reports submitted by the depot's superintendent to the board. There are also a number of reports from the depot's surgeon to the board. The minutes reflect the board's duties as the depot's administrative organ, while the superintendent's reports reflect the day-to-day operation and maintenance of the depot. The surgeon's reports are interesting in that they will occasionally provide information on admissions requiring medical attention as well as a description of types of wounds or illnesses treated.

Finding aids: Bundle listing.

A4117 Records Pertaining to the New York State Soldiers' Depot, ca. 1864–1866. 0.5 c.f.

This series includes correspondence, descriptive rolls of individual soldiers, receipts for claims, inventories of the depot's kitchen and dining room, discharge papers, receipts for official records received from the Adjutant General's Office, certificates of enlistment, matron's reports, list of depot expenditures, receipts for work performed at the depot, and furloughs. The records have little or no relationship to one another and it is unclear why they were originally filed together. It is possible these records were forwarded to Albany after the depot was closed. The presence of discharge papers and furloughs may be explained by the fact that each soldier was strongly urged to place all official records and other valuables on deposit with the proper official at the depot. These were then returned to the soldier upon completion of his stay. It may be that these records were never returned to the soldier but instead remained at the depot and were eventually forwarded to Albany.

A4135 Registers of Soldiers' Claims Expedited by the New York Military Agency, 1866–1868. 24 volumes.

Arrangement: By office and then by original register letter.

These registers describe claims filed by Civil War veterans and actions taken on those claims by both the federal and state govern-

ments. The claims pertain mainly to overdue pension and bounty monies, but there are also claims for commutations of rations and back pay. The registers were compiled by branch offices of the New York Military Agency located in New York, Buffalo, and Washington. Each register, regardless of office, provides the claimant's name (including relation to deceased soldier) and rank; company and regiment; dates of enlistment and discharge; by whom paid and date; by whom discharge was signed; amount of claim; actions taken by the agency (names of official state and federal correspondents; dates correspondence was received or sent, etc.); and a signed receipt or statement that the claimant has received the money due and/or related papers, such as certificate of discharge. The Buffalo Agency registers often provide additional information relating to the claimant's military service record; or if the claimant was filing for an invalid pension, a detailed description of the disability and how it occurred is included.

Indexes: Alphabetical name index for each register, except those of the Washington office, which have a general name index to all of its registers.

Finding aids: Volume listing.

A4136 Register of Soldiers Who Visited the Washington Office of the New York Military Agency, 1863–1865. 1 volume.

Arrangement: Entries are arranged chronologically by the date of the soldier's visit.

This volume contains the names and needs of soldiers who visited the Washington, D.C., office of the New York Military Agency between December 1863 and May 1865. Information provided includes soldier's name, rank, residence (the majority are from New York, but there are some soldiers from other states), regiment, company, location, date of visit, reason for visit, and remarks. The reasons for the visits vary, but they often deal with applications for passes or furloughs; requests for clothing or official papers needed to obtain discharges, pensions, or bounties; inquiries about employment; shipment of personal items back home; transportation to regiment or back home; or requests for medical examinations in order to obtain discharges. The remarks usually refer to the disposition of the soldier's request.

A4137 Case Registers of New York Medical Agents, 1865–1866. 2 volumes.

Arrangement: Entries in Volume One are arranged chronologically by date of filing of claim. Entries in Volume Two are arranged chronologically by date of request.

These registers were compiled by medical agents assigned to the Washington office of the New York Military Agency. The two registers, which date between February 1865 and September 1866, deal with different issues. Volume One relates mainly to the processing of soldiers' claims for back pay, invalid pensions, or other monetary concerns. Volume Two records claims of soldiers in hospitals applying for discharges, transfers, or furloughs. Information provided for each entry in Volume One consists of claimant's name; rank; company and regiment; usually, his residence; description of claim; lists of actions taken to process the claim; and, normally, a notation concerning final disposition. Each entry in Volume Two provides date; soldier's name; occasionally, rank; regiment and company; usually, the name of hospital treating the soldier; soldier's request (discharge, transfer, or furlough); and remarks. The remarks typically refer to actions taken by the medical bureau to process the soldier's request. Occasionally the final disposition of the case is recorded.

Finding aids: Volume listing.

Indexes: Both volumes contain alphabetical name indexes at the fore.

A4138 Superintendent's Ledger Regarding the New York Military Agency Field Offices' Accounts, 1865–1867. 1 volume.

Arrangement: Entries are arranged by field office or individual; therein debits and credits are listed chronologically by date of transaction.

This ledger provides financial information on each of the New York Military Agency's field offices. The ledger also records accounts with individuals with whom the agency had business relationships. Usually, specifics are not included. Rather, general notations such as "expenses," "expenditures," "services," "check," or "voucher" are used when recording debits or credits. Aside from three entries for early 1867, the ledger records accounts only for the year 1865. The location of earlier and later ledgers is unknown.

Paymaster General's Office

The Office of Paymaster General can be traced to 1818, when the legislature made provisions for a Paymaster General's Department within the state's militia. The department was to be headed by a paymaster general with the rank of colonel. The law failed, however, to specify the functions and duties of the paymaster general. Subsequent statutes enacted between 1819 and 1854 also failed to describe the paymaster general's duties. The *General Regulations for the Military Forces of the State of New York* for the year 1858, like the militia-related statutes, also failed to discuss the paymaster general's responsibilities. In all probability, the position was nominal during peace.[34]

During the Civil War, however, the Paymaster General's Office was the scene of intense activity and importance. One of the most important functions the paymaster general performed was the payment of state bounties to recruits and veterans who volunteered or re-enlisted in the army. The first state bounty was authorized by a proclamation issued by Governor Edwin D. Morgan on July 17, 1862. Additional state bounties were authorized in 1863 (Chapter 184) and 1865 (Chapter 29). From July 17, 1862, through January 1, 1866, the paymaster general disbursed more than $35,000,000 to men entitled to receive state bounty payments. This figure does not include local bounties authorized by county, city, and village governments.[35]

In addition to distributing state bounties, the paymaster general was responsible for paying state National Guard (militia) troops activated during the war. National Guard units were called into service for a variety of reasons that included guarding the state's arsenals and armories from unruly mobs, re-pressing the New York City draft riots, and guarding the state's borders from possible invasion. After the Civil War the duties of the Paymaster General's Office consisted mainly of settling claims of unpaid state bounties and paying National Guard troops which had been ordered into service.

Unfortunately, only a small amount of the records pertaining to the payment of state bounties originally filed in the Paymaster General's Office is extant. According to the paymaster general's 1862 Annual Report, for example, the office had collected nearly 89,000 vouchers and copies of original enlistment papers of individuals entitled to state bounties from July through December 1862.[36] Undoubtedly, thousands of similar records were filed in the office after additional bounties were authorized in 1863 and 1865, but for reasons unknown the bulk of these files have been lost. For additional records relating to bounties and the Paymaster General's Office, see the section pertaining to the Comptroller's Office (pp. 79–81).

A4146 Outgoing Correspondence, 1865.
2 volumes.

Arrangement: Chronologically by date.

This series consists of two letterpress volumes containing outgoing correspondence of the Paymaster General's Office dating between April 25, 1865 and September 25, 1865. The correspondence deals mainly with the payment of bounty money and other claims filed against the state by Civil War veterans.

Finding aids: Volume listing.

Indexes: Each volume contains an alphabetical name index.

A4139 Ledgers Pertaining to Bounties Authorized by Chapter 184 of the Laws of 1863, 1863–1866. 3 volumes.

Arrangement: Entries in Volumes One and Two are arranged by regiment number or synonym and therein chronologically by date of payment. Volume Three is arranged alphabetically by last name and therein by branch of service, with payments listed chronologically.

These oversized volumes record bounty payments disbursed by the Paymaster General's Office between 1863 and 1866. Information provided for each entry in Volumes One and Two consists of date of payment, name, company, amount, date, amount (again), and total. The date and amount categories are repeated because soldiers often did not receive their entire bounty at once. Frequently, a portion of the bounty was paid upon enlistment or re-enlistment and the balance paid at a later date. The information in Volume Three differs slightly in that it provides only regiment number and omits company letter. The title of this volume, "List of Partial Payments for All Regiments for 1863 and 1864," suggests it was originally used to record only partial bounty payments. However, many entries contain the dates and amounts of subsequent payments made as late as 1866.

Finding aids: Volume listing.

A4159 Register of Bounty Claims, ca. 1864–1865. 1 volume.

Arrangement: Alphabetically by the first letter of the claimant's last name and therein numerically by each claimant's regiment number.

This volume appears to be a register of bounty claims of New York State soldiers who served during the Civil War and which, for the most part, had yet to be paid. The volume may be only a portion of what was once a larger series,

since it records only claims of men who served in the 106th through 156th volunteer regiments. Each entry provides the claimant's name, regiment and company, amount due, date paid, and remarks. The column recording date paid is almost always blank, which might indicate that these claims remained unpaid when the series was created. The remarks section often contains such notes as: "no roll furnished to Adjutant General," "stricken from roll," or "marked on roll absent without leave."

A4161 Bounty Payment Register, 1865–1867. 1 volume.

Arrangement: Alphabetically by first letter of last name and therein chronologically by date of payment.

This volume records bounty payments disbursed by the Paymaster General's Office between 1865 and 1867. Each entry provides date of payment, name, regiment, and amount. Chapter 29 of the Laws of 1865 authorized these payments, and the regulations and procedures governing their distribution were set forth in General Order No. 6 issued by the Adjutant General's Office on March 1, 1865.

A4164 Register of Bounty Applications, 1876–1882. 1 volume.

Arrangement: Chronologically by month and therein by date of receipt of application.

This volume records applications for state bounty monies received between January 1876 and December 1882. Each entry provides the following information: date application was received, name, company and regiment, bounty claimed, and remarks. The remarks consist of brief statements concerning date of enlistment, desertions, dates of previous bounty payments, or length of service. The number of applications received and amounts awarded are totaled monthly. There is no name index.

A4165 Register of Men Claiming Bounty Money Due, ca. 1865–1868. 1 volume.

Arrangement: Alphabetically by first letter of last name.

This volume records the names of men who filed bounty claims. Each entry provides name, rank, company, and regiment only. No information is provided about the date when the claim was filed, amount claimed, or if the claim was awarded. The volume is undated but it was probably compiled sometime between 1865 and 1868, when the majority of claims were filed.

A4127 Claims Files, 1875–1884. 0.5 c.f.

Arrangement: The series is arranged into bundles according to type of claim. Records within bundles are unarranged.

This series consists of incoming and outgoing correspondence, letters of transmittal, affidavits, questionnaires, and statements of service. The bulk of the series deals with claims submitted by Civil War veterans for bounty money due. A small part of the series deals with claims submitted by National Guard troops called into service during the Buffalo railroad riots in July 1877 and for operating expenses of camps of instruction. Many of the claims pertaining to Civil War bounties contain questionnaires mailed by the Paymaster General's Office to claimants, and statements of service received from the United States War Department. Both of these forms provide basic information on a veteran's military record (i.e., name, rank, company, regiment, dates of enlistment and discharge, etc.).

Finding aids: Bundle listing.

A4118 Assorted Records, ca. 1861–1868. 0.5 c.f.

This series contains correspondence, vouchers, abstracts and statements of receipt, lists of expenditures, copies of special orders, reports, claims, lists of officers and men paid, and volunteer certificates issued for bounty money received under Governor Morgan's proclamation of July 17, 1862. The series contains mixed records from not only the Paymaster General's Office, but also the Offices of the Inspector General, the Quartermaster General, and the New York Military Agency. As a whole, the series pertains mainly to routine administrative duties performed by the Paymaster General's Office, such as certifying the accuracy of accounts submitted for payment and the disbursing of funds to individuals for goods or services purchased by the state's military establishment.

Surgeon General's Office

Although the Office of Surgeon General had been in existence since 1818, the position was purely honorary and without any substantive duties. However, with the outbreak of the Civil War in April 1861, the office was assigned several important responsibilities. These included conducting physical examinations of recruits raised by the state's first call for men (Chapter 277, Laws of 1861); determining the qualifications of men applying for positions as surgeons and assistant surgeons in the newly formed regiments; establishing and maintaining hospitals for sick and disabled men at each of the receiving depots, located in Albany, Elmira, and New York; and vaccinating men before they left the state to begin their terms of service in the federal army.[37]

During the following year the Surgeon General's Office concerned itself with weeding out and replacing incompetent surgeons erroneously commissioned in 1861; appointing and promoting surgeons and assistant surgeons to vacancies; tightening the examination process of new recruits, particularly those trying to enlist under the inducement of bounties authorized by Governor Morgan's July 17, 1862 proclamation; and examining individuals claiming exemption from military duty because of physical disabilities.

In March 1863 the surgeon general was appointd to the Board of Managers of the New York State Soldiers' Depot and became responsible for overseeing the medical department of the facility. The depot was located in New York City and first opened in May of 1863.[38]

In addition to the duties described above, the surgeon general frequently visited hospitals near battlefields to inspect conditions and to assist and comfort wounded soldiers from New York. A considerable amount of time was also expended in helping soldiers obtain furloughs, arranging transfers of sick and wounded men to hospitals nearer their homes, and in responding to inquiries from relatives concerning the location and health of loved ones.

With the end of the war in April 1865, the duties of the Surgeon General's Office lessened, since it was no longer necessary to examine recruits and prospective medical officers or appoint and promote men to vacancies. For the most part the surgeon general was responsible for reorganizing the medical staff of the state's National Guard; establishing and overseeing a temporary home in Albany for indigent, sick, and disabled veterans; and supervising the medical operations of the New York State Soldiers' Depot. Upon the closing of the Soldier's Depot in March 1868, the duties of the Surgeon General's Office diminished even further. Eventually, the position returned to its ante-bellum status as an ornamental and honorary office with few tangible functions.

A4104 Incoming Correspondence Received from Medical Officers of New York State Volunteer Units, 1861–1866. 2 c.f.

Arrangement: Numerically by regiment number and therein chronologically by year.

This series consists of incoming correspondence from various medical personnel affiliated with New York State Volunteer units, directed to the surgeon general. For the most part, the letters are from regimental surgeons and assistant surgeons. The bulk of the correspondence deals with requests for appointments as regimental surgeons or assistant surgeons, the acceptance of commissions, requests to forward commissions, requests for promotions, requests for information pertaining to uniforms, acknowledgements for receipt of commissions, requests for hospital stewards, requests for reappointment or reassignment, and requisitions for medicine. The correspondence from persons requesting appointments is noteworthy because it often provides information pertaining to the applicant's medical education, experience, and other pertinent credentials.

Indexes: See Series B0312 described below.

Finding aids: Folder listing.

B0312 Register of Letters Received by the Surgeon General's Office, 1865–1868.

1 volume.

Arrangement: Chronologically by date of receipt of correspondence.

This register serves as an index to the correspondence described above for the years 1865 and 1866 only. The register provides the following information on each letter received: date of receipt, sender's name, file number assigned, addressee's name, place and date of writing, disposition (where filed), and a one-line summary of contents.

Indexes: Alphabetical name index to senders and names of persons mentioned in the summaries appears at fore of volume.

B0311 Roster of Medical Staff of New York State Volunteer Regiments, 1861–1865.

1 volume.

Arrangement: Numerically by unit.

This volume is a roster of surgeons and assistant surgeons in New York State Volunteer regiments. Each entry provides name, rank, date of rank, and remarks concerning promotions, resignations, and other charges in status.

Indexes: Alphabetical name index contained at end of volume.

A4147 Telegrams Received, 1861–1864.

1 volume.

Arrangement: Chronologically by date of receipt.

This volume contains incoming telegrams received by the Surgeon General's Office between April 26, 1861, and November 26, 1864. The telegrams deal with administrative matters such as the examination of regiments, distribution of medical supplies, appointments of regimental surgeons, and the disposition of wounded soldiers received at New York City and Albany.

Bureau of Military Statistics

The Bureau of Military Statistics[40] was originally established as a part of the Adjutant General's Office on December 20, 1862, pursuant to Special Order No. 866. The order's only other provision was the appointment of Lockwood L. Doty as the bureau's chief. The state legislature recognized the action by enacting Chapter 113 of the Laws of 1863. The statute appropriated $6,000 for the bureau and mandated that it collect and preserve "an authentic sketch of every person from this State who has volunteered into the service of the general government" since April 15, 1861, "and likewise a record of the service of the several regiments, which shall include an account of their organization and subsequent history and generations, together with an account of the aid afforded by the several towns and counties of this State...."

In his first annual report (January 1864) Doty declared his intention to have the bureau collect not only the records required by the legislature, but also "every fact relating to the rebellion, and especially to the part which New York has taken in the war, whether now recorded or printed, or still existing only in memory...." Accordingly, the bureau began to actively collect (mostly through donations) newspapers, sheet music, books, pamphlets, photographs, maps, military reports, federal and state published reports, scrapbooks, and recruiting posters. The bureau also began to acquire artifacts. In its first year, over fifty regimental flags carried by New York State units were deposited in the bureau. In addition, military items such as rifles, carbines, swords, ammunition, knives, and uniforms were acquired. As a result, the bureau began to take on the appearance of a museum.

In March 1864 the legislature repealed the enabling statute of 1863 (Chapter 51) and made the bureau an independent organization separate from the Adjutant General's Office. The law also made the bureau an office of record by authorizing it to procure a seal and issue certified copies of any record in its possession. The bureau was, however, to continue collecting the same information as described in the 1863 legislation.

Chapter 690 of the Laws of 1865 changed the name of the bureau to the Bureau of Military Record and expanded its record-keeping functions. In addition to accumulating the records specified in earlier legislation, the law required various local officials to file certain records with the Chief of the Bureau of Military Record. According to the statute:

- Town clerks were to compile a complete record of all men comprising the town's quota of troops furnished to the United States. These records were to contain biographical material pertaining to each man's civilian and military careers.
- Town supervisors were to furnish detailed statements of monies raised and paid by the town, bounties to soldiers, and the total number furnished.
- County treasurers were to submit a statement of the amount of money raised by taxes and loans as well as a detailed list of expenditures connected with the war.
- Mayors and common councils of cities were to compile biographical registers similar to that of the town

clerks. They were also required to submit accounts of funds raised and expended for war and the total number of men furnished to the federal government.

Furthermore, the law provided for the establishment of auxiliary bureaus of military record on a county level. These bureaus, after being certified by the Bureau of Military Record, were authorized to collect and preserve the same type of data as the state bureau.

Believing the duties and functions of his office were being encroached upon by the bureau, New York's adjutant general, William Irvine, addressed the relationship of the two bodies in his 1865 annual report to Governor Reuben Fenton. Irvine pointed out that under federal law the Adjutant General's Office was the only office duly authorized to maintain official military records and the state legislature could not alter this fact. Irvine argued that without federal approval, all state legislation conferring record-keeping responsibilities upon the Bureau of Military Record was unconstitutional. According to Irvine, the bureau "can not have . . . custody of a single official roster, muster roll, enlistment paper or other document which belongs to the official military records of this State."

The legislature apparently agreed with Irvine because it redesignated the Bureau of Military Record as the Bureau of Military Statistics and organized it as an "additional Military Staff Department" (Chapter 665, Laws of 1866). Two years later the legislature specifically ordered the Bureau of Military Statistics to be "transferred and constituted a bureau in the department of the Adjutant General" (Chapter 717, Laws of 1868).

Between 1868 and 1886 the bureau's duties consisted mainly of displaying the various Civil War regimental flags, artifacts, and books it had acquired. The bureau continued to collect, but on a much smaller scale, photographs and individual histories of soldiers who had fought in the war. In 1887 the bureau was abolished when Chapter 247 required the adjutant general "to establish as part of his office a bureau of records of the war of the rebellion, in which all records in his office relating to said war, and the records and relics of the bureau of military statistics, shall be united and kept."

13774 Town and City Registers of Officers, Soldiers, and Seamen Composing the Quotas of Troops Furnished to the United States During the Civil War, 1861–1865. 35 c.f.

Arrangement: Alphabetically by county and therein alphabetically by name of city, town, or village.

These registers are printed forms issued by the Bureau of Military Record and completed by the state's town and city clerks pursuant to Chapter 690 of the Laws of 1865. The registers provide the individual's full name, residence, date and place of birth, present rank, regiment and company, dates of enlistment and muster, rank, length of enlistment, place of enlistment, race, amount of bounty paid by town or county if disbursed by supervisor, marital status, previous occupation, parents' names, and dates of any promotions, resignations, discharges, or deaths. For seamen, the information is identical, except that the name(s) of the vessel(s) upon which they served is listed.

Indexes: Alphabetical name indexes are found at the end of each volume.

Finding aids: Item listing.

Available on microfilm.

A0389 Registers of Officers and Enlisted Men Mustered into Federal Military or Naval Service During the Civil War, 1861–1865. 6 volumes.

Arrangement: By subseries and then alphabetically by county and therein alphabetically by city, town, or village.

These folio-sized volumes provide both military and civil information on New York men mustered into federal military or naval service during the Civil War. Much of the information in the series was compiled from questionnaires distributed by the bureau to the soldiers themselves, friends, relatives, medical officers in charge of United States hospitals, and local officials. This was probably done sometime between 1863 and 1867. The data were then arranged into three types of categories: New York Volunteers in service, New York Volunteers formerly in service, and New York Volunteers deceased. These categories constitute the three subseries into which the series is arranged.

The first subseries, "Return of Officers and Enlisted Men Who Are Now in the Military or Naval Service," consists of three volumes that provide information on individuals who were still in federal service when the data was collected. Information provided includes: county, town, village, or city (including ward number); name, age, and color; place of birth; marital status; trade or occupation; voter or alien; ability to read or write; regiment first entered; date originally entered service; length of first enlistment; first rank; promotions, transfers, etc.; length of unexpired term till June 1, 1865; current regiment and rank; whether or not drafted; substitute or representative recruit; and remarks. The remarks usually refer to wounds received, hospitalizations, mustering out dates, and whether or

not the person was a prisoner of war or a bounty jumper.

The second subseries, "Return of Officers and Enlisted Men Who Have Been in the Military or Naval Service," consists of two volumes very similar to the subseries described above. The volumes provide the same data pertaining to the individual's birthplace, trade, residence, marital status, education, and original enlistment. However, additional information is provided on how long the individual served; manner of separation (discharged on expiration of term, resigned, deserted, etc.); health (good or permanently impaired); loss of fingers, hands, arms, feet, or legs; other wounds received; and remarks (where killed, reason for discharge, where wounded, health problems, place of capture, place of internment, etc.).

The final subseries consists of one volume entitled "Deaths of Officers and Enlisted Men Which Have Occurred While in the Military or Naval Service of the United States, or From Wounds or Disease Acquired in Said Service since April 1861, Reported by the Families to Which the Deceased Belonged at Home." The volume provides the following information: county, town, village or city (including ward number); name; age at time of death; marital status; citizen or alien upon enlistment; date of entering the service; regiment first entered; original rank; regiment assigned to at time of death; rank at time of death; class on entering the service (volunteer, drafted, substitute, representative recruit, or colored); promotions while in service; date, place, and manner of death (died after leaving service, while a prisoner of war, in battle, of wounds received in battle, by accident or accidental wounds, of sickness, and unknown); surviving relatives and friends; place of burial; and remarks (description of death, comments on moral character, medals received, number of battles participated in, date captured, or various other comments). There are no name indexes.

Finding aids: Volume listing.

Available on microfilm.

A4134 Historical Notes on New York State Volunteer Regiments, 1861–1865.
7 volumes.

Arrangement: By branch of service (infantry, artillery, and cavalry) and therein by unit number.

This series describes the organizational history of New York State Volunteer infantry, artillery, and cavalry regiments that participated in the Civil War. These "historical notes" may have been compiled by the bureau between 1863 and 1866 from information contained in annual reports issued by the adjutant general between 1861 and 1866 (see Appendix F). Each regimental history consists of twenty pages, providing information on the unit's recruitment and organization; terms of enlistment; bounties paid; presentation and final disposition of flags; arms, uniforms, and equipment issued; and mustering out. Unfortunately, the quantity and quality of the information varies widely. Some unit histories are extremely complete and detailed while others contain no information whatsoever. Although much of the information contained in this series can be obtained from Frederick Phisterer's *New York in the War of the Rebellion* (Albany: J. B. Lyon, 1912), there are some topics upon which Phisterer does not touch. These include arms and equipment issued and used by regiments, bounties paid, and aid furnished by federal, state, or local authorities.

Finding aids: Volume listing.

A4111 Administrative Correspondence Files, 1858–1875. 4 c.f.

Arrangement: Files are arranged topically and therein chronologically by date.

Although spanning the years 1858 through 1875, the bulk of this series consists of incoming correspondence received by the bureau between 1863 and 1867. However, for a number of reasons, the series also contains various types of records created before and after these dates. Chief among these is the incoming correspondence directed to the Governor's Office which dates between 1858 (one item) and 1862.[41]

The records dating between 1863 and 1867 consist of questionnaires received from banks concerning amounts of money deposited by soldiers or their families; statements received from district assessors concerning the amount of income taxes assessed; questionnaires received from district provost marshals regarding the draft; correspondence directed to General R. B. Van Valkenburg, Commanding Depot of Volunteers at Elmira; checklists of reports and newspapers received; rough minutes and correspondence of the "Fireman's Zouave Fund Committee"; poetry; battle reports; correspondence received by Colonel John S. Neville, Superintendent of the New York Soldier's Depot; and papers, correspondence, and orders concerning various volunteer regiments.

Subjects documented by these files include the raising and equipping of volunteer regiments; appointments of officers to volunteer units; desertions by soldiers; drafting of men to fill quotas; number of men and financial aid provided by counties during the war; and bounties paid to soldiers. The bulk of the files, however, deal mainly with the acquisition of information needed by the bureau in order to fulfill its mandated duties. Much of the correspondence consists of letters of transmittal from individuals submitting personal histories, photographs, or artifacts; town officials forwarding forms detailing the names of men who served during the war and financial aid provided; or reports from provost marshals providing data on drafted men. The correspondence directed to the Governor's Office and to his aides-de-camp deals mainly with the preparation for public defense and such military affairs as the raising of regiments, applications for and issuance of commissions, and claims for services rendered.

Finding aids: Folder listing.

A4114 Accounts Submitted by Local Officials Detailing Monies Raised and Expended and Men Furnished during the Civil War, 1861–1866. 3 c.f.

Arrangement: By subseries and then alphabetically by county and therein by locality.

This series consists of various types of printed forms, reports, incoming correspondence, lists of men mustered into federal service, and an assortment of printed material submitted by local officials to the bureau between 1863 and 1868. The records are arranged into two subseries: Records Collected Pursuant to Chapter 113 of the Laws of 1863, and Records Collected Pursuant to Chapter 690 of the Laws of 1865. Both sub-series are incomplete and the location of records pertaining to missing counties is unknown.

The subseries collected pursuant to Chapter 113 of the Laws of 1863 contains a variety of records. These include questionnaires entitled "Detailed Account of Aid Afforded by Cities and Counties" (Form C.C.); "Inquiries Relating to Aid furnished by the several towns of the State to Volunteers, the Families of Volunteers, etc." (Form D); "Detailed Ac-

count of Aid Afforded by Towns in Men, Money, Hospital and other Supplies, etc., Since the Commencement of the Rebellion" (Form D.D.); and "Supplemental Inquiries Relating to Men Furnished the Government and Aid Rendered to Soldiers, the Families of Soldiers, etc., by the Several Towns of the State During the Period Between July 1, 1863 and December 31, 1863." (Form H); examples of local bounty posters and bounty bonds; copies of local newspapers; reports from local aid societies; lists of persons to whom various forms were mailed by the bureau; abstracts compiled by the bureau from returned questionnaires; lists of names and addresses of town supervisors; lists of names of deceased soldiers with names and addresses of friends; lists of names of soldiers either discharged or in the service of the United States along with their post office addresses; names of soldiers and their units who died in service from wounds or sickness whose bodies have not been returned home; town lists providing name, rank, company, and regiment of men enlisted up to various dates; and subscription lists providing names and amounts pledged by individuals to defray costs of bounties.

The bulk of the records contained in this subseries are the questionnaires mailed to local officials by the bureau. The forms provide detailed information, usually at the town level on the following: quotas of men assigned by the federal government; number of men furnished; regiments and companies to which they were generally assigned; amounts of moneys raised by taxes, loans, and otherwise on the property of the county; implementation of the draft; meetings, conventions, and fairs held in connection with the raising of volunteers; effects of the war on pauperism, crime, courts, banking interests, and general business interests; amounts of moneys raised by private subscription (including subscribers' names); aid furnished by churches, schools, academies, or literary societies to families of volunteers, volunteers in hospitals, or in the service; names and addresses of men discharged from the service due to wounds; information respecting deceased, returned, and returning volunteers; and biographical material on volunteers.

The records collected pursuant to Chapter 690 of the Laws of 1865 consist mainly of three forms sent by the bureau to town officials. In most respects, this subseries contains the same type of information found in the records collected by the bureau between 1863 and 1865. The main difference in content is that forms in the latter subseries provide information for the years 1865 and occasionally 1866.

Finding aids: Bundle listing.

A4144 Volunteer Relief Payroll of the Joint Volunteer Relief Committee of Albany, 1861–1862. 2 volumes.

Arrangement: Entries in each volume are arranged alphabetically by name.

These folio-sized volumes record relief payments made by the Joint Volunteer Relief Committee of Albany, otherwise known as the Military Relief Committee. The Joint Volunteer Relief Committee was a charitable organization which provided monetary assistance to needy families of men from Albany who had volunteered for service during the Civil War. The committee's payroll provides name of recipient, street address, regiment and company of relative, marital status (including number of children), remarks, amount of weekly allowance, and weekly payments disbursed. The volumes were donated to the bureau in 1864.

Finding aids: Volume listing.

A4149 Telegrams Received and Sent by the Governor's Office, 1861–1862. 10 volumes.

Arrangement: By subseries (Copies of Telegrams Received, Original Telegrams Received, and Telegrams Sent) and therein chronologically by date of telegram.

This series consists of original and duplicate telegrams received and sent by Governor Edwin D. Morgan's office between April 15, 1861, and September 20, 1862. The majority of the telegrams pertain to military matters such as the initial raising and equipping of troops in response to President Lincoln's call for 75,000 volunteers after the attack on Fort Sumter; transportation of troops to the Washington, D.C. area; purchase of arms, uniforms, and accoutrements for New York soldiers; subsequent recruitment of men to satisfy quotas established by the federal government; appointment of officers; and the payment of recruiting bounties. Many of the telegrams in the series were received from and sent to President Lincoln, Lincoln's first Secretary of War, Simon Cameron, and his successor Edwin M. Stanton, and General Henry W. Halleck, who was, essentially, Lincoln's chief of staff.

Indexes: Volumes Seven through Ten contain alphabetical name indexes; Volumes One through Six do not.

Finding aids: Volume listing.

A4112 Examples of State Commissions Issued to Military Officers, 1865. 20 items.

Arrangement: Alphabetically by state.

This series consists of commissions utilized by Northern states in commissioning general officers during the Civil War. The commissions are blank except for signatures of appropriate state officials (i.e., adjutant general or governor) and the state seal. The bureau collected the commissions in 1865.

Finding aids: Item listing.

A4113 Duplicate Thanksgiving Proclamations Issued by Governors of the States and Territories, 1861–1866. 0.5 c.f.

Arrangement: Alphabetically by name of state.

This series consists of proclamations issued by governors of Northern states and territories, plus one received by the bureau from Arkansas. The bulk of the proclamations are printed, but there are a few handwritten items, as well as clippings from newspapers that published the proclamations. Essentially, the proclamations are messages designating a specific day (usually in November) on which prayers and thanksgiving should be offered and the reasons why.

Finding aids: Item listing.

A4119 Enrollment Lists for the Fourteenth District, New York State, 1864. 0.5 c.f.

Arrangement: Alphabetically by county and therein alphabetically by locality. The lists for Albany city are arranged numerically by ward number.

This series consists of printed lists of men enrolled, and therefore liable to military duty, residing in the Fourteenth Enrollment District (Albany and Schoharie counties) of the state. The lists provide the names of all men between the ages of twenty and forty-five who were subject to the draft authorized by an act of Congress entitled "An Act for enrolling and calling out the national forces" approved March 3, 1863, and later amended on February 24, 1864. The lists pertaining to Albany (city) provide not only the enrollee's name but his street address as well. Filed with the enrollment lists is one very oversized list that contains the "names of all drafted men from the 14th District of New York who have failed to report under the draft of September 28, 1863 . . . in accordance with instructions from the Provost Marshal." These men were considered deserters and a reward of thirty dollars was offered for their capture. The list is divided into thirty-six sub-districts. In addition to each deserter's name, the list provides age, marital status, occupation, nativity, place of enrollment, and date drafted.

Finding aids: Item listing.

A4120 Index to Newspaper Articles Concerning New York Volunteer and Militia Units, 1863. 218 items.

Arrangement: Numerically by assigned consecutive numbers.

This index provides references to newspapers containing articles pertaining to military matters in which New York State Volunteer and Militia units were involved. The index, which was probably compiled by the bureau sometime in 1863, consists of handwritten entries recorded on slips of paper. The bulk of the notations are brief summaries of newspaper articles describing various events, occasions, or battles in which New York Volunteer or Militia units participated. There are a small number of references to political events, but for the most part the index pertains to military matters. Newspapers from which articles were abstracted include the *New York Tribune*, *The New York Times*, *New York Herald*, *Newburgh Daily Journal*, and *Albany Evening Journal*. The bulk of the abstracts pertain to articles dating between April and May 1863. Since the index is not arranged alphabetically by subject as one might expect, access is not easily gained to a specific topic. Many of the articles to which the index refers are maintained by the New York State Division of Military and Naval Affairs (see Appendix K) as part of the "The Capital Collection."

A4131 Examples of Ballots and Related Voting Records Issued by Union States to Soldiers During the 1864 Presidential Election, 1864. 0.5 c.f.

Arrangement: Alphabetically by name of state.

This series contains printed tickets and other items pertaining to the 1864 presidential election contested between Abraham Lincoln and George B. McClellan. The tickets usually provide the names not only of the presidential candidates but also of candidates running for various local offices and presidential electors. In many instances the tickets are the only items pertaining to each state. One state, Wisconsin, submitted not only examples of tickets but also copies of its statute authorizing soldiers in the field to vote, copies of legislative proceedings discussing the pros and cons of allowing soldiers to vote, a printed state canvass detailing voting results, and various circulars relating to voting procedures.

Finding aids: Item listing.

A4143 Roster of Staff Officers and Enlisted Men of the 128th Regiment of New York State Volunteers, 1862–1865. 11 volumes.

Arrangement: Alphabetically by company letter and therein alphabetically by name.

In addition to name, the roster provides rank; birthplace; date of discharge; wounds received (usually a brief description); date and place of death, if applicable; date deserted, if applicable; promotions received and dates, if applicable; and date of discharge.

Finding aids: Volume listing.

A4157 Surgeon's Report on Examinations of Applicants in Steuben County Claiming Exemption From Military Duty on Account of Physical Disability, 1862. 1 volume.

Arrangement: None.

This volume is the report of Stephen Hagadorn, examining surgeon for Steuben County, to the commissioner responsible for overseeing the draft in that county. It is a report on men *applying* for military exemption, not a list of men *granted* military deferments, due to physical disabilities. The report provides the names of the men and a brief description of their disability. The information is unarranged and there is no name index.

A4129 Assorted Printed Material, 1861–1864. .5 c.f.

This series consists of unrelated printed material that deals with a variety of topics. These include procedures to collect bounty payments, soldiers relief funds, presidential politics, and the duties of inspectors of electors.

A4207 Register Pertaining to Various Accounts and Subjects, 1859–1868. 1 volume.

Arrangement: See description below.

Although containing several sections dealing with Executive Chamber operations, this volume was used mainly by the Bureau of Military Statistics to document various activities. The bulk of the volume, however, concerns accounts pertaining to the Military Record Fund, administrative expenses of the Bureau of Military Statistics, and the organization and equipment and supplies issued to New York State Militia and Volunteer regiments.

The section dealing with the Military Record Fund lists monies received from individuals and organizations which were then deposited in a bank. Chapter 744 of the Laws of 1865 established the Military Record Fund in order to provide funds for the construction of a Hall of Military Record in Albany (the building was never built). Each entry provides date, name of individual or organization that forwarded funds, address, and amount. The entries date between February 3, 1866, and December 24, 1868, and are arranged chronologically by date of receipt.

The section pertaining to the Bureau of Military Statistics' administrative expenses documents the year 1864 only. The expenditures are routine and concern such items as stationery, travel, salaries, printing, furniture, and fuel. Entries are arranged by type of expenditure and therein chronologically by date.

The section concerning the New York State Militia and Volunteer units consists mainly of the names of the unit's officers, along with an inventory of items issued to the unit prior to its muster into federal service. This section does not contain data on all of the militia and volunteer units raised by the state during the war. Instead, only those units raised pursuant to Chapter 277 of the Laws of 1861, which was passed in response to President Lincoln's initial call for 75,000 men, are documented. The information is arranged by unit.

Other subjects documented by the volume include reports and forms received and mailed by the bureau (1863), articles missing from the bureau (ca. 1864), and general orders sent by the Adjutant General's Office (1864).

A4121 Schuyler County Board of Supervisors Proceedings, 1862. 0.5 c.f.

This series consists of copies of minutes of proceedings of the Schuyler County Board of Supervisors from October through December 1862. The proceedings relate to non-military matters, such as real property valuation and assessment and claims submitted before the board from a variety of people for services rendered or materials sold. It is unclear why these materials, which appear to be unrelated to subject matter Doty normally tried to acquire, was forwarded and retained by the bureau.

Bureau of Records of the War of the Rebellion

Chapter 247 of the Laws of 1887 authorized the adjutant general to establish as part of his office "a bureau of records of the war of the rebellion in which all records in his office relating to said war, and the records and relics of the bureau of military statistics shall be united and kept." Although the statute was passed in April, the bureau was not formally created until December, when the adjutant general issued General Order No. 35. This order limited the bureau's duties to "the perfecting of the records of the [Civil] War on file in this office." Essentially, this task consisted of coordinating the state's effort to have United States War Department clerks provide copies of records on file in that office that were missing from the New York State Adjutant General's Office. This project began in 1887 and lasted until the secretary of war terminated the arrangement in October 1890.[42]

Between 1890 and 1893 the bureau's main duties consisted of arranging and filing the material acquired from the War Department, responding to applications for military service records of Civil War veterans, and caring for the artifacts amassed by the Bureau of Military Statistics. In 1893, however, the legislature appropriated $25,000 to transcribe and publish the military service records of New York State Volunteers who served during the Civil War. This task was undertaken by the bureau in 1893 and completed in 1906. The service records appear as supplements to annual reports issued by the Adjutant General's Office for the years 1893 through 1905 (see Appendix G). The original records from which the publication was compiled are contained in series 13775, Abstracts of Muster Rolls of New York State Volunteers, United States Sharpshooters, and United States Colored Troops, 1861–1865.[43]

In addition to the above project, the bureau transcribed, but never published, military service records of New York State men who were mustered into the United States Navy, Marine Corps, and Veteran Reserve Corps, and of National Guard (State Militia) troops who were temporarily mustered into federal service during the Civil War. These records are described below, along with several other small series pertaining to men who were never assigned to a specific unit.

After the completion of those projects, the bureau's main duties once again consisted of preserving military records on file in its office, responding to questions regarding military service of New York veterans of the Civil and Spanish–American Wars, and caring for the various military artifacts. Shortly after the First World War, the Bureau of Records of the War of the Rebellion was abolished and a Bureau of War Records established. This bureau was to maintain all records, relics, colors, standards, and battle flags relating to all wars in which New York had participated.[44]

13775 Abstracts of Muster Rolls of New York State Volunteers, United States Sharpshooters, and United States Colored Troops, 1861–1865. 1,363 volumes.

Arrangement: By branch of service (artillery, cavalry, infantry) and therein numerically by unit number. Entries for each unit are arranged alphabetically by last name of officer or enlisted man.

The abstracts are printed forms filled out during the late 1880s through the early 1900s from original military records (i.e., muster in rolls, muster out rolls, morning reports, etc.) on file in the state's Adjutant General's Office and the United States War Department. For each individual the following information is included: date of enlistment, age (in years), place of enlistment and for how long, date mustered in, grade, company and regiment, date left organization, how (killed, discharged, deserted, etc.), in what grade, explanation, and remarks. The remarks typically provide information pertaining to promotions, attendance at roll calls, participation in engagements, wounds received, place of incarceration if a prisoner of war, physical appearance (eyes, hair, complexion, and height), and circumstances surrounding dismissal from service.

Indexes: Seventeen-volume unpublished alphabetical name index.

Finding aids: Volume listing.

Abstracts for the 1st through 92nd New York State Volunteers are available on microfilm.

B0803 Abstracts of Muster Rolls for Men Who Served in the United States Navy, 1861–1865. 96 volumes.

Arrangement: By class (see below) and therein alphabetically by last name.

These abstracts document the military service of New York men who served in the United States Navy during the Civil War. The abstracts are arranged in the following manner:
U.S. Navy Regular Officers   Volume 1
U.S. Navy Volunteer Officers   Volumes 2–5
U.S. Navy Enlisted Men   Volumes 6–96
The abstracts pertaining to U.S. Navy Regular Officers provide name, birthplace, from where appointed, date of appointment, rank, promotions, names of vessels on which served, and final disposition (resigned, retired, died, or dismissed). Occasionally, copies of official

reports or orders are included among the abstracts. The abstracts for U.S. Navy Volunteer Officers contain the same categories of information as those for regular officers. The information contained under the heading "final disposition" is similar to that found for regular officers except for the disposition of honorably discharged. The abstracts for enlisted men contain basically the same information as the other abstracts. In addition to service information, many of these abstracts contain physical descriptions that provide eye and hair color, complexion, and height. They may also state age and occupation.

Finding aids: Volume listing.

B0804 Abstracts of Muster Rolls for Men Who Served in the United States Marine Corps During the Civil War, 1861–1865. 4 volumes.

Arrangement: Alphabetically by last name.

These volumes contain abstracts documenting the military service of New York men who served in the United States Marine Corps during the Civil War. The information consists of name, birthplace, to what place credited, date and place of enlistment, term, rank, names of vessels on which served; and final disposition (discharged, deserted, died, etc.).

Finding aids: Volume listing.

B0800 Abstracts of Muster Rolls for National Guard Units Mustered into Federal Service During the Civil War, 1861–1865. 92 volumes.

Arrangement: Numerically by unit and therein alphabetically by name.

These abstracts document the military service of New York National Guard men whose units were temporarily mustered into federal service during the Civil War. The abstracts do not provide service information for periods during which National Guard units were not in federal service. The abstracts provide the following information for each individual: name, date of enlistment, age (in years), place of enlistment and for how long, date mustered in, grade, explanation, and remarks. The explanations usually pertain to the locations where the unit was assigned after it was mustered into federal service. Remarks concern such matters as how officers were paid for their services, promotions, demotions, desertions, variations in spelling of name, and dates of absences. In addition to service data, the abstracts contain spaces where place of birth, age (in years), occupation, eye and hair color, height, and complexion could be recorded. Unfortunately, these data are almost always omitted.

Indexes: Two-volume unpublished alphabetical name index.

Finding aids: Volume listing.

B0806 Abstracts of Muster Rolls of Veteran Reserve Corps Troops from New York State, 1863–1865. 0.5 c.f.

Arrangement: Alphabetically by last name.

This series consists of unbound printed abstract forms which document the military service of New York men who served in the Veteran Reserve Corps.[45] Individual abstracts provide the following information for each corps member: name, date and place of enlistment, age (in years), length of enlistment, date mustered in, grade, company and regiment, date left the organization, how (mustered out, deserted, etc.), in what grade, and explanation (usually cites place mustered out and authorizing general order). The abstracts also contain a section entitled "remarks," which typically provides information on the soldier's military service prior to being mustered into the Veteran Reserve Corps. Many of the abstracts contain categories providing physical descriptions (eye and hair color, complexion, and height), but these are almost never completed.

Finding aids: Folder listing.

B0805 Abstracts of Muster Rolls of Men Unassigned to any State or Federal Unit During the Civil War, 1861–1865. 2 c.f.

Arrangement: Alphabetically by last name.

This series consists of unbound printed abstracts which document the military service of New York men who were mustered into service but were never assigned to either a federal or state unit. The designation "unassigned" refers to men who were located at various recruiting depots and stations when recruiting was ceased by the federal government; men who were permanently assigned to duty at these depots and stations; and men who deserted at the depots or stations before being assigned to a unit, or en route to their unit. Individual abstracts provide the following information: name, date and place of enlistment, age (in years), length of enlistment, date mustered in, grade, place of birth, occupation, eye and hair color, complexion, height, and congressional district number. The form also contains a section about how an individual left his organization, but since these men were never assigned to a unit, this section always appears blank. Finally, the abstract contains a section entitled "remarks." These remarks usually consist of notations stating that the man was drafted, a substitute (often supplies the name of the individual for whom he substituted), or deserted. It is unclear why, but for some reason the great majority of the remarks state that the man was a substitute.

Finding aids: Folder listing.

B0812 Abstracts of Muster Rolls for Colored Enlisted Men Unassigned to any Unit During the Civil War, 1863–1865.
0.5 c.f.

Arrangement: Alphabetically by last name.

These unbound abstracts document the military service of "colored" New York enlisted men who were mustered into service but never assigned to a unit during the Civil War. Individual abstracts provide the following information: name, date and place of enlistment, age (in years), length of enlistment, date mustered in, grade, place of birth, occupation, eye and hair color, complexion, height, and congressional district number. The form also contains a section dealing with how each man left his organization, but since these men were never assigned to a unit, this section always appears blank. Finally, the abstracts contain a section entitled "remarks," which typically consists of notations stating that the man was drafted ("conscript"), a substitute (in many cases, the name and residence of the man for whom he substituted is supplied), enlisted, or deserted. It is unclear why, but for some reason the majority of the remarks state that the man was a substitute.

Finding aids: Folder listing.

B0813 Abstracts of Muster Rolls for Substitutes Unassigned to any Unit During the Civil War, 1863–1865. 1 c.f.

Arrangement: Alphabetically by last name.

These unbound printed abstracts document the military service of substitutes from New York who were mustered into service but never assigned to a unit. Under provisions governing the conscription of men into the army by the federal government during the Civil War, men who had been drafted were allowed to procure substitutes to serve in their places. Individual abstracts provide the following information: name, date and place of enlistment, age (in years), length of enlistment, date mustered in, grade, place of birth, occupation, eye and hair color, complexion, height, and congressional and sub-district numbers. The abstracts typically provide the name and residence of the man who furnished the substitute.

Finding aids: Folder listing.

B0807 Abstracts of Muster Rolls of the 26th Regiment, United States Colored Troops from New York State, 1863–1865. 1.5 c.f.

Arrangement: Alphabetically by last name.

These unbound abstracts document the military service of "colored" New York enlisted men who were mustered into service and assigned to the 26th Regiment, United States Colored Troops during the Civil War. Individual abstracts provide the following information: name, date and place of enlistment, age (in years), length of enlistment, date mustered in, grade, place of birth, occupation, eye and hair color, complexion, height, and congressional district number. The form also contains sections about how each man left his organization (mustered out, discharged, deserted, etc.), in what grade, and "remarks" that occasionally provide information concerning the payment of bounties, pre-service residence, or enlistment status (e.g., substitute). Finally, many of the abstracts contain physical descriptions of the men (eye and hair color, complexion, height, and age) as well as their place of birth and occupation. Although the exact date of the collation of these records is unknown, they were probably produced during the same period as the abstracts for men who served in the New York State Volunteer units, the United States Navy and Marine Corps, or militia (National Guard) units mustered into federal service. It is most likely these abstracts should have been bound and included among the abstracts contained in series 13775, Abstracts of Muster Rolls of New York State Volunteers, United States Sharpshooters, and United States Colored Troops, 1861–1865 (described above), since that series also contains the abstracts of the 20th and 31st United States Colored Troops.

Finding aids: Folder listing.

Available on microfilm.

Military Board

Three days after the bombardment of Fort Sumter on April 12, 1861, the state legislature appropriated $3,000,000 to provide for the "embodying and equipment" of 30,000 volunteer militia that were to serve for two years (Chapter 277). The law also mandated that all expenditures made for arms, supplies, or equipment were to be made under the direction of the governor, lieutenant governor, secretary of state, comptroller, attorney general, state engineer and surveyor, and state treasurer. Although not specifically designated as such, these officials were commonly referred to as the Military Board.[46]

As stipulated in the enabling legislation, the Military Board's authority extended only over the 30,000 men enlisted for two years. The board had no similar authority pertaining to troops raised at later dates. During 1861 the board expended $2,841,205 of the three million dollars appropriated to purchase arms, uniforms, and equipment for the 30,000 men raised between April and the end of June. Once this was accomplished the board had no substantive function to perform until Chapter 397 of the Laws of 1862 empowered it to pay claims of individuals "incurred in the organization, equipment and subsistence of troops" raised since April 16, 1861. Since these claims could only be paid after they were examined by the Auditing Board, the Military Board's role was a mere formality. For the remainder of the war the board's main duty consisted of reviewing and authorizing these claims.[47]

A4204 Proceedings Regarding the Authorization of Payment of Claims Incurred in Raising Troops During the Civil War, 1863–1868. 1 volume.

Arrangement: Chronologically by date of meeting.

These proceedings record the Military Board's decisions to authorize the payment of claims to individuals who incurred expenses while raising troops for service during the Civil War. According to the provisions of Chapter 397 of the Laws of 1862, the Military Board was empowered to authorize these payments only after they had been examined by the Auditing Board. The proceedings usually provide the date and place of meeting, name of claimant, claim number, and amount authorized to be paid. In addition to the claims, the proceedings also contain information regarding the purchase of arms by the state. There is no index.

A4158 Descriptions and Examinations of the Second Deputy Comptroller Pertaining to War Claims Against the State, ca. 1861. 1 volume.

Arrangement: Numerically by voucher number, beside which appears the claimant's name.

It is not entirely certain what office created this series, but informational content suggests it may have been compiled by the Military Board, of which the comptroller was a member. Essentially, the volume is a compilation of explanations describing claims against the state for expenses incurred in the organization, equipment, and subsistence of troops at the beginning of the Civil War. Remarks describe various types of documents filed, amount and nature of the claim, and occasionally a statement as to whether a claim should be disallowed.[48]

A3311 Extracts of Minutes, 1861. 0.5 c.f.

Arrangement: Chronologically.

This series consists primarily of resolutions of the board and brief reports by board members concerning the raising of troops, commissioning of officers, organization of companies into regiments, and mustering regiments into federal service.

Auditing Board

In the course of the Civil War, New York State provided the federal government with over 350,000 men for the Union's cause. During this mobilization, many disputes arose as to whether the state or the federal government should be responsible for specific costs incurred in the raising and organization of the volunteers. For the most part, these disputes can be attributed to the lack of specific policies, rules, and regulations agreed upon by state and federal government officials regarding the raising of volunteers.

To address this problem the legislature constituted the inspector general, judge advocate general, and the quartermaster general "an auditing board" to examine claims "incurred in the organization, pay, equipment, quartering, subsistence and other proper expenses of troops raised . . . for the service of the United States . . . and which . . . have not hitherto been allowed and paid."[49]

The Auditing Board first convened in April 1862 and continued to meet until April 1868. During this period the board examined 1,352 claims, of which 728 were allowed and 624 disallowed. A total of $294,948.32 worth of claims was admitted; the board rejected another $294,800.33. Descriptions of the twenty-six types of claims allowed by the board as well as the eighteen categories of disallowed claims are contained in the board's final report to the governor. The report also provides claimants' names, descriptions of claims, and amounts of all claims allowed and disallowed.[50]

A4116 Claims Submitted for Expenditures Incurred in the Organization, Equipment, and Subsistence of Troops Mustered into Federal Service, ca. 1861–1870. 0.5 c.f.

Arrangement: Originally consecutively by claim number, but this order has been lost. There are also large gaps in the numbering system.

This series consists of assorted claims, correspondence, vouchers, and receipts received and audited by the Auditing Board. It appears these records are only a part of what was once a much larger group of records. The claims are for expenses for goods or services provided to the state while it was organizing and equipping volunteer units to be mustered into federal service. These include providing of uniforms; rations; eating utensils; various supplies (such as stools, lamps, mess pans, stationery, and pails); blankets and tents; shoes, socks, and other clothing accessories; and similar military equipage and accoutrements.

A4141 Record of Claims, 1862–1868.
1 volume.

Arrangement: Numerically by claim number (1–1352), which is essentially a chronological arrangement by filing date.

This volume contains the disposition of every claim presented to the Auditing Board from April 1862 through April 1868. The record for each claim provides claim number, classification (designated by capitalized or lowercase letter), name of claimant, address (usually city or town), by whom claim was presented, date claim was filed, description of claim and amount, description of board's actions, and final disposition.[51]

Indexes: Alphabetical name index at fore of volume.

Board of Commissioners to Examine Militia Claims

Chapter 421 of the Laws of 1862 constituted the comptroller, state treasurer, quartermaster general, and inspector general a board "authorized and required to receive proof, ascertain and determine the sums due to regiments or members of the militia of the State" for clothing and equipment lost or destroyed while in federal service since April 16, 1861. The enabling legislation appropriated $50,000 for this purpose and, by the board's authority, the quartermaster general was made responsible for disbursing funds to individuals whose claims had been allowed.[52]

The board first met on June 13, 1862, and awarded claims until the end of December 1868, when the original appropriation was exhausted. In addition to the records described below, researchers should refer to the quartermaster general's published annual reports (see Appendix F) for the years 1863–1868 for further information regarding the board's activities.

A4115 Affidavits of Claimants for Clothing and Equipment Lost or Destroyed while in the Service of the United States Since April 16, 1861, 1862. 0.5 c.f.

Arrangement: Numerically by regiment and therein by company letter.

This series consists mainly of affidavits submitted by individuals to the board. There are also a few unit rolls and company rosters submitted by commanding officers. The bulk of the affidavits are printed forms which provide the claimant's name, regiment and company, itemized list of clothing and equipment lost or destroyed, amount claimed, and signatures of claimant and notary public. Some forms contain spaces where commanding officers signed their names. The company rosters and unit rolls contain essentially the same information. There is no name index.

Finding aids: Container listing.

A4162 Minutes of Meetings, 1862–1864. 1 volume.

Arrangement: Chronologically by date of meeting.

The minutes in this volume date from June 13, 1862, through December 21, 1864, and consist of resolutions, procedures, abstracts of expenditures of board members, descriptions of claims presented, abstracts of claims allowed, transcriptions of witnesses' testimonies, and descriptions of claims disallowed by the board, along with reasons for rejection. Although the board continued to award claims until its appropriation was exhausted in 1868, it apparently (judging from the minutes) never met formally after 1864.

Indexes: Alphabetical subject index at end of volume.

Board of Commissioners to Examine Militia and National Guard Uniform Claims

Chapter 334 of the Laws of 1864 constituted the comptroller, secretary of state, state treasurer, inspector general, and quartermaster general a board of commissioners mandated "to receive proof, ascertain and determine what regiments of the uniformed militia or National Guard have lost, worn out or destroyed their uniforms in the service of the United States" since April 16, 1861, "and to which uniforms shall be issued by the State."[53]

Between May 1864 and February 1866 the board convened a total of nine times to examine the claims of various state militia and National Guard regiments for uniforms damaged while the units were temporarily mustered into federal service. The board's minutes contain descriptions and amounts of all claims allowed, as well as parts of claims disallowed. The board met for the last time on February 3, 1866.

A4163 Minutes of Meetings, 1864–1866.
1 volume.

Arrangement: Chronologically by date of meeting.

These minutes record the board's resolutions, procedures adopted as to the filing of claims, descriptions of claims submitted by regiments, abstracts of claims audited and allowed, abstracts of claims audited and allowed to clothing manufacturers for uniforms, and descriptions of the board's expenses. The minutes date from May 14, 1864, through February 3, 1866. The minutes are not indexed.

Governor's Office

The Office of Governor was established with the adoption of the state's first constitution in April 1777. The instrument empowered the governor "to take care that the laws are faithfully executed" and "to transact all necessary business with the officers of government." In addition to several other specific duties, the constitution designated the governor as commander in chief of the state's armed forces.

During its first forty years of statehood, New York was involved in two wars with Great Britain in which its armed forces played a significant role. As commander in chief, Governors George Clinton and Daniel Tompkins exercised extraordinary authority over the state's militia during the Revolutionary War and War of 1812, respectively. The two executives not only effectively administered the state's militia during these critical periods, but each personally led troops in the field as well.[54]

The Constitution of 1821 abolished the Council of Appointment, which had been responsible for selecting non-elective public officials whose selection was not provided for in the first constitution. This included the appointment of military officers, over which the council frequently clashed with the governor. However, with its abolition the governor was now free to appoint military officers of his own choosing.

Between the War of 1812 and the Civil War the state's militia was administered by the adjutant general. With the exception of the Mexican War, during which the governor authorized sending two New York State regiments, this period was marked by inactivity and a general decline in the efficiency of the state's militia.

With the commencement of hostilities between the North and South in April 1861, however, the state's militia was shaken from the lethargic state into which it had lapsed. During the war's first months Governor Edwin D. Morgan was actively involved and largely responsible for the rapid organization, supply, and transport of over 13,000 men to the Washington area in response to President Lincoln's call for 75,000 men.

Between 1861 and 1865 New York's three war governors acted very closely with federal authorities to provide men for federal service. On several occasions, the governor exercised his authority as commander in chief by ordering militia units to other states, such as Pennsylvania when it was threatened by invasion from Confederate forces. In addition, the governor worked closely with the state legislature to draft and enact statutes which would more effectively prosecute the war.

As commander in chief the governor authorized the implementation of the state's bounty system, granted individuals the authority to recruit troops, signed legislation which financed the state's war effort through the issuance of bonds, issued promotions and appointments to military officers, and established institutions such as the New York Soldiers' Depot (see section on the Quartermaster General's Office) to tend to the needs of the state's soldiers. In addition, the governor (Morgan) established the Bureau of Military Statistics, which was responsible for documenting New York's participation in the war.

The New York State Archives does not hold the original public papers of New York's Civil War governors. The bulk of Edwin D. Morgan's (1859–1863) papers are held by the New York State Library. Other Morgan papers are located at the New-York Historical

Society. The New York State Library also holds most of Horatio Seymour's (1863–1865) public papers. Additional Seymour material is contained in the New-York Historical Society and the Cornell University Library. The location of the papers pertaining to Reuben E. Fenton's (Fenton was the governor during the last four months of the war) administration (1865–1869) is unknown.

A4205 Abstracts of Vouchers Certified by the Governor, 1861–1862. 1 volume.

Arrangement: Chronologically by date of approval.

This series consists of abstracts of vouchers submitted to and certified by the Governor's Office between May 1861 and December 1862. The abstracts deal with the following five distinct accounts:

- Vouchers authorized by Chapter 277, Laws of 1861;
- Vouchers authorized by Chapter 292, Laws of 1861;
- Vouchers authorized by Chapter 458, Laws of 1862;
- Vouchers authorized by General Order No. 70, 1861; and
- Vouchers pertaining to the New York State Militia.

The bulk of the series relates to the vouchers authorized by Chapter 277 of the Laws of 1861. This act appropriated three million dollars in order to raise and equip 30,000 men to be mustered into federal service. The act also created the Military Board (see pp. 70–71), of which the governor was a member, and made it responsible for all expenditures necessary to arm, supply, and equip the troops raised. Each entry provides date, voucher number (usually), description, and amount. For the most part, the vouchers pertain to expenditures for rations, bedding, eating utensils, uniforms, arms, equipment, accoutrements, and transportation during the initial mobilization. The abstracts date from May 2, 1861, through December 13, 1862, and are contained on pages 2 through 232 of the volume.

The second set of abstracts concerns vouchers paid under the provisions of Chapter 292 of the Laws of 1861. This statute, passed two days later than Chapter 277, appropriated an additional $500,000 in order to provide arms and equipment to the state's militia. Expenditures made pursuant to this act could be paid only upon the certificate of the governor, lieutenant governor, and comptroller. Each abstract provides date, voucher number (usually), description, and amount. Examples of expenditures include the purchase of Enfield rifles, swords, cartridges, fuzes, primers, artillery shells, and powder, plus expenses incurred in testing cannon and powder. The abstracts, which date from January 7 through December 29, 1862, are contained on pages 300 through 304 of the volume. They are arranged chronologically by date of approval.

The third set of abstracts pertains to expenditures authorized by Chapter 458 of the Laws of 1862, which was a general appropriations statute. This law appropriated $30,000 for the purchase of hospital supplies and the transportation and care of sick and wounded New York soldiers for which no provisions had been made by the federal government, as well as for the removal of the remains of officers slain in battle. Expenditures could be paid only after they were certified by the governor. Each abstract provides date, voucher number (usually), description, and amount. The abstracts date from May 29, 1862, through December 31, 1862, and are arranged chronologically by date of approval. They appear on pages 350 through 356 of the volume.

The fourth set of abstracts concerns vouch-

COL. MICHAEL CORCORAN, AT THE BATTLE OF BULL RUN, V^A. JULY 21ST 1861.
The desperate and bloody charge of the "Gallant Sixty Ninth" on the Rebel Batteries.

Corcoran—and Currier & Ives—at Bull Run

*This hand-colored Currier and Ives lithograph depicts Colonel Michael Corcoran leading the
69th New York State Militia, which was part of Brigadier General William T. Sherman's brigade,
in a "desperate and bloody charge . . . on the Rebel Batteries" at the first battle of Bull Run. The
Irish-born Corcoran had created a minor sensation just prior to the Civil War when he refused to
call out the 69th regiment in honor of a visit to New York City by the Prince of Wales. Corcoran was
wounded and captured at Bull Run, along with several of his officers and the regiment's national flag.
Instead of being promptly paroled and exchanged, which was the custom early in the war, Corcoran
was held hostage by the Confederates until August 1862 to bargain for good treatment for Confederate privateers captured by federal authorities. Upon his release, Corcoran was promoted to brigadier
general, but he was killed on December 22, 1863, when his horse fell on him. Currier & Ives, the
most prolific printmakers of the Civil War, operated from Nassau Street in New York City.*
Courtesy New York State Museum

Sarah Rosetta Wakeman (alias Private Lyons Wakeman)

The proud, well-uniformed soldier pictured in this ambrotype was in many ways a typical Union volunteer—except for the fact that she was a woman. By some accounts, as many as 400 females joined the Union and Confederate armed forces, most of them early in the war, when physical examinations for new recruits were not yet stringent. Born on a small, upstate New York farm, Rosetta (as she preferred to be called) enlisted in the 153rd New York Volunteers in October 1862. Like tens of thousands of her "fellow" soldiers, Sarah faithfully performed her duties until she died from chronic diarrhea in the federal army hospital in New Orleans on June 19, 1864. Buried in Chalmette National Cemetery in Metairie, Louisiana, Rosetta's grave marker identifies her by alias: "Lyons Wakeman, NY."

Courtesy of Robert C. Burke

Body Armor Souvenir From Gettysburg

These pieces of body armor, which form the left and right fronts of an iron vest, were worn by a Confederate soldier during the Battle of Gettysburg, according to records accompanying the relic. Such body armor was sold to many naïve soldiers on both sides early in the war, but buyers soon realized that the contraptions were too heavy and cumbersome to carry on long marches. This particular piece was donated to the Bureau of Military Statistics by Captain Angell Matthewson of the 1st New York Artillery. Matthewson himself was wounded in action on May 24, 1864 at North Anna, Virginia, but he survived his wounds and was mustered out with his regiment at Elmira, New York, on June 16, 1865.

Courtesy New York State Division of Military & Naval Affairs

General Warren's Presentation Sword

During the Civil War it was customary for fellow soldiers, local fire companies, state dignitaries, and even local citizens, to award not only generals, but officers of all ranks, presentation swords in recognition of outstanding service. This sword, which was manufactured by the Ames Manufacturing Company of Chicopee, Massachusetts, was presented to Major General Gouverneur K. Warren by two prominent citizens of Cold Spring, New York, on September 30, 1863, at Culpeper Court House in recognition of his services at Gettysburg. The sword, which Warren reportedly refused to wear, in protest at being relieved of command at Five Forks by Major General Phillip Sheridan, was donated to the State of New York by Emily Warren, his daughter, in 1936.

Courtesy New York State Museum

Bounty Payment Bond Issued by the State of New York

For years after the end of the Civil War in 1865, New York State periodically sold bonds in order to eliminate the more than $27 million debt it incurred as a result of offering bounty money to prospective recruits during the war.

Series A1449 Cancelled State Stock Certificates, 1815–1920.

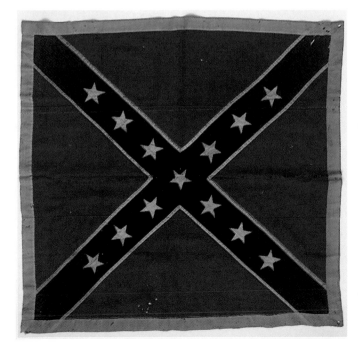

A Captured Confederate Battle Flag

This outstanding example of a Confederate battle flag was reportedly captured by the 3rd New York Cavalry from the "7th Claiborne Cavalry, North Carolina." The flag was subsequently deposited with the Bureau of Military Statistics in Albany. Unfortunately, the precise circumstances of its seizure, and how it actually came into the possession of the bureau, are unknown. The flag is one of several Confederate flags in the custody of the Division of Military & Naval Affairs.

Courtesy New York State Division of Military & Naval Affairs

Confederate Army Surgeon's Kit

On October 9, 1864, Private John S. Robertson of the 8th New York Cavalry captured this complete Confederate Army surgeon's medical kit. Robertson probably obtained his prize at either Tom's Brook or Mt. Olive, Virginia, where his unit engaged Confederate forces under General Jubal Early's command. Robertson then gave the medical kit to Dr. Nelson D. Ferguson, who was the regimental surgeon from March 1862 until he was mustered out of service in December 1862. Ferguson in turn donated the kit to the Bureau of Military Statistics, probably sometime in 1865.

Courtesy New York State Division of Military & Naval Affairs

South Carolina Militia Swallowtail Coat

Exactly how and when this excellent example of a pre-Civil War militia uniform coat came into the possession of the Bureau of Military Statistics remains a mystery. Also called "spiketails" and "claw hammers," swallowtail coats were worn by militia units between 1851 and 1872. Judging from its distinctive buttons featuring Palmetto trees, this outstanding example, which is navy blue with gold facings and red piping, belonged to a South Carolina militia unit.

Courtesy New York State Division of Military & Naval Affairs

Confederate Kepis, Bowie Knives, and Canteens

All of these Confederate items were captured by New York State troops and eventually deposited for safekeeping with the Bureau of Military Statistics. Pictured above is a "Richmond pattern" forage cap (top right) and a standard butternut kepi (top left); a hand crafted "Bowie" knife featuring a bone handle (bottom right); another Bowie knife whose blade measures a massive 11¾ inches long by 2¾ inches wide; and two types of canteens. The canteen at top, which was probably used for carrying kerosene or some other lighting fuel, was reportedly captured from the headquarters of General James Longstreet near Culpeper, Virginia. The other, a water canteen, was imported from England.
Courtesy New York State Division of Military & Naval Affairs

Shako of the 7th New York State Militia

Also referred to as the "Regiment that saved the Capital" because of its timely arrival in Washington after the bombardment of Fort Sumter, the 7th New York State Militia was one of the most celebrated pre-Civil War militia units in the country. Composed of many well-educated men and officered by West Point graduates or former United States Regular Army soldiers, the unit produced hundreds of men who went on to serve as officers during the Civil War. Although the unit did not serve as a whole during the Rebellion, it nonetheless rendered valuable service, most notably during the New York City draft riots. The 7th's Model 1851 shako, shown here, is distinguished not only by the plate featuring the number "7" but also by the distinctive regimental badge appearing just below the pompon.
Courtesy New York State Museum

ers turned over, for the most part, by the state's Quartermaster General's Office to the federal government for payment. The vouchers deal with expenses incurred in the organization, transportation, subsistence, and quartering of an additional 25,000 troops requested by President Lincoln on July 25, 1861. The bulk of the abstracts deal with expenses of the rendezvous camp established at New York City. The abstracts provide date, voucher number (occasionally), description, and amount. They are arranged chronologically by date of approval and appear on pages 382 through 413 of the volume.

The final set of abstracts relates to vouchers certified by Governor Edwin Morgan for expenses incurred by the state's militia. The bulk of these expenses are salaries for staff officers, clerks, messengers, aides-de-camp, secretaries, and other personnel in the military bureaucracy. The abstracts date from July 2, 1862, through December 31, 1862. They are arranged chronologically by date of approval. Each abstract provides date, voucher number, description, and amount.

A4206 Registers of Letters Received Concerning Military Affairs, 1862–1870. 2 volumes

Arrangement: Chronologically by date of receipt.

These registers describe the contents and disposition of letters pertaining to military affairs received by the Governor's Office. Volume One records all incoming correspondence received by Governor Edwin D. Morgan between June 4, 1862, and August 25, 1862. Volume Two records correspondence received by the Governor's Office from March 28, 1865, through October 17, 1870. The bulk of this volume, however, lists letters received between March 29, 1865, and November 13, 1866 (Governor Reuben Fenton's administra-

tion). The majority of the correspondence received pertains to recommendations for promotion of officers; requests for transfers, passes, commissions, etc.; resignations; discharges; and other routine administrative matters. Volume One provides date letter was received, synopsis of contents, and, usually, the office where the letter was forwarded for final disposition. The second volume provides date of letter, author, regiment and company (if applicable), description of contents, and actions taken. The latter category usually states the office where the letter was forwarded for final disposition.

Indexes: Volume Two contains a partial alphabetical name index of individuals who wrote to the Governor's Office.

Finding Aids: Volume listing.

A0623 Registers and Index to Incoming Correspondence, 1861–1862. 2 volumes

Arrangement: Chronologically by date of receipt.

This series consists of two registers recording incoming correspondence received during Governor Morgan's administration and an accompanying index. The registers, which are entitled "Diary of Letters Received at the Executive Department," provide the following information for each letter received: date, from whom received, to whom addressed (usually the governor), to be answered by, date answered, and a brief synopsis of the letter's contents.

The letters received vary in content. Much of the correspondence concerns the issuance of military supplies or the appointment of officers to New York Volunteer regiments. Others pertain to requests for pardons for convicted criminals, applications for appointment to civil offices, invitations to meetings, and other administrative matters. It is unclear how these particular volumes relate to those described above.

The index pertains to both registers. For each letter of the alphabet, all of the correspondence in Volume (or register) One is indexed first, followed by the correspondence of the second volume. The index provides the following information: page, name, date, disposition, and remarks.

Finding Aids: Volume listing.

Comptroller's Office

The Office of Comptroller was first established in 1797 (Chapter 21). The comptroller, as chief fiscal officer of the state, was responsible for overseeing the collection of all state revenues, auditing all claims against the state, prescribing accounting methods, and auditing the records and accounts of the state's administrative departments.[55]

During the Civil War the comptroller was designated a member of the Military Board, Auditing Board, Board of Commissioners to Examine Militia Claims, and Board of Commissioners to Examine Militia and National Guard Uniform Claims (see the respective administrative history of each board for a description of its duties and functions). Furthermore, the comptroller was responsible for issuing the millions of dollars worth of bonds sold to generate revenue for the state's bounty system and for auditing all bounty accounts maintained by the paymaster general. He was also involved, along with the paymaster general, with prosecuting claims against the federal government relating to costs incurred while raising, equipping, and quartering troops during the war.

A1235 Records Pertaining to the Purchase of Firearms by New York State, 1861. 0.5 c.f.

Arrangement: Chronologically by date.

This series consists of correspondence, receipts, affidavits, and an agreement pertaining to the purchase of Enfield rifled muskets from England. Most of the documents are copies of originals. The records were generated pursuant to Chapter 292 of the Laws of 1861, which appropriated $500,000 for the purchase of "arms and equipments" for the use of the state's militia. This money was to be expended by specified members of a Military Board that had been created two days earlier (Chapter 277), of which the comptroller was a member. The bulk of the series consists of correspondence among state officials and representatives of the Bank of Commerce and the firm Schuyler, Hartley, and Graham, outlining details of how the purchase was to be made. The records date from April 20 through December 31, 1861.

A1252 Bonds Issued and Correspondence Relative to the Public Defense, 1862–1863. 0.5 c.f.

This series consists of cancelled bonds, schedules of receipts for the reimbursement of New York State stock, redemption receipts, correspondence, and lists of bonds issued by the comptroller. The bulk of the records in this series was generated pursuant to Chapter 456 of the Laws of 1862. This act authorized a tax to be levied in order to pay the state's direct tax to the federal government, as well as to raise funds for bounties authorized by Governor Morgan's proclamation issued on July 17, 1862. In anticipation of this tax the comptroller's office issued bonds to raise the necessary revenues. The schedules of receipts provide the date of reimbursement, holder's name, name of holder's attorney, and the bond's number, date, amount, and interest rate. The redemption receipts provide basically the same information, except that they pertain to a specific bond. The correspondence is mainly from bankers to the Comptroller's Office regarding the issuance of the bonds. The lists of issued bonds enumerate bonds authorized by Chapter 277 of the Laws of 1861. They are typed and provide bond number, date, to whom issued, and amount. The records contained in this series are only small fragments of what was once a much larger series; the location of the remainder of the bonds is unknown. Similar cancelled bonds for bounties are contained in series A1449 Cancelled State Stock Certificates (see below).

A1253 Records Concerning the Raising of Troops and Payment of Bounties to Volunteers, 1861–1863. 0.5 c.f.

This series consists of requisitions for funds, resolutions and orders of the Military Board, correspondence, memoranda, lists of militia expenditures, lists of war claims filed against the federal government, vouchers, and warrants. Approximately one half of the series pertains to expenses incurred by the state in raising, equipping, and paying troops as authorized by Chapter 277 of the Laws of 1861. Most of the records generated by the Military Board pertain to this subject. The other half of the series pertains to the payment of bounties authorized by Governor Morgan's proclamation issued on July 17, 1862. The bulk of these records consists of requisitions by the paymaster general to the governor asking that certain sums be released to him so that bounty payments could be made. There are also records summarizing amounts of bounty expenditures. The files do not contain genealogical information on individuals who received bounty payments.

A1146 Revenue Bond Stub Books, 1866–1875. 71 volumes.

Arrangement: Numerically by book number with stubs arranged numerically within each volume.

These volumes record revenue bonds issued "to provide for the payment of bounties to volunteers" as authorized by Chapter 56 of the Laws of 1865, Chapter 325 of the Laws of 1865, and Chapter 209 of the Laws of 1866. Each stub provides the certificate number, amount of loan (usually $2,000, $5,000, or $10,000), name of bond holder, date of loan, and signature of comptroller's agent. These particular bonds bore 7 percent interest and were redeemable after April 7, 1877. The series originally consisted of eighty volumes (volumes 1, 12, 15, 16, 23, 24, 27–29 are missing). Many of the cancelled bonds issued in accordance with the statutes above are contained in series A1449, Cancelled State Stock Certificates (see below).

A1449 Cancelled State Stock Certificates, 1815–1920. 14.5 c.f.

This series contains cancelled and unused certificates of state stock issued for a variety of reasons. In addition to certificates issued to finance construction projects such as the state's canals, railroads, and the new capitol, the series contains thousands of bonds issued to finance the state's bounty program. Most of these bonds were authorized by Chapters 325 and 209 of the Laws of 1865 and 1866, respectively. There may be bonds authorized by other statutes, but the lack of arrangement of the series makes it difficult to state so with any certainty. Accompanying many of the certificates are receipts for payment of principal and interest, powers of attorney for transfer of stock, lists of stockholders, and assorted other documents.

A0806 Index to Claims for the "War Account," 1862–1868. 1 volume

Arrangement: Alphabetically by last name of claimant.

This volume is an alphabetical index prepared by the Comptroller's Office and consists of "all claims for the [the] 'war account' presented to the state and upon which determinate action was taken" by the Auditing Board. The index provides the name of the claimant and cross reference to specific records containing detailed information on the claim.

A0910 Claims Examined by the Military Board, 1864–1867. 0.5 c.f.

Arrangement: Chronologically by month.

This series consists of an incomplete set of schedules of claims examined by the Military Board and which were subsequently forwarded to the Auditing Board for their approval between September 1864 and June 1867. Each schedule contains the claim number, name of claimant, dollar amount of claim, and the date of the meeting at which the schedule was prepared and examined by the Military Board.

A1328 Abstracts of Payments of New York State Bounty by the Paymaster General, 1863–1864. 0.5 c.f.

Arrangement: Chronologically by month.

This series consists of monthly statistical summaries of the number of men receiving bounty payments from the Paymaster General's Office for sums varying from $10 to $150. These bounty payments were made in accordance with Chapter 184 of the Laws of 1863 and Chapter 182 of the Laws of 1864 which authorized the payment of bounties to men who enlisted or re-enlisted for military service during the Civil War. Each abstract provides the number of men receiving a specified amount of bounty money and the total amount paid out by the paymaster general for the month.

A1458 Summary Account of Bounties Paid Out by the Paymaster General, 1865. 0.1 c.f.

Arrangement: Chronologically by month.

This is a fragment from an account book of John D. Van Buren, Paymaster General, giving monthly totals of bounties paid out to volunteers by the State of New York between May 1863 and December 1864 pursuant to Chapter 184 of the Laws of 1863 and Chapter 182 of the Laws of 1864. The summary table provides number of bounties paid out to new or re-enlisted men in amounts ranging from $10 to $150. The information contained within the record suggests that this fragment may have originally been filed with series A1328 Abstracts of Payments of New York State Bounty by the paymaster general (see above).

A1460 Vouchers and Bills Submitted and Approved by the Andersonville Monument Dedication Commission, 1914. 0.5 c.f.

Arrangement: Chronologically by date of voucher.

This series consists of receipted vouchers and accompanying bills and invoices incurred by the Andersonville Monument Dedication Commission during the unveiling of the state monument on May 8, 1914, at the Andersonville National Ceremony.[56]

Office of State Historian

The Office of State Historian was created by statute in 1895 (Chapter 393) and filled by appointment of the governor with the advice and consent of the senate. The state historian's official duties were to "collect, collate, compile, edit and prepare for publication all official records, memoranda and data" relative to the war, and state relations of the Colony and State of New York.[57]

Between 1895 and 1911 the Office of State Historian was maintained as a separate administrative unit. During this period the state historian devoted much of his time to publishing documents pertaining to New York's involvement in the Colonial Wars as well as the Civil War. It was during this time that the two series below were compiled, but never published, by the state historian. In 1911 the state historian was placed organizationally within the Education Department (Chapter 380), and the office remains a part of that department.[58]

A0257 Transcriptions of Civil War Records, 1861–1897. 2 c.f.

Arrangement: By branch of service (artillery, cavalry, engineers) and therein numerically by regiment number.

This series consists of transcriptions of official reports, correspondence, and orders primarily relating to volunteer artillery, cavalry, and engineer regiments furnished by New York during the Civil War. Most of these records were transcribed from the multi-volume United States War Department publication *The War of the Rebellion: A Compilation of the Official Records of the Union and Confederate Armies.* Most transcriptions include the serial number of the *Official Records* volume from which they were copied. These transcriptions provide a chronological record of the activities of individual units during the Civil War, as reported in the *Official Records.*

Finding aids: Container listing.

A4170 Memorial Album of the Second New York Veteran Cavalry, 1863–1909.
1 volume.

This album consists of various documents pertaining to the Second New York Veteran Cavalry's organizational history during the Civil War. Included in the album are copies of special orders issued by the New York State Adjutant General authorizing the organization of the unit (1863); copies of the United States Adjutant General's special orders transferring the regiment to the Department of the Gulf (1864); letter from the regiment's officers requesting the resignation of the unit's adjutant (1864); petition to the secretary of war requesting that the regiment be mustered out of service, accompanied by approximately 500 signatures of the unit's enlisted men (1865); copies of two telegrams concerning the mustering out of the regiment (1865); and the statement of former Commissary Sergeant Charles E. Beach presenting this volume to Colonel Morgan H. Chrysler, accompanied by portraits of Beach in 1864 and 1904 (ca. 1909).

Department of State

The Office of Secretary of State was established by the constitution of 1777, which specified that the secretary be chosen by the Council of Appointment. The 1821 constitution vested power to appoint the secretary with the legislature, and the 1846 constitution made the office elective.

Although the Office of Secretary of State was established by the 1777 constitution, the duties and authority of the office were not defined in that document or by statute. The office was apparently inherited from the colonial period, during which the Secretary of the Province of New Netherland and the Secretary of the Colony of New York acted as clerks to the Governor's Council and maintained the records of the colonial governments.

These colonial records were transferred to the custody of the first secretary of state, appointed in 1778. Since then the office has remained responsible for the filing and care of records that form the basic legal foundation of state government. These include state constitutions, original laws, titles and deeds to state-owned land, oaths of office, and other records vital to state government administration. Frequently, laws that established an administrative function in some other government agency specified that records created as a result be filed with the secretary of state. This is the case with the record series described below.

A0468 Title Papers Pertaining to the Erection of Monuments on the Gettysburg and Chattanooga Battlefields, 1887–1898.
1 volume.

This series consists of one bound volume containing letters of transmittal, agreements, typed copies of legislative bills, correspondence, maps, deeds of conveyance and dedications, and a printed copy of *Circular and Instructions of the New York Board of Commissioners, Gettysburg Monuments. . . .*

The majority of the records in the volume pertain to land conveyed and dedicated for the purpose of erecting monuments and markers showing the location of various New York military units during the battle of Gettysburg on July 1–3, 1863. However, the volume also contains a letter of transmittal, maps, a deposition, and a deed of conveyance and dedication pertaining to land in Hamilton County, Tennessee, where the battles of Wauhatchie and Lookout Valley were fought in October 1863. These documents are filed at the end of the volume.

The fore of the volume contains a letter of transmittal from Daniel E. Sickles, chairman of the Gettysburg Monuments Commission, along with the agreement entered into with the Gettysburg Battlefield Memorial Association. This agreement outlines the provisions for the erection of monuments and markers showing the locations of New York units during the battle. Accompanying these two documents are two notarized depositions attesting to the validity of the agreement.

Following the depositions are typed copies of Chapter 466 of the Laws of 1886 and Chapter 269 of the Laws of 1887. The first statute created the commission, which was to determine the position and movements of the military organizations of New York State at the battle of Gettysburg. The second act provided for the erection of the monuments and markers on the battlefield.

Appearing after the typed copies of laws is a letter from the New York State Attorney

General to Sickles stating that the agreement described above is sufficient to provide for the erection of the monuments and markers.

Filed after the attorney general's opinion is a map of the Gettysburg battlefield (including the scene of the cavalry engagement three miles to the east of the town). This map was prepared expressly for the New York State Gettysburg Monument Commission and shows the positions of all New York regiments (both infantry and cavalry) and batteries between July 1 and 3, 1863. In addition, the map depicts land presently (1887) owned by the Gettysburg Memorial Association, land about to be acquired by the association, and lands owned by General Crawford which were dedicated to public use.

The printed copy of the *Circular and Instructions . . .* was published in 1887 and contains the following items: printed copy of the map described above; circulars issued by the New York Board of Commissioners, Gettysburg Monuments, stating its recommendations concerning the monuments and markers to be built upon the battlefield; rules promulgated by the commission for the guidance of the regiments and batteries intending to erect monuments on the battlefield; notice to contractors, specifications, and general provisions detailing the construction methods and materials to be used for the monuments; copies of Chapter 466, Laws of 1886 and Chapter 269, Laws of 1887; report of the commissioners to the legislature; and a table of losses of New York Volunteers engaged at Gettysburg between July 1 and 3, 1863.[59]

The letter of transmittal, agreement, typed copies of legislative bills, attorney general's opinion, map, and *Circular and Instructions* appear to have been filed together in the Secretary of State's Office on September 26, 1887.

Following these documents are four deeds of conveyances and dedications. These are the most important records in the series, and comprise its bulk. The instruments are dated March 28, 1888; March 18, 1889; July 11, 1890; and June 27, 1891. Included with these records are detailed maps depicting the exact location of every monument and marker to be erected upon the battlefield. The instruments themselves contain a narrative description of monument and marker locations as well as a statement of the legal provisions setting aside for public use the land upon which these structures were to be built. The deeds of conveyances and dedications are accompanied by notarized depositions attesting to their validity.

The last seven documents in the volume are the letter of transmittal, deed of conveyance and dedication, deposition, and maps pertaining to the conveyance of land in Hamilton County, Tennessee, for the purpose of erecting markers siting the position of New York regiments and batteries involved in the battles of Wauhatchie and Lookout Valley, October 28–29, 1863. All of the documents are dated 1897 except for the letter of transmittal, directed to the secretary of state, which is dated July 23, 1898.

There is no arrangement to any of the records bound within the volume, except for the documents filed with the Secretary of State's Office in September 1887. These appear in the fore of the volume. The remaining records are filed regardless of date of creation or date of filing.

New York State Civil War Centennial Commission

In addition to records directly relating to New York State's involvement in the Civil War, the State Archives also holds several series of records relating to observances of the centennial of the Civil War. Most of these records were generated by the New York Civil War Centennial Commission, established in 1960 "to provide for appropriate observances, ceremonies and other activities to commemorate the 100th anniversary of the Civil War." The commission was to "prepare an over-all program" and to make plans in cooperation with other similar commissions at the national and state level.[60]

Active from 1961 to 1963, the commission was particularly concerned with the theme of emancipation. Among its activities relating to this theme were the initiation of a movement to create a shrine for the original draft of the Emancipation Proclamation in President Lincoln's hand, which is owned by the State of New York (in the custody of the State Library); arranging for display of the draft Emancipation Proclamation throughout New York State and in Maryland, New Jersey, and Washington, D.C.; sponsoring a New York State Emancipation Proclamation observance in New York City, September 12, 1962, at which Governor Nelson Rockefeller and Dr. Martin Luther King, Jr. were featured speakers; and, with the national centennial commission, co-sponsoring the Washington, D.C. emancipation observance to which Governor Rockefeller conveyed the draft Emancipation Proclamation for month-long display in Washington.

The commission also issued a monthly publication entitled *New York State and the Civil War*, sponsored educational programs for public and private schools throughout the state, and worked with local centennial committees to plan community programs, exhibits, and observances.

Funding for the commission was terminated in 1963, and the commission ceased operations after completing its final report to the legislature on March 31, 1963.

A1444 Office Files, 1961–1964. 1 c.f.

Arrangement: By subject.

This series is apparently the central subject and correspondence files of the commission. It includes correspondence of commission Chairman Bruce Catton and Executive Director Thomas E. Mulligan, with related reports, memoranda, press releases, clippings, and other materials. Most of the records relate to the centennial of the Emancipation Proclamation and a proposed shrine for the original draft of the Emancipation Proclamation.

The series also contains copies of the commission's annual report for 1962–1963; a typescript index to, and mailing list for, its monthly publication, *New York State and the Civil War*; minutes of the "First Assembly" held by the commission on April 17, 1961; correspondence relating to the U.S. Grant Association of Ohio; and a card file index of chairmen of county Civil War Centennial Commissions.

Finding aid: Folder listing.

B0309 Emancipation Proclamation Centennial Motion Picture Film, 1962.

1 c.f. (4 tape reels)

A typed memorandum attached to two film containers indicates that this is the master film and soundtrack of the hour-long ceremonies at the Lincoln Memorial, Washington, D.C., on September 22, 1962, commemorating the centennial of the Emancipation Proclamation. During these ceremonies, the original draft of the proclamation in President Lincoln's hand was publicly displayed in Washington, D.C. for the first time. Both motion picture film and a separate audio soundtrack tape are included in the series. The film is 16 mm black and white and was produced by the New York Civil War Centennial Commission.

A1445 Tape Recordings, 1961–1964.
1.3 c.f. (45 tape reels)

These 7-inch reel-to-reel tape recordings produced for the commission include meetings of the Planning Committee for the Shrine for the Emancipation Proclamation; a panel discussion of the Emancipation Proclamation held at Rutgers University, December 8, 1962; proceedings of the New York State Board of Regents concerning the Emancipation Proclamation, November 16–17, 1961; address by State Historian Albert W. Corey at a meeting of the New England States Civil War Centennial Commission, Montpelier, Vermont, July 8, 1962; address of Dr. David Mearns at a New York State Library Association meeting, Albany, October 19, 1962; remarks of Mason Tolman, Roy C. Van Denbergh, and Thomas E. Mulligan at Utica, May 8, 1962; addresses by Allan Nevins and others at a conference of the Ulysses S. Grant Association in Columbus, Ohio; interviews with the Horseheads, New York, town historian about her collection of Civil War sheet music, and with Harlan Hoyt Horner about the State Capitol fire of 1911; and a press conference with Governor Nelson Rockefeller, June 12, 1962. Some tape reels are not identified.

A0208 Scrapbooks and Clippings, 1961–1962. 2.5 c.f.

Arrangement: Scrapbooks are roughly chronological by date of clipping; unmounted clippings are unarranged.

This series consists of two large scrapbooks of newspaper clippings, along with many unmounted clippings, relating to the activities of the New York Civil War Centennial Commission and of local commissions across the state.

B0928 Plans, Photographs, and Working Files of the Planning Committee for the Shrine for the Emancipation Proclamation, 1961–1963. 3 c.f. (2 oversize folders, 2 boxes)

Arrangement: Working files are roughly alphabetical by subject or type of document; remainder of records are unarranged.

This series contains files kept by the secretary of the Planning Committee for the Shrine for the Emancipation Proclamation, established by law in 1962. These files relate to the committee's activities in designing a shrine for permanent exhibit of Lincoln's draft of the Preliminary Emancipation Proclamation held by the New York State Library. The shrine was designed for the Education Building in Albany but was never built. These files provide information on the work of the committee, design of the proposed shrine, and other displays of the Preliminary Emancipation Proclamation during the centennial of the Civil War.

The following kinds of records are included: newspaper clippings; correspondence of the committee; news releases; minutes of planning committee meetings; photographs of committee meetings and public ceremonies involving the Emancipation Proclamation; final report of the planning committee; New York State and local publications relating to

the centennial of the Civil War; plans, eleva-
tions, and artist's renderings of the proposed
shrine; original governor's proclamation of
Lincoln Memorial Week, February 11–17,
1963; and two original copies of governor's
certificates.

Notes

1. Edgar A. Werner, *Civil List and Constitutional History of the Colony and State of New York* (Albany: Weed, Parsons, 1889), p. 169.

2. New York State Legislature, *Laws of the State of New York Passed at the Sessions of the Legislature Held in the Years 1789 . . . 1796 inclusive [sic], Being the Twelfth . . . and Nineteenth Sessions*, 16th (1793) sess., chapter 45 (March 9, 1793), 5 vols. (Albany: Weed & Parsons, 1887), 3:440–50.

3. In addition to the duties and functions prescribed by federal and state legislation, the *General Regulations for the Military Forces of the State of New York, 1858* (Albany: Weed, Parsons, 1858), pp. 136–38, describe the types of records required to be compiled and filed with the Adjutant General's Office. These regulations were published for the first time in 1858, under the provisions outlined in Section 14 of Chapter 129 of the Laws of 1858 entitled "Act to improve the discipline and promote the efficiency of the Military forces of the state." See New York State Legislature, *Laws of the State of New York*, 81st sess., chapter 129 (April 8, 1858) (Albany: J. Munsell, 1858), pp. 238–43.

4. The figure for the number of troops furnished by New York State during the Civil War is from William F. Fox's *Regimental Losses in the American Civil War, 1861–1865* (1898, reprint, Dayton, Ohio: Morningside Bookshop, 1985), p. 533.

5. For an administrative history of this institution see the section pertaining to the Quartermaster General (pp. 46–50).

6. Researchers interested in the 1862 enrollment should also consult county and town clerks' offices because copies of the enrollment results were required to be filed in these offices.

7. Thomas Hillhouse, New York's Adjutant General at this time, provides a lengthy discussion citing the various reasons why this draft was not implemented in the *Annual Report of the Adjutant General of the State of New York* (Albany: Comstock & Cassidy, 1863), pp. 33–40. This report summarizes the adjutant general's activities for the year 1862. For more on conscription during the Civil War see Eugene C Murdock, *Patriotism Limited, 1862–1865: The Civil War Draft and Bounty System* (Kent, Ohio: Kent State University Press, 1967);

Murdock, *One Million Men: The Civil War Draft in the North* (Madison: State Historical Society of Wisconsin, 1971; and James W. Geary, *We Need Men: The Union Draft in the Civil War* (De Kalb: Northern Illinois University Press, 1991).

8. All of this information, as well as the number of men enrolled in and exempt from the proposed draft, is available from "Table L Statistics of the Draft" contained in the annual report issued by the Adjutant General's Office cited above.

9. It is unclear how this register, which deals with claims filed by United States troops against the federal government, came into the possession of the New York State Adjutant General's Office. No state laws pertaining to the filing or payment of back pay, pension, or bounty claims of this nature can be found. However, in the United States Statutes, Thirty Eighth Congress, Chapter 124, Section 4, Laws of 1864, provision is made for payment of such claims to U.S. Colored Troops.

10. Researchers interested in original records relating to New York State monuments at Gettysburg should also consult series A0468 Title Papers Pertaining to the Erection of Monuments on the Gettysburg and Chattanooga Battlefields, 1887–1898, described on pp. 83–84 of this guide.

11. Normally, the term battalion is not associated with a volunteer regiment. However, this particular usage can be explained by the fact that the 77th New York State Volunteers was originally mustered into federal service on November 23, 1861, for a term of three years. Upon the expiration of the terms of enlistment, the regiment's men eligible for discharge were sent to Saratoga, where they were mustered out on December 13, 1864. The remaining men were subsequently designated a battalion and referred to as such until they were mustered out on June 27, 1865, at Washington (see Frederick Phisterer, *New York in the War of the Rebellion* 6 Vols. 3rd edition (Albany: J. B. Lyon, 1912), 4:2813–14).

12. *Laws of the State of New York*, 74th sess., chapter 180 (April 16, 1851) (Albany: Gould, Banks, 1851), pp. 337–47; General Order No. 368 exact date unknown. Series 14403 General Orders, 1802–1975. New York State Archives and Rec-

ords Administration (hereafter referred to as NYSARA).

13. *General Regulations for the Military Forces of the State of New York, 1858*, pp. 141–42.

14. Special Order No. 317 dated July 30, 1861. Series 14405 Special Orders, 1855–1975. NYSARA.

15. General Order No. 52 dated July 7, 1862 and General Order No. 59 dated July 19, 1862. Series 14403 General Orders, 1802–1975. NYSARA.

16. See "Communication From the Governor Transmitting the Special Report of the Inspector General," in New York State Legislature. Senate. *Documents of the Senate of the State of New York, 1831–1918* (Albany). Senate Document No. 33, 1864.

17. General Order No. 24 dated June 19, 1863, in Series 14403, General Orders, 1802–1975. NYSARA; *Laws of the State of New York*, 85th sess., chapter 477 (April, 1862) (Albany: Wrighton, 1862), pp. 881–946; Ibid., chapter 397 (April 21, 1862), pp. 724–26; Ibid., chapter 421 (April 22, 1862), pp. 753–55; Special Order No. 190 dated April 21, 1863, in Series 14405 Special Orders, 1855–1975, NYSARA; General Order No. 18 dated May 4, 1863, in Series 14403 General Orders, 1802–1975, NYSARA; and Special Order No. 151 dated March 31, 1863, in Series 14405 Special Orders, 1855–1975, NYSARA.

18. *Laws of the State of New York*, 38th sess., chapter 253 (April 18, 1815) (Albany: J. Buel, 1815), pp. 278–79.

19. *Laws of the State of New York*, 46th sess., chapter 244 (April 23, 1823) (Albany: Leake & Croswell, 1823), pp. 329–67.

20. *General Regulations for the Military Forces of the State of New York, 1858*, pp. 143–47.

21. *Laws of the State of New York*, 85th sess., chapter 477 (April 23, 1862), pp. 881–946.

22. Ibid., 41st sess., chapter 222 (April 21, 1818) (Albany: J. Buel, 1818), pp. 210–33.

23. *General Regulations for the Military Forces of the State of New York, 1858*, pp. 160–63.

24. *Laws of the State of New York*, 84th sess., chapter 277 (April 15, 1861) (Albany: Munsell & Rowland, 1861), pp. 634–36.

25. Ibid., 85th sess., chapter 397 (April 21, 1862) and chapter 421 (April 22, 1862), pp. 224–26, 753–55; see the administrative history of the Auditing Board (p. 72) for a description of its duties and functions and p. 73 for the administrative

history of the board constituted to examine clothing and equipment claims; Special Order No. 246 dated May 27, 1863 in Series 14405 Special Orders, 1855–1975, NYSARA; *Laws of the State of New York*, 86th sess., chapter 184 (April 17, 1863) (Albany: Weed, Parsons, 1863), pp. 320–22.

26. U.S. War Department, *The War of the Rebellion: A Compilation of the Official Records of the Union and Confederate Armies*, 127 vols., index, and atlas (Washington, D.C.: GPO, 1880–1901) Series III Vol. 2:211–12 (hereafter referred to as *OR*).

27. Special Order No. 151 dated March 31, 1863 and Special Order No. 204 dated May 8, 1863 in Series 14405 Special Orders, 1855–1975, NYSARA.

28. For additional information on the depot researchers should consult the "Annual Report of the Board of Managers of the New York Soldiers' Depot, 1863–1864" contained in New York State Legislature. Assembly, *Documents of the Assembly of the State of New York* (Albany: various publishers, 1831–1918), Assembly Document No. 184, 1864; *Annual Report of the General Agent for Relief of Sick and Disabled Soldiers, 1865* (Assembly Document No. 140, 1866); and the Quartermaster General's Annual Reports for 1866 (Assembly Document No. 112, 1867) and 1868 (Assembly Document No. 23, 1869).

29. *Laws of the State of New York*, 85th sess., chapter 458 (April 23, 1862), pp. 824–43.

30. Ibid., 86th sess., chapter 224 (April 24, 1863), pp. 404–405.

31. *Report of the General Agent of the State of New York For the Relief of Sick, Wounded, Furloughed, and Discharged Soldiers* (Albany: Comstock & Cassidy, 1864), p. 6.

32. Ibid., 88th sess., chapter 15 (February 2, 1865) (Albany: Van Benthuysen's Steam Printing House, 1865), pp. 23–24. Additional information on the New York Military Agency can be found in the various reports listed in Appendix F under the Board of Managers Soldiers' Depot and the Annual Reports of the Quartermaster General for the years 1866–1868 (Assembly Document No. 112, 1867; Assembly Document No. 47, 1868; and Assembly Document No. 23, 1869 respectively).

33. General Order No. 5 dated March 25, 1868, in Series 14403 General Orders, 1802–1975, NYSARA.

34. *Laws of the State of New York*, 41st sess., chapter 222 (April 21, 1818), pp. 210–33.

35. *Laws of the State of New York*, 86th sess., chapter 184 (April 17, 1863), pp. 320–22; Ibid., 88th sess., chapter 29 (February 10, 1865), pp. 39–46; *Annual Report of the Paymaster General of the State of New York* (Albany: C. Wendell, 1866), p. 29.

36. *Annual Report of the Paymaster General of the State of New York* (Albany: Comstock & Cassidy, 1863), p. 15. George Bliss, the Paymaster General, indicated that these vouchers and papers were to be deposited with the Bureau of Military Statistics and noted that "they will be of use for reference, long after the purpose for which they were originally obtained has been answered. . . ." Unfortunately for today's students of the Civil War, these records are no longer extant.

37. *Annual Report of the Surgeon General of the State of New York* (Albany: Charles Van Benthuysen, 1862), pp. 3–4.

38. Special Order No. 151 dated March 31, 1863, in Series 14405 Special Orders, 1855–1975, NYSARA; *Annual Report of the Surgeon General of the State of New York* (Albany: Comstock & Cassidy, 1864), pp. 8–9.

39. Ibid., pp. 13–14.

40. Much of the following information, including all of the relevant citations, pertaining to the bureau's administrative history is found on pp. 16–22 of this guide. Therefore, for the sake of avoiding unnecessary redundancy, the citations pertaining to this condensed administrative history have been omitted.

41. The presence of this correspondence is explained by the fact that Doty was the chief clerk in the Executive Department from 1859 to November 1860, when he was appointed as Governor Morgan's private secretary. Doty held this position up to his appointment as chief of the Bureau of Military Statistics.

42. *Laws of the State of New York*, 110th sess., chapter 247 (April 30, 1887) (Albany: Banks & Brothers, 1887), pp. 310–11; General Order No. 35 dated December 14, 1887, in Series 14403 General Orders, 1802–1975, NYSARA.

43. *Laws of the State of New York*, 116th sess., chapter 726 (May 18, 1893), 2 vols. (Albany: James B. Lyon, 1893), 2:1803–42 (see specifically p. 1810).

44. Ibid., 142nd sess., chapter 75 (March 20, 1919) (Albany: J. B. Lyon, 1919), pp. 155–58.

45. The corps was created on April 28, 1863, by General Order No. 105 issued by U.S. Acting Adjutant General Edward D. Townsend (*OR*, Series III, Vol. 3, pp. 170–72). The Veteran Reserve Corps was initially called the Invalid Corps of the United States until March 18, 1864, when the name was officially changed to the Veteran Reserve Corps. This organization was composed of men unfit for regular duty in the field but who were healthy enough to perform prison guard, hospital, and military police duties. By carrying out these assignments, the federal government was able to release healthy men previously charged with these tasks for active field duty where replacements were needed.

46. *Laws of the State of New York*, 84th sess., chapter 277 (April 15, 1861), pp. 634–36.

47. For the board's 1861 expenditures see p. 8, "Report of the Board of Officers named in the Act of April 16, 1861, entitled 'An act to authorize the embodying and equipment of a Volunteer Militia, and to provide for the public defence,'" contained in *Documents of the Assembly of the State of New York*, Assembly Document No. 15, 1862. See also *Laws of the State of New York*, 85th sess., chapter 397 (April 21, 1862), pp. 724–26. For the administrative history of the Auditing Board, see p. 72.

48. In addition to this series, researchers should also consult Assembly Document No. 15, 1862 (see above citation), which contains the Military Board's first and only annual report as well as the minutes of meetings held between April 16 and December 31, 1861.

49. *Laws of the State of New York*, 85th sess., chapter 397 (April 21, 1862), pp. 724–26.

50. See pp. 4–24 of the board's final report, "Communication From the Governor Transmitting a Report of the Auditing Board, Relative to the Claims Against the State for Expenses in Connection With Raising Volunteers During the Rebellion," in *Documents of the Assembly of the State of New York*, Assembly Document No. 157, 1868.

51. See Ibid. for a description of the various criteria used to classify each claim, including both those allowed and those disallowed.

52. *Laws of the State of New York*, 85th sess., chapter 421 (April 22, 1862), pp. 753–55.

53. Ibid., 87th sess., chapter 334 (April 23, 1864) (Albany: Banks & Brothers, 1864), pp. 777–80.

54. The public papers of both governors have been published. See *Public Papers of George Clinton, First Governor of New York, 1777–1795; 1801–*

1804, 10 vols. (Albany: State of New York, 1894–1914) and *Public Papers of Daniel D. Tompkins Governor of New York, 1807–1817*, 3 vols. (Albany: State of New York, 1898–1902). These works provide a wealth of information concerning military affairs, both national and local, during these periods. The two publications also document to what extent each governor was involved in the raising, organizing, equipping, supplying, and paying of the militia. In short, they are indispensable sources for studying the administrations of both of these very important governors.

55. *Laws of the State of New York Passed at the Sessions of the Legislature Held in the Years 1797 . . . 1800, inclusive [sic], Being the Twentieth . . . and Twenty-Third Sessions*, 20th sess., chapter 21 (February 17, 1797) (Albany: Weed, Parsons, 1887), pp. 25–27.

56. The Andersonville Monument Dedication Commission was established by Chapter 413 of the Laws of 1913 to "have complete charge of the ceremonies to dedicate the monument erected by the state of New York . . . to commemorate the heroism, sacrifice, and patriotism of more than nine thousand New York soldiers, who were confined as prisoners of war in Andersonville prison. . . ." For a complete account of the dedication of the monument see *Dedication of Monument Erected by the State of New York at Andersonville, Georgia 1914* (Albany: J. B. Lyon, 1916).

57. *Laws of the State of New York*, 118th sess., chapter 393 (April 23, 1895) 2 vols. (Albany: J. B. Lyon, 1895), 1:236–37.

58. Ibid., 134th sess., chapter 380 (June 21, 1911) 3 vols. (Albany: J. B. Lyon, 1911), 1:364–66.

59. Researchers interested in New York State's role in the battle of Gettysburg should consult the three-volume report of the New York Monument Commission for the Battlefields of Gettysburg and Chattanooga, *Final Report on the Battlefield of Gettysburg* (Albany: J. B. Lyon, 1900). Edited by William F. Fox and commonly referred to as "New York at Gettysburg," this indispensable work provides detailed information about every New York State unit that participated in this great battle.

60. *Laws of the State of New York*, 183rd sess., chapter 435 (April 12, 1960), 2 vols. (Albany: n.p., 1960), 1:1496–98.

Appendix A

Conducting Genealogical and Local History Research in Civil War Records in the New York State Archives

Three record series out of the many records described in this guide may be especially helpful to researchers seeking information on individual soldiers or sailors from New York who served in the Civil War. These series are listed below, with an explanation of what information of a personal nature may or, as importantly, may not be found within them. Standard reference works important for regimental and genealogical research are found in Appendix K of this guide. Researchers are strongly advised to use these sources when planning their research.

Of primary importance to personal research is series 13775, Civil War Muster Roll Abstracts of New York State Volunteers, United States Sharpshooters, and United States Colored Troops (see description on pp. 65–66).[1] Series 13775 is organized by regiment, but the New York State Archives maintains a unique, unpublished personal name index to these abstracts.[2] The abstracts of muster rolls provide a basic service record for each Civil War soldier from New York, but it is important to note that, as in many record systems, there are certain omissions. The printed forms on which the data for each individual were entered have places for place of birth, occupation, and physical description of the soldier. In fact, less than 10 percent of the forms contain this information.

The abstracts of muster rolls contain information taken from original reports or rolls created during the Civil War. On the abstract forms the researcher will notice the frequent use of the initials "M.I.R.," "M.R.," and "M.O.R." These abbreviations indicate the source of the data:

- M.I.R. means Mustering-In Report (or Roll)
- M.R. means Muster Report (or Roll)
- M.O.R. means Mustering-Out Report (or Roll)

Another term that appears quite often, and which in context is sometimes quite confusing, is the word "deserted." Evidence indicates that this term had a meaning somewhat different from its modern connotation. Technically, desertion is the act of leaving military service without the intention of returning. The extreme penalty for this act, especially in wartime, is death. Throughout the Civil War, in both the Union and Confederate armies, many men were caught, tried, and executed for desertion. The abstracts of muster rolls use the term "deserted" with alarming frequency. Yet with nearly as great a frequency other entries might appear in the same soldier's record, occurring chronologically later than the so-called "desertion."

The best explanation for this perplexing inconsistency is that the clerks who made the entries on the reports were imprecise, and actually meant that the soldiers were "missing in action" (a term which post-dates the Civil War). While a certain number of "desertions" were desertion in the legal sense, a much larger number do contain later entries within the same service record, such as "a prisoner at Andersonville" or "in hospital at Washington." It seems that the majority of "deserted" notations simply mean that the company officer or clerk could not account for an individual after a battle.[3]

Most of the information in the abstracts was published in forty-three volumes by the Adjutant General's Office as *Registers of New York Volunteer Regiments in the War of the Rebellion* (Albany: J. B. Lyon, 1894–1906). These are commonly referred to as "The Adjutant General Reports" or simply "Annual Reports." The Adjutant General Reports are available in paper copy and on microfiche from the State Library's Manuscripts and Special Collections Unit. These reports are also available through *Civil War Unit Histories: Regimental Histories and Personal Narratives* (see Appendix K for description).[4] For a list of units contained within each volume, see Appendix G.

A second important source of personal information is series 13774, Town and City Registers of Men Who Served in the Civil War (see description on p. 57). This is the only Civil War record in the New York State Archives that contains true genealogical information, such as date and place of birth and full names of parents (including mother's maiden name). However, researchers should note that in many cases, the local officials who prepared these registers simply omitted the genealogical data. Furthermore, registers are lacking for many communities (including major cities such as New York, Brooklyn, Buffalo, Rochester, and Utica). Each register contains an index to names of officers, soldiers, and sailors listed therein. Appendix H provides a listing of all localities contained in this series.

A third series containing summary information on service of individuals is series A0389, Registers of Officers and Enlisted Men Mustered into Federal Military or Naval Service During the Civil War (see pp. 58–59). These registers are arranged by county, then by town or city, but the names in them are *not* indexed. The registers contain only military service information, but they do list servicemen in all communities in the state, including those (such as New York City) for which the Town and City Registers (series 13774) are missing.

These and a number of other record series in this inventory are useful for community as well as family research. Of particular interest for community historians is series A4114, Accounts Submitted by Local Officials Detailing Monies Raised and Expended and Men Furnished during the Civil War (see pp. 60–61). This series includes much information on local efforts to recruit troops, raise money for bounties, and assist soldiers and their families. The documents are arranged by county, then by town or city.

Information on the Civil War military effort may also be found in local government records. The proceedings of county boards of supervisors contain resolutions and votes on borrowing money (repayment being secured by bonds) for recruitment bounties. The board of supervisors' proceedings are in custody of the clerk of the county legislature, and printed copies may be available in local libraries. The New York State Library and the Mann Library, College of Agriculture and Life Sciences, Cornell University, have nearly complete sets of published board of supervisors proceedings from every county in the state. Enrollments of men liable for military duty were taken in 1862, and copies of the enrollments were required to be filed in every town and county clerk's office. These enrollments list men in alphabetical order and give

residence, age, and class (class 1, ages 18–30; class 2, ages 30–45). Finally, town clerk's minute books from the Civil War years record resolutions of the town board authorizing bounties for soldiers credited to the town's quotas of troops, and local relief provided to soldiers' families.[5]

Search Services and Fees

The records described in this appendix and throughout this guide are available to researchers at the New York State Archives' research facility in Albany. The State Archives also offers limited search services for records series which are accessible by name and comprehensive in their coverage.

Search request forms and additional information about State Archives records and research services can be obtained from:

New York State Archives
Cultural Education Center, Room 11D40
Albany, NY 12230
(518) 474–8955
E-mail: archref@mail.nysed.gov
World-Wide Web: www.sara.nysed.gov

Notes

1. The New York State Archives also holds abstracts of muster rolls for those who served in the U.S. Navy, U.S. Marine Corps, and the Veteran Reserve Corps; for those enrolled in National Guard (i.e., militia) units mustered into federal service; and those unassigned to any military unit (including substitutes and "colored" New York enlisted men).

2. Volunteer infantry and cavalry regiments and artillery units were typically raised from one or more counties, and individual companies were often comprised of men from one community. New York military units may be linked to particular communities by consulting C. E. Dornbusch, comp., *The Communities of New York and the Civil War: The Recruiting Areas of the New York Civil War Regiments* (New York: The New York Public Library, 1962), or by consulting Appendix I of this guide.

3. Another possible explanation for this practice may reside with the issuance of General Order No. 92, which was issued by the U.S. War Department on July 31, 1862, under Secretary of War Edwin M. Stanton's signature. This order stipulated that on August 18, 1862, "each Regiment and Corps shall be mustered" and "all officers and pri-

vates fit for duty absent at that time will be regarded as absent without cause" and "treated as deserters." It is possible, therefore, that the company clerks in complying with this order simply marked as deserted many men for whom they could not account. For the full text of the order see U.S. War Department, *The War of the Rebellion: A Compilation of the Official Records of the Union and Confederate Armies*, 127 vols., index, and atlas (Washington, D.C.: GPO, 1880–1901), Series III, 2:286–87.

4. This microfiche publication is available through the New York State Library's Microform Section. The fiche numbers for these reports are #138 through #680.

5. Federal records sources are well described in the following two guides: Kenneth W. Munden and Henry Putney Beers, *The Union: A Guide to Federal Archives Relating to the Civil War* (Washington, D.C.: National Archives and Records Administration, 1986; first published 1962), and *Guide to Genealogical Research in the National Archives* (Washington, D.C.: National Archives Trust Fund Board, 1983).

Appendix B
The Educational Uses of Civil War Records

The ways in which teachers may use Civil War records in the classroom is limited only by their imaginations. The records can be used in several disciplines and by students of widely varying ages and proficiencies. To give a few examples: elementary students can be introduced to the Civil War through photographs from the time period, students in math classes can apply their knowledge of statistics to analyze causes of soldiers' deaths listed in a census record, and art students can study drawings of uniform insignia and regimental flags.

The records that document the Civil War can be a very effective tool for meeting standards of achievement for both content and skills development and can be integrated easily into existing curricula. They provide students with an opportunity for hands-on, experiential learning that cannot be replicated by textbooks or teacher lectures. In the increasingly global and diverse society in which these students live, historical records are an excellent way to promote an understanding and tolerance of multiple perspectives. Furthermore, historical records are inexpensive teaching tools. A master copy of a record can be preserved and all other copies made from it. That costs far less than a new textbook or a field trip.

There are many records series about the Civil War in the State Archives that can be useful to teachers. For example, the State Archives has the military service records of all New Yorkers who fought in the war, including African Americans. Teachers may find the Abstracts of Muster Rolls of New York State Volunteers, United States Sharpshooters, and United States Colored Troops (series number 13775) an especially interesting group of records for students to study as a part of a lesson on the varied experiences of African Americans during the Civil War. The muster rolls contain information on date of enlistment; age of the soldier; place and duration of enlistment; date mustered in; grade, company, and regiment; date left the organization and how (killed, discharged, deserted, etc.). Additional remarks typically provide information about promotions, wounds received, physical appearance, and circumstances surrounding dismissal from service. Because the muster roll contains such detailed information, it can also serve as the beginning of more in-depth research about a particular soldier's life.

Other records series can also be transformed into an educational resource in the hands of a creative teacher. Undoubtedly, bounty payment made to soldiers for military service is an unfamiliar concept to students. The State Archives has many records about the bounty system, including the large, colorful bonds that were issued to finance the system. With guidance from a teacher, students can be led to make their own discoveries about what bounty payments were by studying the historical records. Teachers who organize instructional units around holidays might use the handwritten Thanksgiving proclamations issued by governors as the basis for a lesson on the origins of our national celebration. A holiday usually associated exclusively with the Pilgrims was made a national holiday by Abraham Lincoln.

Of course, there are always practical considerations when selecting a record for classroom use. Is the record readable and will a photocopy of it be readable? Is the length of the record appropriate for the instructional time available? Is the level of difficulty of the record appropriate for the students in the class? Does the content of the record relate to the curriculum?

A most important practical consideration is the location of the record. While the New York State Archives in Albany holds thousands of records about the Civil War, teachers can also find records about the Civil War in their own communities. County governments often have copies of the 1865 New York State census, which provides Civil War statistics for each county, including names of soldiers who died, cause of death, and place of death. The minutes of meetings of town councils and village boards often contain information about the community's response to the war. Many historical societies have personal letters, diaries, and photographs of individual soldiers who fought in the war. Invariably, these records engage students' attention because they are reading about the very place in which they are growing up and often about people very close in age to themselves.

To encourage teachers to use historical records from a variety of time periods, the State Archives has published *Consider the Source: Historical Records in the Classroom*, a 146-page book containing reproductions of 22 historical documents, sample lesson plans, and a how-to-do-it manual. Copies of the book can be obtained by contacting the New York State Archives. The book is also available on the State Archives' web site at:

www.sara.nysed.gov/services/teachers/cts promo.htm.

Appendix C
List of Record Series by Creating Office

ADJUTANT GENERAL'S OFFICE

Page numbers refer to the Series Descriptions section of this volume.

INSPECTOR GENERAL'S OFFICE

COMMISSARY GENERAL'S OFFICE

QUARTERMASTER GENERAL'S OFFICE

PAYMASTER GENERAL'S OFFICE

SURGEON GENERAL'S OFFICE

BUREAU OF MILITARY STATISTICS

BUREAU OF RECORDS OF THE WAR OF THE REBELLION

MILITARY BOARD

AUDITING BOARD

BOARD OF COMMISSIONERS TO EXAMINE MILITIA CLAIMS

BOARD OF COMMISSIONERS TO EXAMINE MILITIA AND NATIONAL GUARD UNIFORM CLAIMS

GOVERNOR'S OFFICE

COMPTROLLER'S OFFICE

OFFICE OF STATE HISTORIAN

DEPARTMENT OF STATE

Appendix D
List of Record Series in Numerical Order by Series Number

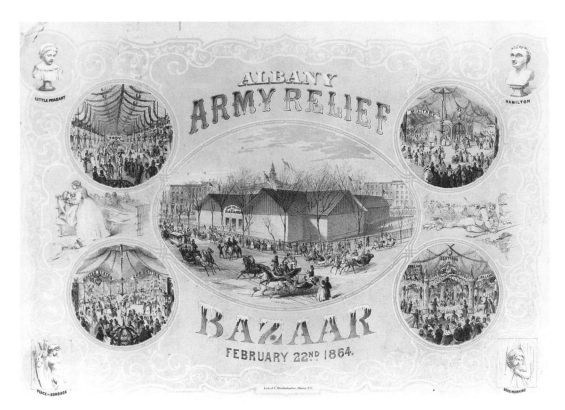

Broadside Advertising a Relief Bazaar

Proceeds from the February 1864 Albany Relief Bazaar, advertised in this broadside, benefited the United States Sanitary Commission, the largest soldiers' relief organization operating during the war. Of all the many booths at the Albany bazaar, it was said that the one earning the most money offered young Irish girls selling kisses for a dollar each.

Courtesy New York State Museum

256

"Group of Ladies With Flags"

Aside from the vague inscription on the back of this albumen photograph, nothing is known about this unusual patriotic image. However, the presence of Union and Confederate flags in the scene, along with the military-style garb of the ladies, suggest the subjects may have been affiliated with one of the many war-charity bazaars or exhibitions held in New York, Albany, and other localities throughout the state. These events, which normally displayed hundreds, and in some instances thousands, of military artifacts, art, and ladies' handiwork, were held to raise funds for such organizations as the United States Sanitary Commission.

Courtesy New York State Division of Military & Naval Affairs

Broadside Proclaiming Republican Victory in 1864

Proclaiming that 1864 polling results showed the Empire State remained true to the Union, this broadside celebrates the re-election of Abraham Lincoln and boldly predicts that there will now be no peace with the so-called Copperheads, who favored making peace with the Confederacy. The 1864 presidential canvas, which historians have called the most important in American history, compelled voters to choose between continuing the costly, three-year-long war and seeking a truce that included reneging on the Emancipation Proclamation. Ironically, the presidential race pitted Lincoln against Democrat George B. McClellan, a onetime Union army commander now running on a peace platform. New York—and the Union—chose Lincoln.

Courtesy Manuscripts and Special Collections Unit, New York State Library

Abstract of Muster Roll for a New York Volunteer

The service record for Harrison Clark, who served in the 125th New York Volunteers, provides a full synopsis of Clark's military history. It shows that he was promoted on the field at Gettysburg from private to sergeant and was subsequently discharged after losing his left leg at the Wilderness in May 1864. After the war, Clark was awarded the Medal of Honor for his deeds at the second day's fighting at Gettysburg.

Series 13775 Abstracts of Muster Rolls of New York State Volunteers, United States Sharpshooters, and United States Colored Troops, 1861–1865.

opposite

Private William Carasaw, United States Colored Troops

This carte-de-visite was initially identified only as "William (?), Co. A., 26th U. S. C. T." But military service records in the New York State Archives make it almost certain that the subject is Private William Carasaw, who joined Company A of the 26th United States Colored Troops in August 1864 at the small Adirondack town of North Elba. Carasaw, who was born in Watervliet, New York, was a married 44-year-old laborer when he enlisted for a three-year term. Like many other men who joined the army at this time, Carasaw received a bounty for his services: the town of North Elba paid him $500, and he collected an additional $100 from the federal government—a significant sum at the time. Carasaw survived the war and was mustered out of service on August 28, 1865.

Courtesy New York State Division of Military & Naval Affairs

Member of the 159th New York Volunteers

According to his service record, Private Edwin Ward Clapp, shown here in a carte-de-visite *portrait, was an 18-year-old machinist from Stuyvesant, New York, when he enlisted in the Union Army in October 1862 for a period of three years. Looking here considerably younger than his officially stated age, Clapp, who stood only 5 feet 3½ inches tall, had the good fortune to serve in the 159th New York Volunteers, which saw relatively little action during the war. During its entire term of service, the regiment suffered only 86 combat casualties. Clapp was mustered out with the rest of his regiment at Augusta, Georgia, on October 12, 1865.*
Courtesy New York State Division of Military & Naval Affairs

Anthony, Thomas,
Co. E, 31st U. S. C. Troops.
Enlisted at Albany, N. Y. for 3 years,
Dec. 14/63. Discharged Aug. 21/45. Paid in
full except bounty and clothing. Mustered with regt every muster day, except July 30/64, when he was wounded
up to that time. Aug. 31/64, Oct., Dec.
Feb. 28/65, a prisoner of war. Paroled
March 4/65, and sent to Annapolis.-
Furloughed from Annapolis, and entered the Ira Harris Hosp, East of Mass,
where he remained up to date of
discharge.
    Addres: 111 Broad St, Albany.

Discharge, P. M. receipts and
statement sent to Capt. Lee,
Aug. 28

$13.88

Received of Maj Wm H. Post U.S. Mil
Agent a check for thirteen & 88/100 dollars
received by him from Paymaster Genl U.f.a
Albany Feby 6/66.

Witness   his
C A Kimberly   Thomas x Anthony
                              mark

Soldier's Claim Filed with the New York Military Agency

The New York Military Agency was established in 1862 to provide sick, wounded, and disabled soldiers with medical and spiritual assistance, and, for those overlooked by federal authorities, with financial assistance as well. The agency functioned until 1868; after the war its main duty was to help soldiers settle claims for back pay or bounty money. The entry in this register indicates that the agency successfully secured for one Thomas Anthony, who served in Company E of the 31st United States Colored Troops, $13.88 from the United States Paymaster General. As the register shows, Anthony was wounded on July 30, 1864 (most likely at the Battle of the Crater before Petersburg) and was a prisoner of war from August 1864 through the end of February 1865, when he was paroled and sent to Annapolis.

Series A4135 Registers of Soldiers' Claims Expedited by the New York Military Agency, 1866–1868.

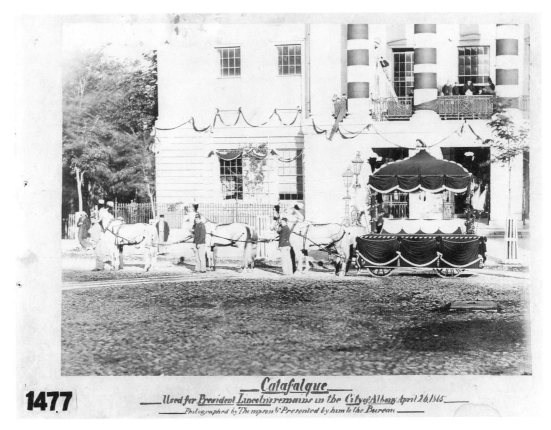

Catafalque.
Used for President Lincoln's remains in the City of Albany April 26, 1865
Photographed by Thompson & Presented by him to the Bureau

1477

Catafalque for a Martyred President

On April 26, 1865, Abraham Lincoln's remains were paraded through Albany, and citizens of the capital city lined the streets for a final opportunity to pay respects to the slain President. Some time before the parade got underway at noon, a local photographer named Thompson took this image of the catafalque and six white horses that would be used to transport the President's body through the city. The catafalque, without the President's coffin (which was still lying in state at the State Capitol at the time the photograph was exposed) rests in front of Albany's old City Hall, which no longer stands.

Courtesy New York State Division of Military & Naval Affairs

Appendix E
Record Series Available on Microfilm

The Civil War records listed below are available on microfilm from the New York State Archives either through interlibrary loan or by direct purchase. Researchers interested in borrowing individual reels of microfilm can do so by contacting their local library and completing an interlibrary loan request. This request can either be mailed to the State Archives (see address below) or faxed (518 473–9985). Individual rolls of microfilm are also available for purchase.

Interlibrary loan requests and payment for the purchase of microfilm rolls can be mailed to:
New York State Archives
Cultural Education Center, Room 11D40
Albany, NY 12230
(518 474–8955)

Page numbers refer to the Series Descriptions section of this volume.

A0389 Registers of Officers and Enlisted Men Mustered into Federal Military or Naval Service During the Civil War, 1861–1865 (7 reels) — p. 58

B0807 Abstracts of Muster Rolls of the 26th Regiment, United States Colored Troops from New York State, 1863–1865 (2 reels) — p. 68

B0812 Abstracts of Muster Rolls for Colored Enlisted Men Unassigned to any Unit During the Civil War, 1863–1865 (1 reel) — p. 68

13774 Town and City Registers of Officers, Soldiers, and Seamen Composing the Quotas of Troops Furnished to the United States During the Civil War, 1861–1865 (37 reels) — p. 57

13775 Civil War Muster Roll Abstracts of Muster Rolls of New York State Volunteer Units, United States Sharpshooters, and United States Colored Troops [1st through 92nd New York Volunteer Regiments only], 1861–1865 (358 reels) — p. 65

Appendix F
List of New York State Agency Annual Reports

This appendix is a listing of annual reports published by the various state military agencies, boards, and commissions already in existence or constituted by the state legislature during the Civil War. Researchers interested in the functions and duties of these administrative bodies are strongly encouraged to consult these reports, as they often contain detailed information concerning agency activities during any given year. These reports are available from the New York State Library as well as from many major research institutions. Many of the reports were issued as separate publications, while others were published only as part of the New York State Senate and Assembly Documents series. Moreover, some reports were published as separate documents as well as in the Senate and Assembly series. The full citations for these two important collections of government documents are as follows: New York State Legislature: Assembly. *Documents of the Assembly of the State of New York* (Albany: various publishers, 1831–1918) and New York State Legislature: Senate. *Documents of the Senate of the State of New York* (Albany: various publishers, 1831–1918). The New York State Library maintains a complete set of these documents. Commonly referred to as the "Senate and Assembly Documents," these publications are also available on microfiche from the State Library.

ADJUTANT GENERAL'S OFFICE

Annual Report of the Adjutant General of the State of New York [for 1861]. Albany: C. Van Benthuysen, 1862 (also published as Assembly Document No. 25, 1862).

Annual Report of the Adjutant General of the State of New York [for 1862]. Albany: Comstock & Cassidy, 1863 (also published as Assembly Document No. 49, 1863).

Annual Report of the Adjutant General of the State of New York [for 1863]. 2 vols. Albany: Comstock & Cassidy, 1864 (also published as Assembly Document No. 80, 1864).

Annual Report of the Adjutant General of the State of New York [for 1864]. 2 vols. Albany: C. Van Benthuysen, 1865 (also published as Assembly Document No. 22, 1865).

Annual Report of the Adjutant General of the State of New York [for 1865]. 2 vols. Albany: C. Wendell, 1866 (also published as Assembly Document No. 24, 1866).

AUDITING BOARD

Communication From the Governor Transmitting the Report of the Auditing Board, Constituted by Chapter 397, Laws of 1862 (available only in Senate Document No. 69, 1864).

Communication From the Governor Transmitting a Report of the Auditing Board, Relative to the Claims Against the State for Expenses in Connection with Raising Volunteers During the Rebellion (available only in Assembly Document No. 157, 1868).

BUREAU OF MILITARY STATISTICS [MILITARY RECORD]

First Annual Report of the Chief of the Bureau of Military Statistics. Albany: Comstock & Cassidy, 1864 (also published as Assembly Document No. 56, 1864).

Second Annual Report of the Chief of the Bureau of Military Statistics. Albany: C. Wendell, Legislative Printer, 1865 (also published as Assembly Document No. 64, 1865).

Third Annual Report of the Bureau of Military Record [Chief of the Bureau of Military Statistics] of the State of New York. Albany: C. Wendell, 1866. (Also published as Assembly Document No. 71, 1866).

Fourth Annual Report of the Bureau of Military Statistics. State of New York. Albany: C. Van Benthuysen & Sons, 1867 (also published as Assembly Document No. 235, 1867).

Fifth Annual Report of the Chief of the Bureau of Military Statistics, with Appendices. Albany: C. Van Benthuysen & Sons, 1868 (also publshed as Assembly Document No. 148, 1868).

BOARD OF MANAGERS, SOLDIERS' DEPOT

Report of the Board of managers of the New York state Soldiers' Depot, and of the fund for the relief of sick and wounded, furloughed and discharged soldiers. . . . Albany: n.p., 1864.

Report of the General Agent of the State of New York, for the Relief of Sick, Wounded, Furloughed and Discharged Soldiers. Albany: Comstock & Cassidy, 1864.

Annual Report of the General Agent for the Relief of Sick and Wounded Soldiers (avaliable only in Senate Document No. 83, 1865).

Annual Report of the New York State Soldiers' Depot, and of General Agent for the Relief of Sick and Disabled Soldiers of the State of New York (available only in Assembly Document No. 140, 1866).

MILITARY BOARD

Report on "An act to authorize the embodying and equipment of volunteer militia," etc., with minutes of their meetings from April 16-Dec. 16, 1861. n.p., n.d. Assembly Document No. 15, 1862.

Report of the Minority of the Select Committee on so much of the Governor's Message as Relates to the Transactions of the Military Board, April 17, 1862 (available only in Assembly Document No. 233, 1862).

Report of the Majority of the Select Committee on so much of the Governor's Message as Relates to the Transactions of the Military Board (available only in Assembly Document No. 194, 1862).

Report of the Select Committee Appointed to Investigate the Transactions of the State Military Board (available only in Assembly Document No. 242, 1862).

COMMISSARY GENERAL'S OFFICE

Annual Report [for 1860] of the Commissary General, January 31, 1861 (available only in Assembly Document No. 14, 1861).

Annual Report [for 1861] of the Commissary General of the State of New York. Albany: Charles Van Benthuysen, 1862 (also published as Assembly Document No. 248, 1862).

Annual Report [for 1862] of the Commissary General of the State of New York. Albany: Comstock & Cassidy, 1863 (also published as Assembly Document No. 66, 1863).

Annual Report [for 1863] of the Commissary General of Ordnance of the State of New York (available only in Assembly Document No. 142, 1864).

Annual Report [for 1864] of the Commissary General of the State of New York (available only in Assembly Document No. 21, 1865).

Annual Report [for 1865] of the Commissary General of Ordnance of the State of New York (availble only in Assembly Document No. 48, 1866).

INSPECTOR GENERAL'S OFFICE

Annual Report [for 1861] of the Inspector General's Office (available only in Assembly Document No. 13, 1862).

Annual Report [for 1862] of the Inspector General's Office (available only in Assembly Document No. 47, 1863).

Annual Report [for 1863] of the Inspector General's Office. Albany: Comstock & Cassidy, 1864 (also published as Senate Document No. 28, 1864).

Communication from the Governor Transmitting the Special Report of the Inspector General (available only in Senate Document No. 33, 1864).

Annual Report [for 1865] of the Inspector General of the State of New York. For the Year Ending December 31,1865. Albany: C. Wendell, Legislative Printer, 1866 (also published as Assembly Document No. 45, 1866).

PAYMASTER GENERAL'S OFFICE

Annual Report [for 1862] of the Paymaster General of the State of New York. Albany: Comstock & Cassidy, 1863 (also published as Assembly Document No. 187, 1863).

Annual Report [for 1865] of the Paymaster General of the State of New York. Albany: C. Wendell, 1866 (also published as Assembly Document No. 39, 1866).

Communication From the Governor Transmitting a Communication From the Paymaster General Relative to the Payment of Bounties to Volunteers (available only in Assembly Document No. 183, 1864).

QUARTERMASTER GENERAL'S OFFICE

Annual Report [for 1861] of the Quartermaster General of the State of New York. Albany: Charles Van Benthuysen, 1862 (also published as Assembly Document No. 245, 1862).

Annual Report [for 1862] of the Quartermaster General of the State of New York for the Year Ending December 31, 1862, with Accompanying Documents. Albany: Comstock & Cassidy, 1863 (also published as Assembly Document No. 198, 1863).

Annual Report [for 1863] of the Quartermaster General of the State of New York for the Year Ending December 31, 1863, with Accompanying Documents. Albany: Comstock & Cassidy, 1864 (also published as Assembly Document No. 127, 1864).

Annual Report [for 1864] of the Quartermaster General of the State of New York for the Year Ending December 31, 1863, with Accompanying Documents. Albany: Comstock & Cassidy, 1865 (also published as Assembly Document No. 53, 1865).

Annual Report [for 1865] of the Quartermaster General of the State of New York for the Year 1865. Albany: C. Wendell, 1866 (also published as Assembly Document No. 36, 1866).

Annual Report of the Transactions of the Quartermaster General's Department for the year 1866, Including also Reports of Military Agencies, and in Relation to the Sick, Wounded, and Disabled Soldiers Cared for by the State of New York for the same period (available only in Assembly Document No. 112, 1867).

Annual Report of the Transactions of the Quartermaster General's Department for the year 1867, Including also Reports of Military Agencies, and in Relation to the Sick, Wounded, and Disabled Soldiers Cared for by the State of New York for the Same Period (available only in Assembly Document No. 47, 1868).

Annual Report of the Transactions of the Quartermaster General's Department for the year 1868, Including also Reports of Military Agencies, and in Relation to the Sick, Wounded, and Disabled Soldiers Cared for by the State of New York for the Same Period (available only in Assembly Document No. 23, 1869).

SURGEON GENERAL'S OFFICE

Annual Report [for 1861] of the Surgeon General of the State of New York. Albany: Charles Van Benthuysen, 1862 (also available as Assembly Document No. 12, 1862).

Annual Report [for 1862] of the Surgeon General of the State of New York. Albany: Comstock & Cassidy, 1863 (also available as Assembly Document No. 44, 1863).

Annual Report [for 1863] of the Surgeon General of the State of New York. Albany: Comstock & Cassidy, 1864 (also available as Assembly Document No. 110, 1864).

Annual Report [for 1864] of the Surgeon General of the State of New York. Albany: C. Wendell, 1865 (also available as Assembly Document No. 113, 1865).

Annual Report [for 1865] of the Surgeon General of the State of New York. Albany: C. Wendell, 1866 (also available as Assembly Document No. 129, 1866).

Appendix G
Adjutant General's Annual Reports

The following is a list of supplements to annual reports issued by the New York State Adjutant General's Office between 1893 through 1905. These supplements provide summary information on the military service records of individuals who served in volunteer regiments during the Civil War. These volumes were compiled from Series 13775 (see p. 65), Civil War Muster Roll Abstracts of New York State Volunteers, United States Sharpshooters, and United States Colored Troops. For many researchers, the information contained in these publications will serve to meet their immediate needs concerning the service of New Yorkers who served during the Civil War. However, these volumes do not contain all of the information that is frequently provided in Series 13775 (e.g., physical description, occupation, etc.). Nevertheless, they remain a readily accessible source of data on more than 360,000 men from New York who served during the war. This appendix is intended to assist researchers in identifying specific volumes containing information about units in which they are interested. The serial number referred to in each entry is more commonly known as the volume number for the report.

These volumes are available at many major research institutions in New York State. The New York State Library's Manuscripts and Special Collections Unit maintains a complete set of the reports, both in paper and on microfiche, which researchers may use in its reference room on the 11th floor of the Cultural Education Center in the Empire State Plaza. The volumes are also available on microfiche as part of the *Civil War Unit Histories: Regimental Histories and Personal Narratives*, a micro publication issued by University Publications of America. *Civil War Unit Histories* is available from the State Library's Microforms Section, which is located on the 7th floor of the Cultural Education Center. This micro publication is not available through interlibrary loan. It is, however, available from many major research institutions nationwide.

Annual Report of the Adjutant General of the State of New York for the Year 1893, Volume II. Registers of New York Regiments in the War of the Rebellion [Supplementary Volumes to the Annual Report of the Adjutant General for 1893–1905. Serial 1]. Registers of the 1st, 2nd, 3d, and 4th Regiments of Cavalry, N.Y. Vols., in War of the Rebellion (Albany: James B. Lyon, 1894). 1,266 pages.

Annual Report of the Adjutant General of the State of New York for the Year 1894, Volume II. Registers of New York Regiments in the War of the Rebellion [Supplementary Volumes to the Annual Report of the Adjutant General for 1893–1905. Serial 2]. Registers of the 5th, 6th, 7th, and 8th Regiments of Cavalry, N.Y. Vols., in War of the Rebellion (Albany: James B. Lyon, 1895). 1,148 pages.

Annual Report of the Adjutant General of the State of New York for the Year 1894, Volume III. Registers of New York Regiments in the War of the Rebellion [Supplementary Volumes to the Annual Report of the Adjutant General for 1893–1905. Serial 3]. Registers of the 9th, 10th, 11th, and 12th Regiments of Cavalry, N.Y. Vols., in War of the Rebellion (Albany: James B. Lyon, 1895). 1,324 pages.

Annual Report of the Adjutant General of the State of New York for the Year 1894, Volume IV. Registers of New York Regiments in the War of the Rebellion [Supplementary Volumes to the Annual Report of the Adjutant General for 1893–1905. Serial 4]. Registers of the 13th, 14th, 15th, 16th, and 18th Regiments of Cavalry, N.Y. Vols., in War of the Rebellion (Albany: James B. Lyon, 1895). 1,369 pages.

Annual Report of the Adjutant General of the State of New York for the Year 1894, Volume V. Registers of New York Regiments in the War of the Rebellion [Supplementary Volumes to the Annual Report of the Adjutant General for 1893–1905. Serial 5]. Registers of the 20th, 21st, 22d, 23d, 24th, 25th, and 26th Regiments of Cavalry, N.Y. Vols., in War of the Rebellion (Albany: James B. Lyon, 1895). 1,269 pages.

Annual Report of the Adjutant General of the State of New York for the Year 1895. Registers of New York

Regiments in the War of the Rebellion [Supplementary Volumes to the Annual Report of the Adjutant General for 1893–1905. Serial 6]. Registers of the First and Second Veteran Cavalry, First and Second Mounted Rifles, in War of the Rebellion (Albany: Wynkoop, Hallenbeck, Crawford, 1896). 1,059 pages.

Annual Report of the Adjutant General of the State of New York for the Year 1895. Registers of New York Regiments in the War of the Rebellion [Supplementary Volumes to the Annual Report of the Adjutant General for 1893–1905. Serial 7]. Registers of the First Dragoons, Oneida Independent Company Cavalry, First, Second, Third, and Fourth Provisional Cavalry in the War of the Rebellion (Albany: Wynkoop, Hallenbeck, Crawford, 1896). 1,077 pages.

Annual Report of the Adjutant General of the State of New York for the Year 1896. Registers of New York Regiments in the War of the Rebellion [Supplementary Volumes to the Annual Report of the Adjutant General for 1893–1905. Serial 8]. Registers of the First and Second Regiments of New York Artillery, in the War of the Rebellion (Albany: Wynkoop, Hallenbeck, Crawford, 1897). 1,085 pages.

Annual Report of the Adjutant General of the State of New York for the Year 1896. Registers of New York Regiments in the War of the Rebellion [Supplementary Volumes to the Annual Report of the Adjutant General for 1893–1905. Serial 9]. Registers of the Third and Fourth Artillery in the War of the Rebellion (Albany: Wynkoop, Hallenbeck, Crawford, 1897). 1,209 pages.

Annual Report of the Adjutant General of the State of New York for the Year 1896. Registers of New York Regiments in the War of the Rebellion [Supplementary Volumes to the Annual Report of the Adjutant General for 1893–1905. Serial 10]. Registers of the Fifth and Sixth Artillery in the War of the Rebellion (Albany: Wynkoop, Hallenbeck, Crawford, 1897). 1,286 pages.

Annual Report of the Adjutant General of the State of New York for the Year 1897. Registers of New York Regiments in the War of the Rebellion [Supplementary Volumes to the Annual Report of the Adjutant General for 1893–1905. Serial 11]. Registers of the Seventh and Eighth Artillery in the War of the Rebellion (Albany: Wynkoop, Hallenbeck, Crawford, 1898). 828 pages.

Annual Report of the Adjutant General of the State of New York for the Year 1897. Registers of New York Regiments in the War of the Rebellion [Supplementary Volumes to the Annual Report of the Adjutant General for 1893–1905. Serial 12]. Registers of the Ninth and Tenth Artillery in the War of the Rebellion (Albany: Wynkoop, Hallenbeck, Crawford, 1898). 812 pages.

Annual Report of the Adjutant General of the State of New York for the Year 1897. Registers of New York Regiments in the War of the Rebellion [Supplementary Volumes to the Annual Report of the Adjutant General for 1893–1905. Serial 13]. Registers of the Thirteenth and Fourteenth Artillery in the War of the Rebellion (Albany: Wynkoop, Hallenbeck, Crawford, 1898). 831 pages.

Annual Report of the Adjutant General of the State of New York for the Year 1897. Registers of New York Regiments in the War of the Rebellion [Supplementary Volumes to the Annual Report of the Adjutant General for 1893–1905. Serial 14]. Registers of the Fifteenth and Sixteenth Artillery in the War of the Rebellion (Albany: Wynkoop, Hallenbeck, Crawford, 1898). 926 pages.

Annual Report of the Adjutant General of the State of New York for the Year 1897. Registers of New York Regiments in the War of the Rebellion [Supplementary Volumes to the Annual Report of the Adjutant General for 1893–1905]. Registers of the Marine Artillery and First to Thirty-Fourth Batteries. Serial No. 15 (Albany: Wynkoop, Hallenbeck, Crawford, 1898). 1,431 pages.

Annual Report of the Adjutant General of the State of New York for the Year 1898. Registers of New York Regiments in the War of the Rebellion [Supplementary Volumes to the Annual Report of the Adjutant General for 1893–1905]. Registers of the First, Fifteenth, and Fiftieth Engineers, and First Battalion Sharpshooters. Serial No. 16 (Albany: Wynkoop, Hallenbeck, Crawford, 1898). 1,282 pages.

Annual Report of the Adjutant General of the State of New York for the Year 1898. Registers of New York Regiments in the War of the Rebellion [Supplementary Volumes to the Annual Report of the Adjutant General for 1893–1905]. Registers of the First, Second, Third, Fourth, Fifth, and Fifth Veteran Infantry. Serial No. 17 (Albany: Wynkoop, Hallenbeck, Crawford, 1899). 1,244 pages.

Annual Report of the Adjutant General of the State of New York for the Year 1899. Registers of New York Regiments in the War of the Rebellion [Supplementary Volumes to the Annual Report of the Adjutant General for 1893–1905]. Registers of the Sixth, Seventh, Seventh Veteran, Eighth, Ninth, Tenth, and Eleventh Regiments of Infantry. Serial No. 18 (Albany: James B. Lyon, 1900). 1,222 pages.

Annual Report of the Adjutant General of the State of New York for the Year 1899. Registers of New York Regiments in the War of the Rebellion [Supplementary Volumes to the Annual Report of the Adjutant General for 1893–1905]. Registers of the Twelfth, Thirteenth, Fourteenth, Sixteenth, Seventeenth, Seventeenth Veteran, and Eighteenth Regiments of Infantry. (Fifteenth Infantry, *see* Fiftieth Engineers.) Serial No. 19 (Albany: James B. Lyon, 1900). 1,083 pages.

Annual Report of the Adjutant General of the State of New York for the Year 1899. Registers of New York Regiments in the War of the Rebellion [Supplementary Volumes to the Annual Report of the Adjutant General for 1893–1905]. Registers of the Twentieth, Twenty-First, Twenty-Second, Twenty-Third, Twenty-Fourth, and Twenty-Fifth Regiments of Infantry. (Nineteenth Infantry, *see* Third Artillery.) Serial No. 20 (Albany: James B. Lyon, 1900). 811 pages.

Annual Report of the Adjutant General of the State of New York for the Year 1899. Registers of New York Regiments in the War of the Rebellion [Supplementary Volumes to the Annual Report of the Adjutant General for 1893–1905]. Registers of the Twenty-sixth, Twenty-seventh, Twenty-eighth, Twenty-ninth, Thirtieth, Thirty-first, and Thirty-second Regiments of Infantry. Serial No. 21 (Albany: James B. Lyon, 1900). 1,024 pages.

Annual Report of the Adjutant General of the State of New York for the Year 1900. Registers of New York Regiments in the War of the Rebellion [Supplementary Volumes to the Annual Report of the Adjutant General for 1893–1905]. Registers of the Thirty-third, Thirty-fourth, Thirty-fifth, Thirty-sixth, Thirty-seventh, and Thirty-eighth Regiments of Infantry. Serial No. 22 (Albany: James B. Lyon, 1900). 961 pages.

Annual Report of the Adjutant General of the State of New York for the Year 1900. Registers of New York Regiments in the War of the Rebellion [Supplementary Volumes to the Annual Report of the Adjutant General for 1893–1905]. Registers of the Thirty-ninth, Fortieth, Forty-first, Forty-second, and Forty-third Regiments of Infantry. Serial No. 23 (Albany: James B. Lyon, 1901). 1,361 pages.

Annual Report of the Adjutant General of the State of New York for the Year 1900. Registers of New York Regiments in the War of the Rebellion [Supplementary Volumes to the Annual Report of the Adjutant General for 1893–1905]. Registers of the Forty-fourth, Forty-fifth, Forty-sixth, Forty-seventh, Forty-eighth, and Forty-ninth Regiments of Infantry. Serial No. 24 (Albany: James B. Lyon, 1901). 1,374 pages.

Annual Report of the Adjutant General of the State of New York for the Year 1900. Registers of New York Regiments in the War of the Rebellion [Supplementary Volumes to the Annual Report of the Adjutant General for 1893–1905]. Registers of the Fifty-first, Fifty-second, Fifty-third, Fifty-fourth, Fifty-fifth, and Fifty-sixth Regiments of Infantry. Serial No. 25 (Albany: James B. Lyon, 1901). 1,239 pages.

Annual Report of the Adjutant General of the State of New York for the Year 1900. Registers of New York Regiments in the War of the Rebellion [Supplementary Volumes to the Annual Report of the Adjutant General for 1893–1905]. Registers of the Fifty-seventh, Fifty-eighth, Fifty-ninth, Sixtieth, Sixty-first, and Sixty-second Regiments of Infantry. Serial No. 26 (Albany: James B. Lyon, 1901). 1,297 pages.

Annual Report of the Adjutant General of the State of New York for the Year 1901. Registers of New York Regiments in the War of the Rebellion [Supplementary Volumes to the Annual Report of the Adjutant General for 1893–1905]. Registers of the Sixty-third, Sixty-fourth, Sixty-fifth, Sixty-sixth, Sixty-seventh, and Sixty-eighth Regiments of Infantry. Serial No. 27 (Albany: James B. Lyon, 1902). 1,339 pages.

Annual Report of the Adjutant General of the State of New York for the Year 1901. Registers of New York Regiments in the War of the Rebellion [Supplementary Volumes to the Annual Report of the Adjutant General for 1893–1905]. Registers of the Sixty-ninth, Seventieth, Seventy-first, Seventy-second, Seventy-third, and Seventy-fourth Regiments of Infantry. Serial No. 28 (Albany: James B. Lyon, 1902). 1,291 pages.

Annual Report of the Adjutant General of the State of New York for the Year 1901. Registers of New York Regiments in the War of the Rebellion [Supplementary Volumes to the Annual Report of the Adjutant General for 1893–1905]. Registers of the Seventy-fifth, Seventy-sixth, Seventy-seventh, Seventy-eighth, Seventy-ninth, and Eightieth Regiments of Infantry. Serial No. 29 (Albany: James B. Lyon, 1902). 1,357 pages.

Annual Report of the Adjutant General of the State of New York for the Year 1901. Registers of New York Regiments in the War of the Rebellion [Supplementary Volumes to the Annual Report of the Adjutant General for 1893–1905]. Registers of the Eighty-first, Eighty-second, Eighty-third, Eighty-fourth, Eighty-fifth, Eighty-sixth, and Eighty-seventh Regiments of Infantry. Serial No. 30 (Albany: James B. Lyon, 1902). 1,446 pages.

Annual Report of the Adjutant General of the State of New York for the Year 1901. Registers of New York Regiments in the War of the Rebellion [Supplementary Volumes to the Annual Report of the Adjutant General for 1893–1905]. Registers of the Eighty-eighth, Eighty-ninth, Ninetieth, Ninety-first, Ninety-second, and Ninety-third Regiments of Infantry. Serial No. 31 (Albany: James B. Lyon, 1902). 1,333 pages.

Annual Report of the Adjutant General of the State of New York for the Year 1902. Registers of New York Regiments in the War of the Rebellion [Supplementary Volumes to the Annual Report of the Adjutant General for 1893–1905]. Registers of the Ninety-fourth, Ninety-fifth, Ninety-sixth, Ninety-seventh, Ninety-eighth, and Ninety-ninth Regiments of Infantry. Serial No. 32 (Albany: The Argus Company, 1903). 1,382 pages.

Annual Report of the Adjutant General of the State of New York for the Year 1902. Registers of New York Regiments in the War of the Rebellion [Supplementary Volumes to the Annual Report of the Adjutant General for 1893–1905]. Registers of the 100th, 101st, 102d, 103d, 104th, 105th, and 106th Regiments of Infantry. Serial No. 33 (Albany: The Argus Company, 1903). 1,381 pages.

Annual Report of the Adjutant General of the State of New York for the Year 1903. Registers of New York Regiments in the War of the Rebellion [Supplementary Volumes to the Annual Reports of the Adjutant General for 1893–1905]. Registers of the 107th, 108th, 109th, 110th, 111th, 112th, and 113th Regiments of Infantry. Serial No. 34 (Albany: Oliver A. Quayle, 1904). 1,138 pages.

Annual Report of the Adjutant General of the State of New York for the Year 1903. Registers of New York Regiments in the War of the Rebellion [Supplementary Volumes to the Annual Reports of the Adjutant General for 1893–1905]. Registers of the 114th, 115th, 116th, 117th, 118th, 119th, and 120th Regiments of Infantry. Serial No. 35 (Albany: Oliver A. Quayle, 1904). 1,189 pages.

Annual Report of the Adjutant General of the State of New York for the Year 1903. Registers of New York Regiments in the War of the Rebellion [Supplementary Volumes to the Annual Reports of the Adjutant General for 1893–1905]. Registers of the 121st, 122d, 123d, 124th, 125th, 126th, and 127th Regiments of Infantry. Serial No. 36 (Albany: Oliver A. Quayle, 1904). 1,161 pages.

Annual Report of the Adjutant General of the State of New York for the Year 1903. Registers of New York Regiments in the War of the Rebellion [Supplementary Volumes to the Annual Reports of the Adjutant General for 1893–1905]. Registers of the 128th, 129th, 130th, 131st, 132d, 133d, 134th, 135th, 136th, 137th, 138th, and 139th Regiments of Infantry. Serial No. 37 (Albany: Oliver A. Quayle, 1904). 1,172 pages.

Annual Report of the Adjutant General of the State of New York for the Year 1904. Registers of New York Regiments in the War of the Rebellion [Supplementary Volumes to the Annual Reports of the Adjutant

General for 1893–1905]. Registers of the 140th, 141st, 142d, 143d, 144th, 145th, and 146th Regiments of Infantry. Serial No. 38 (Albany: Brandow Printing Company, 1905). 1,220 pages.

Annual Report of the Adjutant General of the State of New York for the Year 1904. Registers of New York Regiments in the War of the Rebellion [Supplementary Volumes to the Annual Reports of the Adjutant General for 1893–1905]. Registers of the 147th, 148th, 149th, 150th, 151st, 152d, 153d, 154th, and 155th Regiments of Infantry. Serial No. 39 (Albany: Brandow Printing Company, 1905). 1,376 pages.

Annual Report of the Adjutant General of the State of New York for the Year 1904. Registers of New York Regiments in the War of the Rebellion [Supplementary Volumes to the Annual Reports of the Adjutant General for 1893–1905]. Registers of the 156th, 157th, 158th, 159th, 160th, 161st, 162d, 163d, 164th, 165th, 166th, and 167th Regiments of Infantry. Serial No. 40 (Albany: Brandow Printing Company, 1905). 1,436 pages.

Annual Report of the Adjutant General of the State of New York for the Year 1905. Registers of New York Regiments in the War of the Rebellion [Supplementary Volumes to the Annual Reports of the Adjutant General for 1893–1905]. Registers of the 168th, 169th, 170th, 171st, 172d, 173d, 174th, 175th, 176th, and 177th Regiments of Infantry. Serial No. 41 (Albany: Brandow Printing Company, 1906). 1,199 pages.

Annual Report of the Adjutant General of the State of New York for the Year 1905. Registers of New York Regiments in the War of the Rebellion [Supplementary Volumes to the Annual Reports of the Adjutant General for 1893–1905]. Registers of the 178th, 179th, 180th, 181st, 182d, 183d, 184th, 185th, 186th, and 187th Regiments of Infantry. Serial No. 42 (Albany: Brandow Printing Company, 1906). 908 pages.

Annual Report of the Adjutant General of the State of New York for the Year 1905. Registers of New York Regiments in the War of the Rebellion [Supplementary Volumes to the Annual Reports of the Adjutant General for 1893–1905]. Registers of the 188th, 189th, 190th, 191st, 192d, 193d, 194th Regiments of Infantry and Independent Battalion, Light Infantry. Serial No. 43 (Albany: Brandow Printing Company, 1906). 805 pages.

Appendix H

List of Town and City Registers Contained in Series 13774

This appendix lists all of the towns and cities referenced in series 13774, Town and City Registers of Officers, Soldiers, and Seamen Composing the Quotas of Troops Furnished to the United States During the Civil War, 1861–1865. For a complete description of this series see p. 57 of this guide. All of the registers, with the exception of the one for Warren (Herkimer County), are available on microfilm.

ALBANY	Wirt	Otto	Dunkirk	Oxford
		Portville	Ellery	Pharsalia
Albany		Randolph	Ellicott	Pitcher
Berne	BROOME	Salamanca	Ellington	Plymouth
Bethlehem		South Valley	French Creek	Preston
Coeymans	Barker	Yorkshire	Hanover	Sherburne
Knox	Binghamton		Gerry	Smithville
New Scotland	Chenango		Kiantone	Smyrna
Rensselaerville	Colesville	CAYUGA	Mina	
Westerlo	Conklin		Poland	
	Kirkwood	Aurelius	Portland	CLINTON
	Lisle	Brutus	Sheridan	
ALLEGANY	Maine	Cato	Sherman	Altona
	Nanticoke	Conquest	Stockton	Ausable
Alfred	Port Crane	Fleming	Villanova	Beekmantown
Allen	Sanford	Genoa		Black Brook
Alma	Triangle	Ira		Champlain
Almond	Union	Ledyard	CHEMUNG	Chazy
Amity	Vestal	Locke		Clinton
Andover	Windsor	Mentz	Baldwin	Dannemora
Angelica		Montezuma	Big Flats	Ellenburgh
Belfast		Moravia	Catlin	Mooers
Birdsall	CATTARAUGUS	Niles	Chemung	Peru
Bolivar		Scipio	Elmira	Plattsburgh
Burns	Allegany	Sempronius	Erin	Saranac
Caneadea	Ashford	Sennett	Horseheads	Schuyler Falls
Centreville	Coldspring	Sterling		
Clarksville	Connewango	Summer Hill		
Cuba	East Otto	Throop	CHENANGO	COLUMBIA
Genesee	Ellicottville	Victory		
Granger	Farmersville		Afton	Ancram
Grove	Franklinville		Columbus	Austerlitz
Hume	Freedom	CHAUTAUQUA	Coventry	Canaan
Independence	Hinsdale		German	Chatham
Rushford	Humphrey	Arkwright	Lincklaen	Claverack
Scio	Ischua	Busti	McDonough	Clermont
Ward	Leon	Carroll	New Berlin	Copake
Wellsville	Little Valley	Charlotte	North Norwich	Germantown
West Almond	Lyndon	Chautauqua	Norwich	Ghent
Willing	Mansfield	Cherry Creek	Otselic	Greenport

Hillsdale
Kinderhooke
Livingston
New Lebanon
Stockport
Stuyvesant
Taghkanick

CORTLAND

Cincinnatus
Harford
Scott
Solon
Taylor
Virgil
Willett

DELAWARE

Andes
Delhi
Franklin
Hamden
Hancock
Masonville
Meredith
Middletown
Roxbury
Sidney
Stamford
Tompkins
Walton

DUTCHESS

Beekman
East Fishkill
Fishkill
Hyde Park
La Grange
Milan
North East
Pawling
Pine Plains
Pleasant Valley
Poughkeepsie

Red Hook
Stanford
Union Vale
Washington

ERIE

Amherst
Aurora
Boston
Brant
Buffalo
Clarence
Colden
Eden
Evans
Grand Island
Hamburgh
Holland
Marilla
Newstead
North Collins
Sardinia
Tonawanda
Wales

ESSEX

Chesterfield
Crown Point
Elizabethtown
Lewis
Minerva
North Elba
St. Armand
Schroon
Westport

FRANKLIN

Bellmont
Brandon
Brighton
Burke
Constable
Dickinson
Duane

Franklin
Harrietstown
Malone
Moira

FULTON

Bleecker
Broadalbin
Ephratah
Mayfield
Oppenheim
Perth

GENESEE

Alabama
Alexander
Batavia
Bergen
Bethany
Darien
Elba
LeRoy
Oakfield
Pavilion
Pembroke
Stafford

GREENE

Ashland
Athens
Cairo
Catskill
Coxsackie
Durham
Greenville
Halcott
Hunter
Jewett
Lexington
New Baltimore
Prattsville
Windham

HAMILTON

Lake Pleasant
Long Lake
Morehouse
Wells

HERKIMER

Columbia
Frankfort
German Flats
Litchfield
Little Falls
Manheim
Norway
Ohio
Russia
Salisbury
Stark
Warren
Wilmurt

JEFFERSON

Adams
Alexandria
Brownville
Champion
Clayton
Henderson
Honnsfield
Le Ray
Lorraine
Lyme
Orleans
Pamelia
Rodman
Rutland
Watertown
Worth

KINGS

Flatbush
Flatlands
Gravesend

New Lots
New Utrecht

LEWIS

Denmark
Diana
Greig
Harrisburgh
Leyden
Lowville
Montague
New Bremen
Oscoly
Pinckney
Turin
West Turin

LIVINGSTON

Caledonia
Conesus
Leicester
Lima
North Dansville
Nunda
Ossian
Portage
Sparta
Springwater
West Sparta
York

MADISON

Cazenovia
De Ruyter
Fenner
Georgetown
Hamilton
Lebanon
Smithfield
Stockbridge

MONROE

Brighton
Chili

Clarkson
Gates
Greece
Henrietta
Irondequoit
Ogden
Parma
Penfield
Perinton
Sweden
Webster

MONTGOMERY

Amsterdam
Canajoharie
Florida
Glen
Mohawk
Palatine
Root
St. Johnsville

NIAGARA

Hartland
Newfane
Pendleton
Somerset

ONEIDA

Annsville
Augusta
Bridgewater
Florence
Floyd
Marcy
Marshall
Remsen
Rome
Sangerfield
Steuben
Trenton
Vernon
Verona
Vienna

Westmoreland
Whitestown

ONONDAGA

Camillus
Cicero
De Witts
Elbridge
Fabius
Lafayette
Manlius
Otisco
Pompey
Salina
Skaneateles
Spafford
Syracuse, 1st
  Ward
Syracuse, 2nd
  Ward
Syracuse, 3rd
  Ward
Syracuse, 4th
  Ward
Syracuse, 5th
  Ward
Syracuse, 6th
  Ward
Syracuse, 7th
  Ward
Syracuse, 8th
  Ward
Tully
Vanburen

ONTARIO

Bristol
Canadice
Canandaigua
East Bloomfield
Gorham
Hopewell
Naples
Phelps
Richmond
Seneca

Victor
West Bloomfield

ORANGE

Blooming Grove
Chester
Crawford
Deerpark
Goshen
Greenville
Hamptonburgh
Minisink
Monroe
Montgomery
Mount Hope
Newburgh
Wallkill
Warwick
Wawayanda

ORLEANS

Barre
Carlton
Clarendon
Gaines
Kendall
Murray
Ridgeway
Shelby
Yates

OSWEGO

Albion
Amboy
Constantia
Hastings
Orwell
Oswego, 1st Ward
Oswego, 2nd
  Ward
Oswego, 3rd Ward
Oswego, 4th Ward
Palermo
Parish
Redfield

Richland
Sandy Creek
Schroeppel
Scriba
Williamstown

OTSEGO

Burlington
Butternuts
Cherry Valley
Decatur
Edmeston
Exeter
Hartwick
Laurens
Maryland
Milford
Morris
Oneonta
Otego
Plainfield
Springfield
Westford
Worcester

PUTNAM

Carmel
Kent
Patterson
Phillipstown
Putnam Valley
South East

QUEENS

Hampstead

RENSSELAER

Berlin
Brunswick
East Greenbush
Grafton
Greenbush
Lansingburgh
Nassau

North Greenbush
Petersburgh
Pittstown
Sand Lake
Schodack

RICHMOND

Southfield

ROCKLAND

Clarkstown
Haverstraw
Ramapo
Stoney Point

ST. LAWRENCE

Brasher
Canton
Colton
De Kalb
De Peyster
Edwards
Fine
Fowler
Gouverneur
Hammond
Hopkinton
Lawrence
Lisbon
Louisville
Macomb
Morristown
Norfolk
Oswegatchie
Parishville
Pierrepont
Pitcairn
Potsdam
Stockholm
Waddington

SARATOGA

Ballston
Charlton

Clifton Park
Corinth
Edinburgh
Galway
Greenfield
Halfmoon
Providence
Saratoga Springs
Stillwater
Waterford
Wilton

SCHENECTADY

Duanesburg
Glenville
Niskayuna
Rotterdam

SCHOHARIE

Blenheim
Broome
Carlisle
Conesville
Esperance
Fulton
Gilboa
Middleburg
Richmondville
Schoharie
Seward
Sharon
Summit
Wright

SCHUYLER

Cayuta
Hector
Montour
Reading

SENECA

Fayette
Junius
Lodi
Ovid
Romulus
Seneca Falls
Varick
Waterloo

STEUBEN

Addison
Avoea
Bradford
Cameron
Campbell
Caton
Cohocton
Greenwood
Hartsville
Hornellsville
Jasper
Lindley
Prattsburgh
Pultney
Rathbone
Thurston
Troupsburgh
Tuscarora
Urbana
Wayland
Wayne
West Union
Wheeler
Woodhull

SUFFOLK

Brookhaven
Easthampton
Huntington
Riverhead
Shelter Island
Smithtown
Southold

SULLIVAN

Bethel
Cochecton
Collicoon
Fallsburgh
Forestburg
Fremont
Highland
Liberty
Lumberland
Mamakating
Neversink
Rockland
Thompson

TIOGA

Berkshire
Candor
Nichols
Richford
Spencer
Tioga

TOMPKINS

Caroline
Danby
Enfield
Groton
Ithaca
Newfield
Ulysess

ULSTER

Denning
Esopus
Hardenburgh
Kingston
Lloyd
Marlborough
New Paltz
Olive
Plattekill
Rochester
Saugerties
Shandaken
Wawarsing
Woodstock

WARREN

Bolton
Caldwell
Chester
Hague
Horicon
Johnsburgh
Luzerne
Queensbury
Stony Creek
Thurman
Warrenburgh

WASHINGTON

Argyle
Easton
Dresden
Granville
Greenwich
Hampton
Hebron
Jackson
Putnam
White Creek

WAYNE

Butler
Galen
Huron
Lyons
Macedon
Marion
Ontario
Rose
Savannah
Walworth
Williamson
Wolcott

WESTCHESTER

Bedford
Poundridge

WYOMING

Attica
Covington
Eagle
Genese Falls
Java
Middleburg
Pike
Warsaw
Wethersfield

YATES

Barrington
Benton
Italy
Potter
Starkey
Torrey

Appendix I
Where the Men Came From

Many researchers are interested in knowing the localities from which military units were recruited during the Civil War. As Frederick Phisterer commented in his monumental *New York in the War of the Rebellion* (3rd ed., Vol. I. p. 72), "It is impracticable, in fact impossible, to obtain any accurate figures of the number of men furnished during the war by each county, city, town and village." However, Phisterer was able to list under each regimental summary the places at which respective companies "were recruited principally." Charles E. Dornbusch then systematically tabulated this information to produce *The Communities of New York and the Civil War: The Recruiting Areas of the New York Civil War Regiments*. Originally published in 1962 by the New York Public Library, this invaluable reference aid has long been out of print and is difficult to find in the used book market. In fact, many researchers are unaware of the existence of the publication. This appendix is intended to make much of the information contained in Dornbusch's publication once again readily available to the research community. The New York State Archives and Records Administration gratefully acknowledges the cooperation and assistance of the New York Public Library in making this information available once again to researchers interested in the Civil War.

Entries within the appendix are listed by county and therein alphabetically by community. Each community's contribution is then listed by arm of service, in this order: Art(illery), Cav(alry), Eng(ineers), and M(ounted) R(ifles). For some localities only a unit designation appears, with no reference to specific companies. This is due to the fact that some of the regimental summaries prepared by Phisterer contain no specific references to the localities from which individual companies were recruited. Consequently, Dornbusch was able to supply only the regiment number.

ALBANY
COUNTY: Art 7LM, 9L Inf 22, 44
Albany: Art 1M, 4BD, 7A-GIK, 13ACEI, 14C, 16A-CEF, Btty 11, 12 Cav 2G-I, 2(Veteran) BEI, 3D, 6E, 7E, 9F, 12B, 13G-I, 16F, 18 CGILM, 20GKM, Eng 15F, 50M, Inf 3CDFGI, 7(Veteran)BD-K, 18BFHI, 20D, 25(Militia), 43A-D, 61I, 63K, 91A-FH-K, 93B, 175, 177, 186G MR 1E
Bethlehem: Art 7K Inf 3G
Coeymans: Inf 177
Cohoes: Art 4E Cav 6A, 21F, Inf 2C-EHI, 3CF, 104K
Green Island: Inf 2H
Knox: Art 7K Inf 175
New Scotland: Inf 177
Rensselaerville: Art 7K Inf 177
Watervliet: Cav 21F Inf 175, 177
Westerlo: Art 7K Inf 177
West Troy: Art 4BGH, 7H Cav 12B Inf 34A

ALLEGANY
COUNTY: Inf 67C, 76, 189I
Alfred: Cav 1DragoonsH Inf 160G
Allen: Inf 136E, 160I

Alma: Inf 160H, 189B
Almont: Cav 1DragoonsH, 1(Veteran)L Inf 160G
Amity: Cav 1DragoonsH, 1(Veteran)D Inf 179H
Andover: Cav 1DragoonsE Inf 160GI, 179C
Angelica: Cav 1DragoonsG, 6I Inf 27I
Belfast: Art 13D Inf 160I
Birdsall: Cav 1DragoonsH
Black Creek: Cav 5E Inf 85F
Bolivar: Inf 136K, 189B
Burns: Cav 1DragoonsI Inf 104E, 136B
Caneadea: Eng 15F Inf 160I, 189B
Centerville: Cav 1DragoonsF Eng 1I Inf 104C, 149H MR 2B
Clarksville: Inf 136K, 184E, 189B
Cuba: Art 13D Cav 1(Veteran)G, 5E, 6I, 12B, 15L, 22D, Inf 23B, 136K
East Rushford: Cav 5E
Friendship: Cav 5E Inf 85CF, 136K, 189B
Genesee: Cav 5E
Granger: Art 4D Inf 85E, 184A
Grove: Cav 1DragoonsI
Hume: Cav 1DragoonsF, 5F MR 2B
Independence: Cav 1DragoonsE Inf 160HI
Little Genesee: Inf 85D
New Hudson: Inf 136K, 189B MR 2H

Oramel: Cav 1DragoonsCFH, 5F
Richburgh: Cav 5E Inf 85I
Rushford: Art 13D Inf 64D, 160I MR 2B
Scio: Cav 5E Inf 67C, 160H
Ward: Cav 1DragoonsH
Wellsville: Art 13D Cav 1DragoonsE, 5EF Inf
    64G, 85H, 160G-I
West Almond: Inf 160H, 136K
Wirt: Inf 160H, 189B

BROOME
Binghamton: Art 16Btty Cav 1(Veteran)FM, 6GI,
    8LM, 11C, Inf 27CDF, 89BH, 109DEH,
    137ABEF, 155F, 161EG, 168H
Chenango: Cav 2GH Inf 109E, 137BEF, 161E
Colesville: Cav 1DragoonsC Inf 137F, 161E
Conklin: Inf 137BF
Corbettsville: Inf 89K
Kirkwood: 137BF
Lisle: Cav 11FG Inf 137E, 168AH
Maine: Eng 50EH Inf 137E
Nineveh: Inf 90E
Port Crane: Inf 137K, 179K
Sanford: Art 3M Inf 109E, 137AF, 179K
Triangle: Inf 137E
Union: Eng 15G, 50CFIK Inf 137 BE, 168H,
    179K
Vestal: Inf 179K
Whitney's Point: Inf 89F, 137E
Windsor: Inf 89G, 124I, 137BF

CATTARAUGUS
Allegany: Cav 5E Inf 37H, 154CGI, 188A
Ashford: Cav 9B Inf 116F, 154DG, 187AC
Carrolton: Inf 154AH, 179D
Cattaraugus: Inf 100E
Cold Spring: Art 14G Inf 154AH
Conewango: Inf 154AK, 179D
Dayton: Inf 154BK
East Otto: Cav 9B Inf 154G
East Randolph: Cav 9E
Ellicottsville: Art 13C Cav 5E Inf 37I, 154AG,
    179DH, 187CDG
Farmersville: Art 13C Cav 5E Inf 105K, 122C MR
    2B
Franklinville: Cav 6I Inf 100A, 154D, 187A
Freedom: Cav 5F Inf 154DF, 179D, 188A
Gowanda: Inf 64A
Great Valley: Art 14G Cav 5E Inf 71I, 154AHI,
    187ADEH

Hinsdale: Inf 85K, 154CI, 179D, 187C
Humphrey: Inf 154ACI
Ischua: Inf 154C
Leon: Inf 64K, 154BK
Little Valley: Cav 5E, 9B Inf 64F, 154AH
Lyndon: Inf 154D
Machias: Inf 154DI
Mansfield: Cav 9B Inf 154BG, 187H, 188A
Napoli: Cav 9E Inf 154AH
New Albion: Art 13E Inf 154BIK, 187I
Olean: Cav 1(Veteran)G Inf 64I, 71H, 85A,
    154CGI
Otto: Art 14G Cav 10M Inf 64C, 154B
Perrysburg: Art 13C Inf 154BK
Persia: Cav 10L Inf 100B, 154BK, 160K
Portville: Eng 15G Inf 154CI, 179D
Randolph: Art 13E Inf 64B, 154AH
Salamanca: Art 13B Inf 154AHI
South Valley: Inf 154AH
Yorkshire: Inf 105K, 154DI, 188A

CAYUGA
COUNTY: Inf 75
Auburn: Art 3ABDEGI, 4B, 9FI, 16CDLM, 1st
    Btty Cav 8ILM, 11K, 22IM, 24BCLM Eng
    15HLM, 50D Inf 111CF-H, 160ACEFHI
Aurelius: Art 9F, 16L
Brutus: Art 16LM
Cato: Art 9C, 16LM, Inf 111H
Conquest: Art 9C, 16M Inf 111H
Fleming: Art 9E
Genoa: Inf 111GK
Ira: Art 9K, 16L Inf 111H
Ledyard: Inf 111IK
Locke: Inf 111I, 160F
Mentz: Art 9F, 16L
Montezuma: Art 9E, 16LM Cav 8G Inf 111C
Moravia: Art 3F, 9E Inf 111IK, 160F
Niles: Art 9EF, 16M Inf 111I
Owasco: Art 9FI Inf 160BEFI
Port Byron: Inf 111F
Scipio: Art 9E Inf 111IK
Sempronius: Inf 111I, 160F
Sennett: Art 9FI, 16M Inf 160F
Springport: Cav 11K Inf 111K
Sterling: Art 9G, 16LM Inf 111CH, 160F
Summerhill: Art 9E Inf 111C, 160F
Union Springs: Art 3K Cav 11K Inf 111K
Venice: Art 9E Inf 111I, 160F
Victory: Art 9CH, 16LM Cav 10A Inf 111C, 160F
Weedsport: Art 3H Inf 111F

CHAUTAUQUA

COUNTY: Inf 49AGIK, 68 (Militia), 90H

Arkwright: Inf 100H, 112C, 154F

Ashville: Cav 9F

Brockton: Cav 9D Inf 100E

Busti: Cav 9F Inf 112D

Carroll: Inf 112A

Charlotte: Inf 112B, 154F

Chautauqua: Inf 112EH, 154E

Cherry Creek: Art 13F Cav 9K Inf 100H, 112CK

Clymer: Cav 9E Eng 15G Inf 112D, 179D

Dunkirk: Art 14G Cav 9H, 15L, 22FK Eng 15H
    Inf 72DEH, 90H, 100E, 112G, 179D, 187AI

Ellery: Inf 112E

Ellicott: Inf 112AF

Ellington: Inf 100H

Forestville: Cav 9K

Fredonia: Cav 9K

French Creek: Eng 15G Inf 112D, 154F

Gerry: Inf 112ABF, 154F

Hanover: Art 13M Inf 100H, 112CK, 187E

Harmony: Cav 9E Eng 15G Inf 112DF, 187E

Irving: Cav 9H Inf 100H

Jamestown: Cav 9C, 15L Inf 72B, 100B, 154GH

Kennedy: Cav 5E

Kiantone: Inf 112D

Mayville: Cav 9I Inf 100E

Mina: Inf 112D

Panama: Cav 9F

Poland: Inf 112A

Pomfret: Cav 22K Inf 112BI, 187H

Portland: Cav 22K Inf 100E, 112G, 154E

Ripley: Cav 9I Inf 112E, 154E

Sheridan: Inf 112G

Sherman: Cav 9E Inf 112E

Silver Creek: Cav 9H Inf 100H

Sinclairsville: Inf 72L

Smith Mills: Cav 9D Inf 100H

Stockton: Cav 9D Inf 112BI

Villanova: Inf 100H, 112CK, 188A

Westfield: Cav 9CDF-I, 15L Inf 72G, 100E, 112E,
    154E, 156HI

CHEMUNG

COUNTY: Inf 23

Baldwin: Cav 24D

Big Flats: Art 5C Inf 179H

Catlin: Cav 24D

Chemung: Art 14M Eng 50C Inf 141C, 179H

Elmira: Art 1BFI-L, 3M, 5C, 13D, 16D, 33Btty,
    Cav 1(Veteran) ABF-HL, 2FK, 3EK, 5G, 7G,

8LM, 10B-H, 15LM, 21B, 24D, Eng 15HIL-M
    Inf 23FK, 35D, 86E, 103B-K, 107A-EGHK,
    137L, 141CGIK, 161BC, 179ABGH, 187H

Horseheads: Cav 5C, 14D Inf 38I, 179H

Millport: Inf 3K

Southport: Art 1F Cav 24D Inf 179F

Van Etten: Inf 141C

Veteran: Art 14D

CHENANGO

Afton: Art 5E

Bainbridge: Art 3M Inf 168H

Columbus: Inf 161K

Coventry: Cav 10K Inf 168A

German: Cav 10M, 22L

Greene: Cav 10K, 22L Inf 114E, 168H

Guilford: Inf 161K

McDonough: Cav 10K

New Berlin: Art 1A Inf 114F

Norwich: Art 2IL Cav 8K, 20LM, 22L Inf 17H,
    89E, 90B, 114BC, 161K

Otselic: Inf 114I

Oxford: Cav 10KM, 22L Inf 89E, 114AH

Pharsalia: Cav 8K

Pitcher: Cav 8K, 10LM Inf 157C

Plymouth: Cav 22L

Preston: Cav 10K

Sherburne: Art 1A Cav 8K, 10K Inf 114F, 157A,
    161K, 176B

Smyrna: Inf 157F

CLINTON

COUNTY: Inf 22

Altona: Inf 60H, 153GK

Au Sable: Inf 118K, 153I

Black Brook: Inf 118K

Champlain: Cav 11H, 16A Inf 34D, 60H, 118I,
    153I

Chazy: Inf 60H, 96F, 118BI

Dannemora: Inf 118I

Ellenburg: Cav 15M Eng 1I, Inf 60H, 118B, 153K

Mooers: Art 13GH, Cav 16A Inf 16K, 60H, 96F,
    118I, 153GK

Mooers Forks: Eng 1I

Peru: Inf 118K

Plattsburg: Cav 2EM, 2(Veteran)H, 12F, 16AE-I,
    22G, 25LM Eng 1I Inf 16CE, 72L, 96B-DHK,
    118AH, 153GI, 186G

Redford: Inf 91C

Rouse's Point: Art 16A Cav 9M, 12F

Saranac: Eng 1I Inf 60H, 118B

Schuyler's Falls: Eng 1I
West Chazy: Inf 16K

COLUMBIA
Ancram: Art 5H Inf 128G
Austerlitz: Cav 12C Inf 128AE
Canaan: Inf 128A MR 1I
Chatham: Cav 2(Veteran)I, 12C Inf 9I, 128AEK, 159G MR 1GIM
Claverack: Cav 12B Inf 128AGK, 159ACEG
Clermont: Inf 128G
Copake: Cav 12B Inf 128K, 159CE
Gallatin: Inf 128G, 159CI
Germantown: Inf 128AK, 159C
Ghent: Inf 128AG, 159ADEG
Greenport: Inf 128K, 159AE
Hillsdale: Cav 12C Inf 91H, 128EG, 154G, 156H-K, 159E, 187E
Hudson: Cav 2L, 5L, 6M, 12BCG Eng 1C Inf 14K, 20H, 91EI, 128AFGK, 159ACDEGI
Kinderhook: Cav 4L, 6M Inf 30K, 128E, 159G
Livingston: Inf 128D, 159ACEI
New Lebanon: Inf 128AG, 159AG
Stockport: Inf 3F, 128G, 159CG
Stuyvesant: Art 16EK Cav 4L Inf 128G, 159CE
Taghkanick: Inf 128G, 159CEGI
Valatie: Cav 2(Veteran)I Inf 128E

CORTLAND
COUNTY: Inf 23, 76
Baltimore: Inf 156H
Cincinnatus: Cav 10A Inf 157B, 185G
Cortland Village: Inf 93E
Cortlandville: Inf 157EHK, 185E
Cuyler: Cav 10L Inf 157C
Freetown: Cav 10AM Inf 157CK, 185G
Harford: Inf 157EK
Homer: Inf 12D, 157DH, 185E
Laper: Cav 10M
McGrawville: Cav 10A
Marathon: Inf 157CK, 185G
Preble: Inf 157D
Scott: Art 16H Inf 157D
Solon: Inf 157C
Taylor: Cav 10L Inf 157C, 185EF
Truxton: Inf 157H, 185E
Virgil: Cav 10LM Inf 157EK, 185F
Willet: Inf 157C, 185G

DELAWARE
Andes: Art 8Btty Inf 144E
Bloomville: Art 8Btty

Bovina: Art 8Btty Inf 144E
Clark's Factory: Art 8Btty
Colchester: Inf 71I, 144K
Davenport: Inf 144I
Delhi: Art 8Btty Cav 3E Inf 72IL, 89I, 144CIK
Deposit: Cav 1(Veteran)H, 3E
Downsville: Art 8Btty
Fergusonville: Art 8Btty
Franklin: Cav 1(Veteran)H Inf 142D, 144DK
Hamden: Inf 144CK
Hancock: Art 8Btty Cav 1(Veteran)H, 25AB Eng 50I Inf 101DFG, 144F
Harpersfield: Inf 144CHK
Hobart: Art 8Btty
Kortright: Art 8Btty Inf 144CI
Lumberville: Art 8Btty
Margaretville: Cav 3E
Masonville: Inf 144BDK
Meredith: Art 8Btty Inf 144CI
Middletown: Art 7Btty Cav 3E Inf 18D, 124K, 144GK, 156HK, MR 1CD
North Hamden: Inf 93D
Roxbury: Art 8Btty Inf 144H
Sidney: Inf 144DI
Stamford: Inf 144CH
Tompkins: Art 13E Cav 1(Veteran)H Inf 144AK
Walton: Art 8Btty Cav 3E Inf 143B

DUTCHESS
COUNTY: Art 5F Inf 21(Militia), 38G, 57H-AK
Amenia: Inf 128BF, 150AI
Beekman: Inf 128DH, 150G
Clinton: Inf 128CDK, 150CH
Dover: Inf 128B, 150E
Dover Plains: Cav 6H
Fishkill: Inf 3B, 18C, 128DFH, 150GK, 159DEGH, 168BFHK
Hyde Park: Inf 128CDHK, 150DH
La Grange: Cav 9AH Inf 128D, 150I
Matteawan: Inf 3B
Milan: Inf 128C, 150F, 176C
North East: Inf 128BF, 150D
Pawling: Art 4A Inf 128BF, 150E
Pine Plains: Inf 128BDF, 150D
Pleasant Valley: Inf 128D, 150AC, 159I
Poughkeepsie: Art 5H, 16BK, 7Btty Cav 2IK, 4L, 6F, 18G, 25I Eng 1E Inf 5C, 7(Veteran)D-K, 20D, 30E, 87FG, 128DHI, 150, 159G-I, 168FK
Red Hook: Inf 128CK, 150F
Rhinebeck: Inf 128C, 150DFK
Stanford: Inf 128BC, 150CI

Stormville: Inf 143B
Union Vale: Inf 150GI
Washington: Cav 6H Inf 128BF, 150ACI

ERIE
COUNTY: Inf 21, 44, 49BD-F, 67(Militia),
    98(Militia)
Alden: Inf 116BC, 187D
Amherst: Art 1I Inf 116CEH MR 2HK
Angola: Inf 116A
Aurora: Cav 23A Inf 111K, 116BDH
Boston: Inf 93H, 116F
Brant: Inf 116AK
Buffalo: Art 1Marine, 1I, 4IK, 13ABILM,
    14BCEGH, 15GKL, 15DF, 11Btty, 27Btty,
    33Btty Cav 1(Veteran)CG, 8I-M, 10B-FLM,
    11LM, 12DEHK-M, 13I, 14HI, 16B-EG-L,
    18I, 24CDFKM Eng 50ELM Inf 35D, 36A,
    65(Militia), 69K, 74(Militia), 78E, 100AC-K,
    116ACDEG-I, 132GH, 151K, 155IK, 160K,
    164B-D, 176CGH, 178A, 179AD-G, 187AH
    MR 1FHK, 2AC-FH-KM
Cheektowaga: Cav 23A
Clarence: Inf 116BH MR 2D
Colden: Cav 23A Inf 116D MR 2H
Collins: Inf 160K, 116F MR 2D
East Hamburg: Inf 187A
Eden: Inf 116DHK, 151K, 160K
Elma: Inf 116BI
Evans: Inf 116AK
Grand Island: Inf 100D MR 2FHK
Hamburgh: Inf 116AHK, 160K
Holland: Inf 116I
Lancaster: Art 1I Cav 23A Inf 116BI, 187C
Marilla: Inf 116IK, 160K
Newstead: Art 14L Cav 3F, 23A Inf 116B
North Collins: Inf 151K
North Hamburgh: Cav 3I
Sardinia: Cav 5F Inf 116CFI
Springville: Inf 100A
Tonawanda: Cav 23A Inf 100D, 187A, MR 2CDHK
Wales: Inf 116I
Walesville: Inf 3I
West Seneca: Inf 116DH
White's Corners: Inf 100C

ESSEX
COUNTY: Art 23Btty Cav 11I Inf 22
Ausable Forks: Cav 11K
Chesterfield: Cav 2(Veteran)L Inf 153I
Crown Point: Cav 5H Inf 34H, 118E

Elizabethtown: Inf 38K, 118F
Essex: Inf 118F, 153G
Jay: Cav 2 (Veteran)L, 11K Inf 118C
Keene: Inf 118C
Keeseville: Inf 77I
Lewis: Cav 11L
Minerva: Inf 93C
Moriah: Cav 2(Veteran)K Inf 118EF
Newcomb: Inf 118E
North Elba: Inf 118C
North Hudson: Inf 118E
Port Henry: Cav 2M, 2(Veteran)E
St. Armand: Inf 118C
Schroon: Cav 2(Veteran)D Inf 118E
Ticonderoga: Cav 2E Inf 96G, 118E
Westport: Cav 11L Inf 77A, 118F
Wilmington: Inf 118C

FRANKLIN
COUNTY: Inf 92
Bangor: Inf 60E, 98DG, 142DF
Belmont: Art 13GH Cav 1DragoonsH, 5E Inf
    142DH
Bombay: Inf 142G
Brandon: Inf 60E, 142FH
Burke: Inf 142DH
Burkfield: Art 14L
Chateaugay: Art 13GH Inf 96A
Constable: Inf 142DH
Dickinson: Cav 12F Inf 142F
Fort Covington: Cav 12F Inf 98H, 142G
Malone: Art 13GH, 14C, 16E Cav 2(Veteran)H,
    13GH Eng 15GH, 50H Inf 16I, 60E, 98A-CE,
    106HI, 164A
Moira: Inf 142F
Westville: Inf 142DG

FULTON
Broadalbin: Art 3M, 13FM Cav 7F, 10I Inf 115K
Ephratah: Art 13E Inf 115EK, 153F
Garoga: Inf 115K
Gloversville: Cav 7F Inf 77K
Johnstown: Art 13E-HM, 14M Cav 10I Inf 32C,
    115EK, 153AD
Lassellsville: Inf 153F
Mayfield: Art 13GH Cav 7F, 10I Inf 115E, 153D
Northampton: Art 4D
Northville: Art 4D
Oppenheim: Art 13E, 16H Inf 115E, 153F
Perth: Cav 10I
Stratford: Inf 115E

GENESEE

COUNTY: Art 8 (3 companies)

Alabama: Art 8L, 19Btty, 25Btty Inf 104G

Alexander: Art 9M, 22Btty Inf 187E

Batavia: Art 4I, 8L, 9M, 22Btty Cav 8K, 15EF Inf 12K, 28F, 100B, 105E, 151C, 179C MR 2AM

Bergen: Art 8L, 9M, 22Btty Cav 8H Inf 100B

Bethany: Art 8L, 9M, 22Btty Cav 23A

Byron: Art 25Btty

Darien: Art 8L, 9M, 22Btty

East Pembroke: Inf 100B

Elba: Art 25Btty

Le Roy: Art 4L, 8L Cav 14F, 23A Inf 100B, 105DK

Linden: Cav 9A, 22D

Oakfield: Art 8L, 9M, 22Btty

Pavilion: Art 8L Cav 9A, 23A Inf 100B

Pembroke: Art 8L, 25Btty Inf 100C

Stafford: Art 8L, 25Btty

GREENE

COUNTY: Cav 25A Inf 20(Militia)

Ashland: Inf 120DK

Athens: Cav 5L Eng 1C

Cairo: Inf 120K, 156C

Catskill: Art 5C, 15KL Cav 5L Inf 120F

Coxsakie: Inf 120D

Durham: Inf 120K, 156C

Greenville: Inf 120K, 156HI

Hunter: Inf 120F

Jewett: Inf 120F

Lexington: Inf 120F

New Baltimore: Inf 120D

Prattsville: Inf 120D

Windham: Inf 120K

HAMILTON

Wells: Inf 115K

HERKIMER

COUNTY: Inf 44, 97G

Columbia: Cav 18LM Inf 121BD, 152EK

Danube: Art 13GF Inf 121B, 152EI MR 2M

Fairfield: Art 13GH, 14M Inf 121C, 152F

Frankfort: Art 2KL Inf 121D, 152K

German Flats: Art 2L Inf 121BI, 152K

Graysville: Inf 34C, 186G

Herkimer: Art 2K, 16DF Cav 20M Inf 34FG, 121CG, 152AK, 186G

Litchfield: Cav 2L Inf 121B, 152E

Little Falls: Art 1A, 2M, 16B-DF Inf 34B, 97I, 121AH,152AFK MR 2M

Mannheim: Art 14L Cav 18LM Inf 121AD, 152AF

Newport: Inf 121C, 164H, 152BF

Norway: Art 16F Inf 34C, 152B

Ohio: Art 5E

Russia: Art 2M Inf 121C, 152B

Salisbury: Cav Oneida Independent Cavalry Inf 34K, 97DF, 121ADH

Schuyler: Art 2L Inf 121D, 152E

Stark: Art 2L Inf 121B, 152DI

Warren: Art 2L Inf 121D, 152DK

Wilmurt: Inf 152B

Winfield: Cav 18LM Inf 121B, 152E

JEFFERSON

COUNTY: Inf 59B, 94

Adams: Art 10BHL, 14M Cav 1(Veteran)ABFL Inf 35G, 186CI

Alexandria: Art 1C, 8L, 10F, 14K Cav 18K-M, 20C Inf 186E

Antwerp: Art 1D, 10C, 14AK Cav 20CH

Belleville: Inf 24K

Brownsville: Art 10I Cav 20B Inf 35K, 186HI

Cape Vincent: Art 1D, 10K-M, 28Btty Cav 6E, 18IK, 20DGI Inf 186E

Carthage: Art 2H Cav 7E

Champion: Art 1C, 5M, 10D Cav 20AE Inf 186AH

Clayton: Art 10GK, 14IM Cav 20BD Inf 186D

Dexter: Cav 20B

Ellisburg: Art 10EL, 14M Cav 1 (Veteran)ABL, 20D

Evan's Mills: Art 10C Cav 20G

Henderson: Art 10EL

Houndsfield: Art 10HIL, 20Btty Inf 186HI

LaFargeville: Cav 20D

Le Ray: Art 1C, 10CK, 14IL Cav 20C

Lorraine: Art 10B Cav 24G Inf 186CI

Lyme: Art 10LM, 28Btty Cav 20B

Mannsville: Cav 20DM

North Adams: Inf 2I

Orleans: Art 10GK, 14I Inf 186E

Pamelia: Art 10KM, 13GH, 14M Cav 18LM Inf 186I

Philadelphia: Art 1C, 10C, 14IK Cav 20B Inf 186D

Redwood: Cav 20F Inf 35I

Rodman: Art 10B, 14M

Rutland: Art 1C, 10DK Inf 186D

Sackett's Harbor: Art 28Btty Cav 20ABDI-M Inf 186BHI

Stone Mills: Art 1D

Theresa: Art 5K, 10F, 14K Cav 20 CM Inf 35C, 186D

Watertown: Art 1CDH, 2L, 10AHKL, 13A-CI,

14C-EHILM, 16ACF, 20Btty, 28Btty Cav 2B,
6E, 11H, 13HI, 18HLM, 20B-DGKM, 25H Inf
35AE, 186G-K

Wilna: Art 1C, 5M, 10D, 14K Cav 20AEK Inf
186AH

Worth: Art 10BH Inf 186CI

KINGS
COUNTY: Inf 57C, 59B
Brooklyn: Art 4BDGHK, 5A-D, 13M, 16E, 20Btty
Cav 2LM, 4LM, 5I, 11FH, 13K-M, 25HILM
Eng 1FM, 15B-DI-K Inf 3AI, 4E, 5ABD-I,
7(Veteran), 13(Militia), 20H-K, 23(Militia),
28(Militia), 36I, 47, 47(Militia), 48A-CE-K,
53(Militia), 54, 56(Militia), 63C, 67ABE-GIK,
69F, 84, 87B-DFH, 88DI, 90F-K, 95E, 102F,
127DI, 132ABDFGI, 133BF-K, 139A-K,
155DEG, 158, 159BDFHK, 163, 164E-K,
165F, 170, 173, 176BDIK, 186G
East New York: Inf 90FIK
Flatbush: Inf 139AI
Greenpoint: Inf 5H
Williamsburg: Cav 11G, 25H Eng 15H Inf 3A,
5EI, 20I, 31I, 87CIK

LEWIS
COUNTY: Inf 59BG, 97B
Belfort: Cav 1DragoonsI
Copenhagen: Cav 20F Inf 35B
Croghan: Art 5M, 10D Cav 20E Inf 186AF
Denmark: Art 5LM, 14KL Cav 20A Inf 186F
Diana: Art 1D, 5L 10D, 14K Cav 20E
Greig: Art 5IK, 14H
Harrisburg: Art 5M Inf 186A
Highmarket: Art 5K
Leyden: Art 5K, 14K Cav 3G Inf 186F
Lowville: Art 1H, 5IL, 14FHK Cav 3G, 7E Inf 14I,
97H
Martinsburg: Art 5IL, 14FH
Montague: Art 5LM Inf 186H
New Bremen: Art 5I, 14F Inf 186F
Osceola: Art 10K
Pinckney: Art 5M, 13GH Cav 20A Inf 186DF
Port Leyden: Inf 14F
Turin: Art 5FK, 14I
Watson: Art 5L, 14L Cav 3G
West Turin: Art 14G Inf 186F

LIVINGSTON
COUNTY: Inf 58(Militia)
Avon: Art 1E, 8M Cav 2K, 8B, 22G Eng 15I-L Inf
136G, 188B-EG-K, 189K

Caledonia: Art 13GH Inf 100B
Conesus: Cav 1DragoonsG Inf 136I, 188IK
Fowlerville: Inf 104G
Geneseo: Art 14HIL Cav 1(Veteran)M, 6CK Inf
33E, 104D, 136CG, 188BD
Greigsvile: Inf 100B
Groveland: Art 14L Cav 1Dragoons B Inf 104E,
136C, 187DH, 188IK
Leicester: Art 14L Cav 1DragoonsA Inf 136C,
188EG
Lima: Art 8M Cav 1DragoonsG, 1(Veteran)E, 8B
Eng 15K Inf 27G, 102D, 136E
Livonia: Art 14L Cav 1DragoonsG Inf 136C, 188I
Mt. Morris: Art 14D Cav 1DragoonsB, 2K, 24H
Inf 27H, 89C, 136F, 188DGI
North Dansville: Inf 136BI, 188KD
Nunda: Art 4L Cav 1DragoonsI, 1(Veteran)D Inf
33F, 104A, 136I, 188I
Ossian: Inf 136B
Portage: Cav 1DragoonsABI Inf 136HI, 188DE
Portage Station: Inf 136A
Scottsburg: Cav 1DragoonsB
Sparta: Inf 136I, 189 DGH
Springwater: Cav 1DragoonsG Inf 104B, 136BCI,
188C-EGH MR 1K
Tuscarora: Inf 141G, 188F
West Sparta: Cav 10M
York: Inf 136G, 188DEI

LONG ISLAND
Inf 74C, 90FIK, 165G-K *See Also: Kings, Queens,
and Suffolk Counties*

MADISON
COUNTY: Inf 26
Brookfield: Inf 114G, 176A, 189D
Canastota: Inf 12G, 101C, 157G, 176A
Cazenovia: Cav 18H, 22E Inf 35H, 114K, 161K
Chittenango: Cav Oneida Independent Cavalry
Clockville: Inf 157G
DeRuyter: 184BD
Eaton: Cav Oneida Independent Cavalry Inf
114D, 157F, 176F, 184D
Fenner: Inf 184DK
Georgetown: Inf 157AF, 176F, 184B
Hamilton: Art 2L Cav Oneida Independent
Cavalry Inf 26D, 61C, 114G, 157ACFGI,
176A, 189D
Lebanon: Inf 114D, 157F, 174D
Lennox: Cav 22K Inf 157G MR 1L
Madison: Cav 22E Inf 157AF, 176A, 188A

Nelson: Inf 176F

Nelson Flats: Cav Oneida Independent Cavalry

Oneida: Cav 15A, 22M, Oneida Independent
  Cavalry Inf 3I, 157BG

Smithfield: Cav 22EK Inf 157FI

South Brookfield: Art 1A

Stockbridge: Art 1K Cav Oneida Independent
  Cavalry Inf 176F

Sullivan: Inf 157I

Wampsville: Inf 157G

MONROE

COUNTY: Art 24Btty Inf 26

Brighton: Cav 8B Inf 100C, 140D

Brockport: Cav 3KM, 8HK, 22C Inf 13K, 105F,
  140AH

Bushnell's Station: Cav 1(Veteran)I

Chili: Inf 140I

Churchville: Cav 22C Inf 140G

Clarkson: Cav 8H

Fairport: Cav 8H Inf 140H

Gates: Inf 140D

Greece: Eng 50G Inf 140I

Henrietta: Inf 140I

Honeoye Falls: Cav 8B

Mumford: Art 4C

Ogden: Inf 140I

Parma: Inf 140I

Penfield: Cav 8AI, 22A Inf 140DI

Perrinton: Cav 22A

Pittsford: Cav 1(Veteran)I

Riga: Cav 22C

Rochester: Art 1LM, 2M, 4CDG-M, 8LM, 14B-
  GIKM, 18Btty, 26Btty, 33Btty Cav
  1(Veteran)C-GIKM, 2GH, 3ACHKM, 6CG, 8,
  14E, 15EF, 16GK, 21CGKL, 22A-DFGIKM,
  24HL Eng 1F, 15M, 50L Inf 13AC-K, 20G,
  26GH, 27E, 54(Militia), 67H, 78H, 89D, 100C,
  104F, 105G-I, 108, 140B-K, 150E, 164B, 178A,
  188BCFH-K

Rush: Cav 8B

Scottsville: Art 4C

Spencerport: Cav 8K

Sweden: Cav 22C

Union Hill: Inf 20H

West Webster: Inf 140D

MONTGOMERY

Amsterdam: Art 13E, 12Btty Cav 2(Veteran)B Inf
  32BD, 115BDGHK

Canajoharie: Art 16FH Inf 43E, 115ABI, 153F

Charleston: Art 13F Inf 115D, 153C

Florida: Art 13F Inf 115BD, 124AB, 153C

Fonda: Inf 115ABGI

Fort Plain: Art 1K

Glen: Inf 115AK, 134I, 153C

Minden: Art 16H Inf 115BH, 153E

Mohawk: Art 2K Inf 15ADK, 152C, 153B

Palatine: Art 13F Inf 115AK, 153B

Root: Art 13F Cav 25BD Inf 115A, 153BCH

St. Johnsville: Art 16FH Inf 115BI, 153E

NEW YORK

Artillery: 1 Marine, 2C-FI, 4ABDE-L, 5A-H,
  13A-CI-M, 15A-L, 16ABDEG

Batteries: 2, 3, 4, 5, 9, 10, 13, 14, 15, 20, 28, 29, 30,
  31, 32, Varian's Battery

Cavalry: 1ABDEG-ILM, 2AEGLM, 2(Veteran)M,
  4AD-M, Captain de Rosencrantz's Company,
  5A-DKM, 6ABD-FHIL, 8K, 9M, 11A-CE-L,
  12CFGIM, 13A-HK-M, 14, 16AH-M, 18A-K,
  23B, 25C-M, Captain Devin's Company,
  Captain Sauer's Company

Engineer: 1ABD-IM, 15AD-K

Infantry: 1, 3I, 4A-DF-K, 5A-K, 5(Militia), 6, 7A-
  HK, 7(Militia), 7(Veteran), 8, 8(Militia), 9, 10,
  11, 11(Militia), 17DEG, 20B-HK, 22(Militia),
  25, 29, 31A-HK, 32E-GK, 35D, 36C-K, 37A-
  GK, 37(Militia), 38A-DF, 39, 40AD-EI, 41, 42,
  43HI, 45, 46, 47, 48EF, 51, 52, 53, 54, 55,
  55(Militia), 57AD-G, 58, 59A-GI, 61ABD-K,
  62, 63, 65ACD-K, 66, 68, 69, 69(Militia),
  70ABDG, 71BCF, 71(Militia), 72AHK, 73,
  74BEG-K, 77(Militia), 78A-C, 79, 82, 83,
  84(Militia), 87ADEGIK, 88, 90A-CGH,
  93(Militia), 95A-E, 99, 99(Militia), 101A,
  102ACD-FHK, 102(Militia), 103A, 119A-GI-
  K, 125GI, 127A-DFG, 131, 132A-CE-K,
  133A-FHK, 145, 155A-GK, 156H, 158C, 162,
  163, 164E-K, 165, 168AFK, 170, 173, 174,
  175, 176B-EG, 178B-K, 182, 186G

Mounted Rifles: 1ABEKM, 2ABE-KM

NIAGARA

COUNTY: Art 8 (four companies), 23Btty
Inf 49H, 151GH

Cambria: MR 2CE

Hartland: Art 12Btty, 25Btty Cav 8E

La Salle: Inf 100D

Lewiston: Art 8L, 14M Inf 132D MR 2I

Lockport: Art 1M, 8M, 14F, 12Btty, 17Btty,
  19Btty, 25Btty, 33Btty Cav 7G, 8K-M, 15EF

Inf 28A-CK, 105B, 151FIK, 179A, 187DG MR
A-CE-FI

Middleport: Cav 8E

Newfane: Art 12Btty Cav 3F Inf 151K, 164B MR
2E

Niagara: Art 4K, 14B Cav 12M **Inf** 178A, 179CH
MR 2C

Niagara Falls: Cav 10M Eng 50E Inf 28I, 151B

Olcott: Inf 151K MR 2C

Porter: Art 19Btty

Royalton: Cav 8E Inf 179C, 187GH

Somerset: Art 12Btty Inf 151K

Suspension Bridge: Art 14F Inf 78I, 132G

Wheatfield: Inf 100D

Wilson: Art 12Btty, 19Btty Inf 153H, 187G MR 2E

ONEIDA

COUNTY: Inf 26, 81

Annsville: Inf 146AF, 189K

Augusta: Inf 3I, 117K, 146E

Ava: Inf 117I, 146F

Booneville: Art 10H, 14GHK Cav 3G, 7H Inf 14F,
97AC, 117IK, 146D, 189K

Bridgewater: Art 1A Inf 117C, 146G

Camden: Art 2L, 14AEM Inf 117BH, 146E, 189K

Clayville: Inf 117GI, 146K MR 1CD

Clinton: Art 1A Cav 8I Inf 117K, 146GK

Deansville: Cav 8I Inf 117K, 146K

Deerfield: Art 14M Inf 117F

Florence: Inf 146F, 189K

Forestport: Inf 14F

Floyd: Art 14M Inf 117F

Hawkinsville: Inf 146D

Holland Patent: Art 2M

Kirkland: Art 14M Inf 146G

Lee: Inf 146F, 189K

Lowell: Inf 146I

Marcy: Inf 146FK

Marshall: Inf 117K, 146EK

New Hartford: Inf 117D, 164H

North Bay: Cav 8I

Oriskany: Cav 15M Inf 26I, 117F

Paris: Art 13GH, 14M Cav 8I Inf 117G, 146K,
189K

Prospect: Inf 97E

Remsen: Inf 117K, 146I

Rome: Art 4D, 14C, 16C-E Cav 13F, 20GIM, 22C,
24F Eng 50CE Inf 14G, 97K, 117ACE-I,
146B-FHI, 189K

Sangerfield: Inf 117F, 146H

Sauquoit: Art 1A

Steuben: Inf 117F, 146I

Taberg: Art 2M Cav 24F

Trenton: Art 14M Inf 117F, 146I

Trenton Falls: Art 2M

Utica: Art 1A, 2GLM, 4L, 13GH, 14CEGM,
16ACDI Cav 3G, 11C, 13F, 15KM, 22BM,
24BFLM Eng 15IL Inf 14A-CE, 26A-E, 57B,
78D, 97II, 101E, 117A-DF-I, 146ACEFHK,
164H, 189K

Vernon: Cav 15M Inf 3I, 117AK, 146BI, 189K

Verona: Inf 117B, 146I, 189K MR 1L

Vienna: Cav Oneida Independent Cavalry Inf
117BDH, 189K

Waterville: Cav 8I

Western: Inf 117I, 146I

Westmoreland: Cav 15M Inf 3I, 117C, 146I, 189K

Whitesboro: Inf 146K

Whitestown: Cav 15M Inf 26F, 117D, 146DF

ONONDAGA

Amber: Inf 122D

Baldwinsville: Art 1B Inf 3E, 122A, 149K, 185HI

Brewerton: Inf 149H

Camillus: Inf 101I, 122H

Cicero: Cav 2GH Eng 15K Inf 122K, 149H

Clay: Inf 185D

De Witt: Cav 2GH Inf 149F

Elbridge: Art 16LM Cav 2GH Inf 122G, 149G

Fabius: Inf 149FI, 185I

Fayettville: Inf 122C

Geddes: Cav 2GH Inf 3E, 149E, 185D

Jordan: Art 1A, 12Btty Cav 10A MR 2M

Lafayette: Cav 2GH

Liverpool: Inf 12F

Lysander: Cav 15H Inf 149G, 185A

Manlius: Art 14F Cav 2GH, 22E Inf 149FG

Marcellus: Art 16L Inf 122F

Onondaga: Cav 2GH, 24KM Inf 122D, 149E, 179D

Otisco: Cav 15H, Oneida Independent Cavalry Inf
149I, 185D

Pompey: Cav 2GH Inf 149E

Salina: Cav 2GH Eng 15F Inf 3E, 185BD

Skaneateles: Art 16LM Cav 2GH Inf 3E, 122K,
149G, 185K

Spafford: Cav 2GH Inf 122D, 185H

Syracuse: Art 13GH, 16CH Cav 1F, 1(Veteran)CM,
2F-H, 3BI, 8LM, 10A, 12GI, 15A-K, 16A,
20FGIL, 22BEHI, 24KM Eng 15HK-M, 50BD
Inf 3EGI, 12A-CEHI, 14H, 20G, 86A,
101BHK, 122BDEFH-K, 149A-EG-K, 176H,
185A-FH-K, 187G MR 1HL

Tully: Inf 122K, 149K
Van Buren: Inf 149G

ONTARIO
COUNTY: Inf 38H, 126DFHK
Bristol: Inf 148K, 160E
Canandaigua: Art 1K, 4M, 16DH Cav
    1(Veteran)E, 8AK-M, 15C, 24HL Eng 1FG,
    50LM Inf 28E, 33D, 85B, 148G, 160E, 188FG
East Bloomfield: Inf 148K, 160E
Farmington: Cav 2K, 9F Inf 154H
Geneva: Art 4DM, 9F Cav 1(Veteran)C-EG-ILM,
    9M, 14E, 15C Eng 50BDFI Inf 33H, 38H,
    85G, 126E, 148ACDFGI, 160E
Gorham: Inf 148F, 188G
Hopewell: Cav 2K Inf 148CK, 179E
Manchester: Inf 148K
Naples: Inf 148G, 188B
Phelps: Cav 8D Eng 50L Inf 148C, 179E, 188BI
Richmond: Inf 188E MR 1K
Seneca: Art 13B Cav 1(Veteran)L Eng 15GI Inf
    148I, 188E
Victor: Inf 100B, 188B
West Bloomfield: Inf 148K

ORANGE
COUNTY: Inf 19(Militia), 56, 70F
Blooming Grove: Inf 124G, 176C
Bullville: Inf 124E
Buttermilk Falls: Art 7Btty
Chester: Art 16K Cav 15L Inf 93A, 124AG, 176D
Cornwall: Art 15M Inf 3B, 124AC
Craigsville: Inf 124G
Crawford: Art 15M Inf 124E, 168G
Deerpark: Art 15M Cav 15L Inf 124F
Goshen: Art 13M, 15M Cav 2K, 7D, 15L,
    25CEHILM Eng 1I, 15KL Inf 7(Veteran)D-K,
    124A-EHK, 168H
Monroe: Art 15M Inf 124CG, 176D
Montgomery: Art 15M Cav 25CD Inf 124H, 168AK
Mt. Hope: Inf 124E, 168A
Newburgh: Art 15M, 7Btty Cav 2BGM, 5I, 7D,
    15M Eng 1I Inf 3B, 36B, 56A-E, 124A-
    CEGIK, 168B-GI MR 1CD
New Windsor: Art 15M Inf 124CEG
Otisville: Inf 124E
Port Jervis: Cav 2B, 15L Inf 70F, 124EF
Walden: Inf 124H, 168B
Walkill: Art 15M Inf 124EK, 168A, 176CEG
Warwick: Art 15M Inf 124BD, 176C
West Point: Inf 5H

ORLEANS
COUNTY: Art 8(three companies) Inf 151G
Barre: Art 14BE, 17Btty Cav 22F MR 2L
Carlton: Cav 8F Inf 154A MR 2EL
Gaines: MR 2L
Holley: Inf 105C
Kendall: Art 12Btty Cav 8F MR 2L
Medina: Art 17Btty, 25Btty Cav 3F Inf 28E, 90I,
    151A
Ridgeway: Art 14B, 17Btty, 25Btty Inf 90I, 164B
Shelby: Art 17Btty, 25Btty Inf 90I

OSWEGO
COUNTY: Inf 81, 189E
Albion: Art 14K, 16A Cav 6G, 8F, 22F Inf 27K,
    28G, 110B, 147C
Amboy: Art 2M, 14K Cav 24G Inf 110GK, 147H
Boyleston: Inf 110C, 147E, 184G
Constantia: Art 13GH Inf 110K, 184I, 189F
Fulton: Cav 12A, 24AI Eng 50D Inf 24EH, 147DK
Granby: Inf 147D, 184ACE
Greenborough: Art 6L
Hannibal: Cav 24E Inf 110F, 184CEI
Hastings: Art 21Btty Cav 24EI Inf 110D, 184H
Mexico: Art 1G, 13GH, 14M Inf 110E, 147F, 184DI
New Haven: Cav 24G Inf 110E, 147F, 184DI
Orwell: Cav 20B, 24EG Inf 110C, 147E
Oswego: Art 1F, 4CK, 16D, 21Btty Cav
    1(Veteran)M, 5G, 8LM, 12AGI, 15BI, 16G,
    20ILM, 21BD, 24CE-GIK Eng 50DF Inf 24A-
    CFI, 110G-I, 147ABG-K, 184B-DF, 189D
Palermo: Cav 24I Inf 110E, 147F, 184I
Parish: Cav 24EI Inf 24D, 110K, 147H, 184HK
Phoenix: Art 1A, 21Btty Cav 24A
Pulaski: Inf 37K
Redfield: Inf 110C, 147E
Richland: Art 14K Inf 110B, 147C, 184GK
Sand Bank: Art 2M
Sandy Creek: Cav 7B, 20K, 24G Inf 24G, 110C,
    147E, 184G
Schroepel: Inf 110DI, 184K
Scriba: Cav 24E Inf 110G, 147GK, 184BG
Volney: Cav 24C Inf 110AI, 147D, 184AE
West Monroe: Inf 110GK, 147H, 184HK
Williamstown: Art 14K Inf 110B, 147C

OTSEGO
COUNTY: Eng 1G Inf 76
Burlington: Art 1A, 2L Inf 121K, 152I
Butternuts: Inf 121K, 152G, 179C
Cherry Valley: Art 3M Cav 6DE Inf 121G

Cooperstown: Eng 1C Inf 43K, 176G
Decatur: Inf 121G
Edmeston: Art 1A Inf 121F
Exeter: Art 2L Inf 121F, 152G
Hartwick: Art 3M Inf 121EI, 152HI
Laurens: Inf 121IK, 152HI
Maryland: Inf 121F, 152H
Middlefield: Cav 22L Inf 121EG MR 2M
Milford: Art 3M Inf 121EI, 152H
Morris: Inf 121I, 152C
New Lisbon: Inf 121K, 152HI, 176G
Oneonta: Inf 43C, 121K, 152G
Otego: Inf 90E, 121EFHK, 144D, 152G
Otsego: Art 2L Cav 22L Inf 3C, 152DGI, 176G
Pittsfield: Inf 3G, 121IK, 152H
Plainfield: Art 13M Inf 121BK, 146G, 152BDIK
Richfield: Art 2L, 16F Inf 121H
Richfield Springs: Cav 2FK
Roseboom: Inf 121EG, 152IK
Salt Springs: Cav 6E
Schenevus: Cav 3D
Springfield: Cav 24B Inf 121E, 152DEI
Unadilla: Art 3M Cav 3D, 10K, 22L Inf 90E, 121F
Westford: Inf 121G
Worcester: Inf 121GI, 152IK

PUTNAM
COUNTY: Inf 18(Militia)
Brewster: Art 4A
Carmel: Art 6GL Inf 95K MR 1I
Cold Spring: Art 6L
Kent: Art 6G
Dykemans: Art 4A
Patterson: Art 6L
Southeast: Art 6G

QUEENS
COUNTY: Inf 15(Militia)
Astoria: Inf 5C
College Point: Inf 20I
Flushing: Art 2L, 34Btty Cav 14B Eng 15H Inf 5H
Hempstead: Cav 14A Inf 119H, 139AI, 145K,
   155DE
Jamaica: Cav 2I, 25ILM Inf 5I, 7(Veteran)BD-K,
   139AI, 158C, 163, 165B
Newtown: Inf 132A, 156HK
Oyster Bay: Cav 14B Inf 145K, 155DE, 176CD

RENSSELAER
Berlin: Cav 7C Inf 2I
Brunswick: Inf 2C, 169C

Castleton: Inf 175
Eagle Bridge: Inf 30H
Grafton: Cav 7C Inf 2C
Greenbush: Inf 3G
Hoag's Corner: Inf 125E
Hoosick: Art 16K Inf 169C
Hoosick Falls: Cav 2(Veteran)H, 7C Inf 30H, 125A
Lansingburgh: Inf 2CEH, 30A, 125C, 169K, 177
Nassau: Cav 7H Inf 125E, 169A
Petersburgh: Art 16K Cav 7C Inf 2I
Pittstown: Art 13M, 16K Cav 7H Inf 2FHI, 125C,
   169C
Poestenkill: Art 12Btty, Inf 2C, 125F, 169AC
Sand Lake: Inf 3G, 125CE
Schaghticoke: Cav 3D Inf 2I, 125CK
Schodack: Inf 169A
Stephentown: Inf 125E
Troy: Art 4BD, 15KL, 16FHK, 12Btty Cav
   2BEFKL, 2(Veteran)E, 5C, 6D, 7C-H, 9M,
   11G, 12GIM, 16FK, 18G, 21A-IL, 25ILM Inf
   2A-K, 3CG, 7(Veteran)D-K, 30BI, 65D, 93K,
   104H-K, 125B-DF-K, 169A-CG-K, 175 MR
   1E-H

RICHMOND (STATEN ISLAND)
COUNTY: Art 2AB, 4F Inf 132BFIK, 145GK,
   186CDI
Castleton: Inf 91I, 156H-K
Long Neck: Inf 5I
Northfield: Inf 156H-K
Port Richmond: Art 4DEGH
Southfield: Inf 156HI
Tompkinsville: Art 2K Cav 11ACE Eng 1M

ROCKLAND
Clarkstown: Art 6K
Haverstraw: Art 6M, 7Btty Inf 95F
Nyack: Inf 17G
Orangetown: Art 6K, 20Btty
Piermont: Eng 1I Inf 141A

ST. LAWRENCE
COUNTY: Cav 11I, 20I Inf 92
Brasher: Inf 60I, 106F
Canton: Art 14EG-I Cav 6K, 11CDLM Inf 106K,
   142AGK, 164A
Colton: Art 14H Cav 11D Inf 60A, 106K, 142A
DeKalb: Art 14I Cav 20H Inf 142A
Depeyster: Art 14I Inf 16G, 60B, 106C, 142E
Edwards: Cav 20H Inf 60CD, 106K
Fine: Inf 142A

Fowler: Cav 11M, 20H Inf 60C, 142B

Gouverneur: Art 1D, 14HK Cav 6I, 11M, 20H Inf 16D, 60AB, 142AB

Hammond: Inf 60C, 142BEI

Hermon: Art 14HIL Inf 60A, 142A

Heuvelton: Inf 60F

Lawrence: Inf 60I, 106H, 142F

Lisbon: Cav 6K Inf 60H, 142CEGK, 169F

Louisville: Inf 60G, 106F, 142CI

Macomb: Art 14IK Inf 16B, 60B, 106C, 142ABDH

Madrid: Art 14M Inf 60AG, 106G, 142CI

Massena: Cav 16AE, 18LM Inf 60G, 106F, 142I

Morristown: Inf 60C, 106B, 142B

Norfolk: Art 14EI Inf 60G

Ogdensburg: Art 14ACE-I, 16A Cav 6K, 7D, 11D, 12B, 13H, 16F, 24C Eng 50DH Inf 16A, 18K, 60F, 100A, 102K, 160DI, 142CK

Oswegatchie: Art 14A-CI Cav 13G Inf 60C, 106AC, 142AEG, 164A

Parishville: Inf 60A

Pierrepont: Inf 60D, 142IK, 164A

Pitcairn: Art 1D Cav 11D

Potsdam: Art 13GH, 14AEHIM Cav 11D, 13GH Eng 50FH Inf 16BF, 60A, 106E, 142I, 164A

Richville: Art 1D Inf 60K

Rossie: Art 14I-L Inf 60C, 142B

Russell: Art 1D, 14EH Cav 9L Inf 60ACD, 142K

Stockholm: Art 14HM Inf 16H, 60IK, 106G

Waddington: Art 14B Inf 60G, 142CI

SARATOGA

COUNTY: Inf 22

Ballston: Art 13EFM Cav 7FH Inf 2C, 77B, 115CI

Ballston Spa: Art 4D Inf 153H

Charlton: Art 13F Cav 12B **nf** 115GI MR IK

Clifton Park: Art 13EF Cav 12B Inf 115CH, 153FH

Corinth: Inf 115FG

Day: Inf 115C

Edinburgh: Art 4GH Inf 115C

Galway: Art 13E Inf 115C, 153H

Greenfield: Inf 115CFG, 153H

Hadley: Inf 115FG

Halfmoon: Art 13FM Cav 25C Inf 115H

Malta: Art 13F Inf 115CI

Milton: Art 13F Inf 115CI, 153H, 176E

Moreau: Inf 115FG, 153H

Northumberland: Cav 2(Veteran)L Inf 115CF

Providence: Art 13EF Inf 115I

Saratoga: Art 13E Cav 2(Veteran)CDFGI-L, 13G, 25C-F Inf 2C, 77C-GK, 115FG

Saratoga Springs: Cav 25A Inf 30DFG

Schuylerville: Cav 7H

Stillwater: Art 13F Cav 25B Inf 3G, 115H

Waterford: Art 13EFM Inf 115H

West Day: Art 4DGH

Wilton: Cav 2(Veteran)L Inf 77D, 115F

SCHENECTADY

Duanesburgh: Art 13F Inf 134HI

Glenville: Art 13E Cav 2(Veteran)K

Schenectady: Art 4A, 13E, 16CDFH Cav 2(Veteran)BG, 7C, 25DLM Inf 2C, 3G, 7(Veteran)DK, 18AE, 30C, 43G, 91G, 134ABFHI, 177 MR 1E

SCHOHARIE

COUNTY: Inf 76

Blenheim: Art 4B Inf 134E

Broome: Inf 134DEI

Cobleskill: Cav 3D Inf 134G

Conesville: Inf 134EI

Fulton: Cav 11F Inf 134DI

Gallupsville: Cav 3D

Gilboa: Art 4B Inf 134EGI

Jefferson: Inf 134E

Middleburg: Art 8L Cav 1Dragoons Inf 134DI

Richmondville: Inf 134G

Schoharie: Cav 3D, 16L Inf 3C, 134CK

Seward: Inf 134G

Sharon: Inf 134G

Sharon Springs: Inf 102I

Summit: Inf 134E

Wright: Inf 134I

SCHUYLER

COUNTY: Inf 23

Alpine: Inf 3K

Beaver Dams: Inf 3K

Burdette: Inf 3K

Catharine: Art 14D Inf 3K, 141AB, 161E

Cayuta: Art 3M Inf 141AB

Dix: Art 14D Inf 3K, 141AB, 161B, 179C

Havana: Art 14G Inf 3K, 89A, 107H, 141AB

Hector: Eng 15G Inf 141AB, 161BE

Monterey: Art 5C Inf 3K

North Hector: Eng 50E Inf 100B

Odessa: Art 14D Inf 3K

Orange: Art 20Btty Cav 24D Inf 3K, 141AB

Reading: Inf 141A, 161B, 179C

Reynoldsville: Inf 161G

Tyrone: Inf 141B, 161B, 179C

Watkins: Art 14F Eng 50DH Inf 23I, 161BG

SENECA
COUNTY: Inf 75, 126CFGI
Canoga: Inf 148A, 189C
Covert: Art 16L Inf 148E
Fayette: Art 16LM Inf 148AD
Junius: Art 16L
Lodi: Art 16M Eng 15G, 50A Inf 100B, 148E
Ovid: Eng 50K Inf 148E
Romulus: Art 16L Inf 148E
Seneca Falls: Art 3C Cav 1(Veteran)K, 8G, 11K,
    22I Eng 50K Inf 33AK, 148AH, 160E
Tyre: Inf 148H, 160E
Varick: Art 16L Inf 148D
Waterloo: Art 2H, 4I Cav 1(Veteran)K, 8G Eng
    50B Inf 33C, 148H

STEUBEN
COUNTY: Inf 23, 86I
Addison: Cav 2(Veteran)G Eng 50A Inf 34E, 86B,
    107F, 141G
Avoca: Art 28Btty Inf 102D, 141E, 161I, 189CG
Bath: Art 1E, 14D, 16D Cav 2(Veteran)G, 22GM
    Eng 50A Inf 23A, 78F, 107G, 141EH, 161DF,
    189ACH
Bradford: Inf 141B, 179H
Cameron: Inf 107F
Campbell: Art 28Btty Inf 107F, 141E
Canisteo: Art 4C Inf 86G, 107K, 141H
Cohocton: Art 28Btty Cav 6C Inf 104E, 161I,
    179C, 189G
Corning: Art 14DF Inf 23D, 35F, 86CF, 107I,
    141DE, 161G, 188F
Dansville: Art 14DFG Cav 1DragoonsBK, 6C Eng
    15G Inf 138BG, 141F, 179H, 188HI
Erwin: Inf 141E
Fremont: Art 15M Cav 25AB Inf 141F, 143AFG
Greenwood: Art 13D Inf 100B, 141H, 161H
Hammondsport: Inf 34I, 35F, 107G
Hornby: Inf 141B, 188F
Hornellsville: Art 4C Cav 1(Veteran)L, 6CG, Eng
    50G Inf 23G, 86D, 107K, 141F, 161E, 179CFH
Howard: Art 28Btty Inf 107K, 141H, 161F
Jasper: Art 1K Inf 161H
Lindley: Eng 15G
Mitchelsville: Art 1E
Painted Post: Eng 50A
Prattsburgh: Art 14F Cav 1(Veteran)D Inf 161A
    MR 2M
Pultney: Inf 161A
Rathbone: Inf 141G
Savona: Eng 50AK

Thurston: Inf 141E
Troupsburg: Inf 86H, 161H
Urbana: Art 28Btty Cav 22G Inf 161A, 189C
Wayland: Art 28Btty Inf 107I, 189G
Wayne: Inf 141B
West Union: Inf 107I, 141H
Wheeler: Inf 141E, 161A, 189C
Woodhull: Inf 86K, 141G, 161H

SUFFOLK (see also Long Island)
Amityville: Inf 127E
Babylon: Inf 127E
Bridgehampton: Cav 11E Inf 127K
Brookhaven: Inf 139A, 159F
Cold Spring Harbor: Inf 102C
Coram: Cav 11E
Greenport: Inf 127DGHK
Huntington: Inf 127DEI, 155D
Islip: Inf 139I, 155DE
Mattituck: Inf 127H
Orient: Inf 127H
Patchogue: Inf 146G
Quogue: Cav 11E
Riverhead: Inf 127GK
Sag Harbor: Inf 127GK
Smithtown: Inf 131K, 139H
Southampton: Cav 11E Inf 127DK, 155E, 176G
Southold: Inf 127H, 155D
Waverly: Inf 23E, 109I

SULLIVAN
COUNTY: Art 5F Inf 18D, 56
Beaver Kill: Inf 143A
Bethel: Art 15M Inf 143AB MR 2G
Bloomingburgh: Cav 15L Inf 143G
Bridgeville: Inf 143E
Callicoon: Art 15M Inf 143FK MR 2G
Callicoon Depot: Inf 56HL
Cochecton: Art 15M Inf 143GIK
Fallsburg: Inf 143BC MR 1CD, 2G
Forestburg: Inf 143AB
Fremont Center: Art 5H
Grahamville: Inf 143C MR 1CD
Highland: Inf 143K
Jeffersonville: Inf 143F
Liberty: Art 5FH, 15M Inf 56F, 143AH MR 2G
Mamakating: Art 15M
Monticello: Inf 28H, 56IK, 143AE-HK MR 1CD,
    2G
Neversink: Cav 25C Inf 143CG
Phillipsport: Inf 143E

Rockland: Art 8Btty Inf 143ACFH
Thompson: Inf 143BGK MR 2G
Tusten: Inf 143GK
Wurtsborough: Inf 143E

TIOGA
COUNTY: Inf 23, 26
Berkshire: Inf 109B, 137G
Candor: Art 13D Inf 26K, 109BCK, 137GH, 179K
Halsey Valley: Inf 3H
Newark: Cav 8CF Inf 17I, 109B
Newark Valley: Eng 15G Inf 137G
Nichols: Inf 109K
Owego: Eng 15G-IM, 50IM Inf 3H, 23C, 64H, 109BCHK, 137CH
Richford: Inf 109B, 137BG
Smithsboro: Inf 109I
Spencer: Inf 3H, 109I, 137H
Tioga: Inf 3H, 179K
Tioga Center: Inf 109I

TOMPKINS
COUNTY: Inf 23, 32E
Caroline: Cav 15G Eng 50G Inf 109AB, 137GK, 179I
Danby: Inf 109A, 137K, 179I
Dryden: Cav 21M Inf 109F, 143I
Enfield: Cav 21M Inf 109G
Groton: Art 4A Cav 21M Inf 109F, 137GK
Ithaca: Cav 15G-K, 21BM Inf 32AI, 50(Militia), 64E,137DI,143D, 179I
Jacksonville: Inf 109G
Lansing: Art 9F Cav 15IK Inf 109G, 143D
Newfield: Art 3M Inf 109A, 137I, 179I
Trumansburg: Inf 109G
Ulysses: Inf 50(Militia) 109G, 137I

ULSTER
COUNTY: Eng 1E Inf 20(Militia), 56, 80
Denning: Inf 120E
Ellenville: Art 7Btty Inf 56F, 120E MR 1CD
Esopus: Inf 156CG
Gardiner: Inf 120C, 156AE
Hurley: Inf 120A, 156CF
Kingston: Cav 2I, 5C, 15M, 25ELM Eng 1M, 15EF Inf 7(Veteran)D-K, 71K, 120A-GI, 132H, 156B-DFG, 178A
Lloyd: Inf 120G, 156B
Marbleton: Inf 120C, 156BDF
Marlborough: Inf 120A, 156G
New Paltz: Inf 156AE

Olive: Inf 120A, 156BF
Plattekill: Inf 156AE
Quarryville: Art 5C
Rochester: Inf 120C, 156H
Rosendale: Inf 120C, 156CE
Rondout: Art 5D Inf 102BG, 120H, 168G
Saugerties: Art 7Btty Cav 7D Inf 20H, 120G, 156CF
Shandaken: Art 4B Inf 120BF
Shawangunk: Inf 156ADE
Wawarsing: Inf 120AE, 156CD
Woodstock: Inf 156B

WARREN
COUNTY: Art 23Btty Inf 22
Bolton: Inf 118G
Caldwell: Inf 2E, 118G
Chester: Inf 118D
Glens Falls: Cav 2(Veteran)AEG Inf 175
Horicon: Inf 118D
Johnsburgh: Art 16I Cav 2(Veteran)K Inf 118DG
Luzerne: Inf 118DG
Queensbury: Cav 2(Veteran)K Inf 118A, 153K
Stony Creek: Cav 2(Veteran)K Inf 118G
Warrensburg: Inf 96I, 118G

WASHINGTON
COUNTY: Inf 22
Argyle: Art 16H Inf 93I, 123F
Cambridge: Art 16K Cav 2E Inf 93G, 123I
Dresden: Inf 87A, 123D
Easton: Art 16IK Inf 123I, 169C, 177
Fort Ann: Art 16I Cav 2L, 2(Veteran)L Inf 123D, 169F
Fort Edward: Art 5H, 16HI Cav 2EGL Inf 93F, 96E, 169DE MR 1E
Galesville: Inf 48K
Granville: Art 16I Cav 2(Veteran)KL, 6D Inf 123K
Greenwich: Art 16IK Inf 123AF-H
Hampton: Art 16I Inf 3I, 123K, 161E
Hartford: Inf 123EHI
Hebron: Art 16I Inf 123EHI
Jackson: Inf 123G
Kingsbury: Art 16HI Inf 123B, 169D
North Greenwich: Art 4D
Putnam: Inf 123D
Salem: Art 16K Cav 2(Veteran)D, 7A Inf 123GH MR 1E
Sandy Hills: Inf 43F, 169D
Shushan: Cav 2(Veteran)D Inf 123H
Union Village: Inf 2C

White Creek: Art 16IK Inf 123G, 176E
Whitehall: Cav 2(Veteran)DF Inf 87A, 123C, 169F, 176E

WAYNE
COUNTY: Inf 67D
Arcadia: Cav 22H Inf 17I, 111E, 160A MR 2F
Butler: Art 9GH
Clyde: Art 9K Cav 8D Inf 67D, 90D, 111B
Galen: Art 9DHK Inf 111D
Huron: Art 9ADG Cav 22H
Lyons: Art 9DK, 14BG Cav 10L, 22DH Eng 15L Inf 27B, 98FIK
Macedon: Inf 160B
Marion: Cav 8C Inf 111AE, 160D
Ontario: Art 9BK Cav 8I Inf 111A
Palmyra: Art 1L, 14B Cav 1(Veteran)IM, 8C, 15C, 22H Inf 33B, 111ACE, 160BI MR 2F
Red Creek: Art 9A Cav 10A
Rose: Art 9DGH
Rose Valley: Inf 111C
Savannah: Art 9GH Inf 111B
Sodus: Art 9D Cav 8C, 22H Inf 17I, 111DE, 160D
South Butler: Art 9A
Walworth: Art 9B Cav 8I Inf 111A, 160B
Williamson: Art 9BK Cav 8C Inf 111DE, 160D
Wolcott: Art 9AGK

WESTCHESTER
COUNTY: Inf 17(Militia), 18(Militia), 38EG, 49C
Armonk: Art 5C
Bedford: Art 6DIM
Cortland: Art 6I **Cav** 10ALM Inf 23H, 157E, 185F
Croton Falls: Art 4GH
Fordham: Inf 5F
Greenburg: Art 6BK Cav 16K-M Inf 164GI
Harrison: Art 6E, 13I
Hart's Island: Cav 2I
Mamaroneck: Art 6E, 13I
Morrisania: Art 6H Inf 17C, 20H
Mount Pleasant: Art 6BIM Cav 16K MR 1H
New Castle: Art 6IM
New Rochelle: Art 6E Inf 5G
North Salem: Art 6DM
Ossining: Art 6I
Peekskill: Art 6AF Inf 48B, 95K, 168E
Pelham: Inf 176G
Port Chester: Art 6E Inf 17B
Pound Ridge: Art 6DM
Rye: Art 6E
Scarsdale: Art 6BK

Sing Sing: Eng 1E Inf 17F, 95IK, 176D
Somers: Art 6DM
Tarrytown: Art 7Btty Cav 2I, 11A, 25ILM Eng 1M, 15F Inf 5H, 7(Veteran)BD-K, 32H, 186G MR 1H
Valhalla: Art 5C
Washingtonville: Inf 124G
West Farms: Art 6CK
White Plains: Art 6BK Cav 16L Inf 27A, 95K
Yonkers: Art 6AFM Cav 4BC, 16K Inf 5F, 17A
Yorktown: Art 6IL Inf 168E

WYOMING
COUNTY: Art 24Btty
Arcade: Cav 1DragoonsC
Attica: Cav 1DragoonsC, 5F Inf 100B, 160G MR 2CM
Bennington: Art 8L Cav 1DragoonsC Inf 136H, 187G
Castile: Cav 1DragoonsA, 5F, 9H Inf 136D
China: Art 8M Cav 1DragoonsC, 5F Inf 78G, 136H
Covington: Cav 1DragoonsD Inf 136E
Eagle: Cav 1DragoonsC Inf 104C, 136D MR 2B
East Gainesville: Cav 5F
East Pike: Cav 5F
Gainesville: Cav 1DragoonsA Inf 104G, 136D MR 2B
Genesee Falls: Cav 1DragoonsAGHK Inf 136D
Hermitage: Cav 9H
Java: Art 8M Cav 1DragoonsC, 9G Inf 136H, 187G MR 2CL
Orangeville: Inf 136DH MR 2K
Pearl Creek: Inf 100B
Perry: Art 24Btty Cav 1DragoonsAD, 9A Inf 136H
Pike: Cav 1DragoonsA, 1(Veteran)D, 5G Inf 104C, 136D MR 2B
Portageville: Cav 1DragoonsCFH
Sheldon: Art 8M Cav 9GH Inf 136H, 187G
Warsaw: Art 8M Cav 1DragoonsD, 1(Veteran)D, 9AH Inf 17K, 136DE, 179F MR 2CK
Wethersfield: Art 8M Cav 1Dragoons Inf 136H
Wyoming: Cav 1DragoonsD, 9AH Inf 105A

YATES
COUNTY: Inf 44, 76, 126ABG
Barrington: Inf 148B, 188G
Benton: Inf 3K, 148I, 179F
Branchport: Inf 3K, 148I
Dundee: Inf 148B

Italy: Inf 179C, 188BCG

Jerusalem: Art 14L Cav 22A Inf 148I, 179F, 188CE

Middlesex: Inf 148F, 179F, 188CGK

Milo: Art 14IL Inf 148BI, 179F, 188CK

Penn Yan: Art 14HL Cav 8A, 20L, 22A Eng 50E Inf 3K, 33I, 148F, 188B

Potter: Cav 15C Inf 179F, 188DE

Potter Center: Inf 148F

Rushville: Cav 8G Inf 126E, 148F

Starkey: Art 13GH Inf 3K, 148B

Torrey: Inf 148I, 188K

INDIAN RESERVATIONS

Allegany: Inf 132D

Cattaraugus: Inf 132D

Tuscarora: Inf 53(one company), 132D

From Outside the State

CONNECTICUT: Inf 48E, 65E

Hartford: Cav 2ACD

DISTRICT OF COLUMBIA: Art 1Marine

ILLINOIS

Chicago: Art 1Marine Inf 69D

INDIANA

Chambersburg: Cav 2H

Covington: Cav 2F

Lafayette: Cav 2I

MAINE: Inf 65B

MASSACHUSETTS: Inf 48E, 72L

Arlington: Inf 40H

Ashford: Art 7Btty

Boston: Cav 6A Inf 63AE, 70F

Cambridgeport: Inf 74D

Lawrence: Inf 40K

Milford: Inf 40G

Newburyport: Inf 40B

Springfield: Cav 5D

West Cambridge: Inf 40H

MICHIGAN: Inf 78K

Grand Rapids: Cav 1K

Paw Paw: Inf 70C

NEW JERSEY: Art 5GH Eng 15D Inf 20DK, 48DE, 72L

Blairstown: Cav 11C

Deckertown: Cav 2B

Dover: Eng 1K

Hampton: Cav 2K

Jersey City: Inf 5K, 88G, 102K

Kent: Art 6L

Monmouth County: Inf 48H

Morristown: Eng 1K

Newark: Art 1Marine Cav 2K, 11G Eng 1CEF Inf 20AG, 70K, 71AD, 72F

Newton: Cav 2AB Eng 1K

Orange: Inf 5I, 71E

Passaic: Cav 5I

Paterson: Art 4A, 6A Eng 1K Inf 70AI

Perth Amboy: Inf 5I

Plainfield: Cav 5I Inf 5I

Princeton: Cav 5I

Rahway: Art 6Btty

Rockaway: Cav 2K Enf 1K

Stanhope: Eng 1K

Warren County: Cav 11C

OHIO: Inf 59HI, 65K

Ashtabula: Art 11Btty

Cincinnati: Cav 3L

Cleveland: Cav 4H

Warren: Inf 152B

Xenia: Cav 3L

PENNSYLVANIA: Eng 1C

Honesdale: Eng 50BF

Kingston: Eng 1C

Moscow: Eng 50F

Mt. Pleasant: Eng 50F

Northeast: Cav 9I

Philadelphia: Art 15B Cav 1C, 4 Capt. McDonnell's Co. Inf 40CF, 71G

Pittsburgh: Inf 70E, 74AB

Scranton: Cav 2K Eng 50FI

Tidooute: Inf 74F

Williamsport: Eng 50H

RHODE ISLAND: Inf 65B-FH

VERMONT: Inf 72C

Fairhaven: Cav 2F

Pownal: Inf 2G

Salisbury: Inf 3G

Appendix J

Synonyms of New York State Volunteer and Militia Regiments

Frequently, researchers will encounter references to regiments not by their numerical designation (e.g., 125th New York Volunteer Regiment), but by their synonym. Most of the organizations raised by New York State had some name derived from local influences, commanding officer, or other cause, and were known almost entirely by these names. This appendix is intended to assist researchers in determining a unit's numerical designation when only the synonym is known. Researchers who know a unit's numerical designation and wish to determine its synonym can find this information in the unit histories contained in Phisterer's *New York in the War of the Rebellion*. This appendix was compiled from John T. Fallon's *List of Synonyms of Organizations in the Volunteer Service of the United States During the Years 1861, '62, '63, '64 AND [sic] '65* (Washington, D.C.: Government Printing Office, 1885) and Frederick Phisterer's "Index of Synonyms," contained in his *New York in the War of the Rebellion* (Albany: J. B. Lyon, 1912).

Researchers should be aware that this appendix is not an exhaustive listing of all synonyms but rather an amalgamation of the information compiled by Fallon and Phisterer.

A

Aberdeen's (David L.) Battery
  3rd Light Artillery (Battery G)
Abohbots' (D.O) Cavalry Battalion
  12th Cavalry (Co. D) and 14th Cavalry
  (part)
Adirondack Regiment
  118th Infantry
Advance Guard Zouaves
  5th Infantry
Advanced Zoos
  62nd Infantry
Albany and Yates Rifles
  43rd Infantry
Albany County Regiment
  113th Infantry, afterwards 7th
  Artillery
Albany Regiment, 1st
  3rd Infantry
Albany Republican Artillery
  25th Militia (Co. A)
Albany Zouave Cadets
  10th Militia (Co. A) and 177th Infantry
  (Co. A)
American Guard
  71st Militia
American Guard
  124th Infantry
American Rifles
  71st Militia

Ames's (Nelson) Battery
  1st Light Artillery (Battery G)
Ammons's (John H.) Battery
  3rd Light Artillery (Battery I)
Anderson's Zouaves
  62nd Infantry
Angel's (James R.) Battery
  3rd Light Artillery (Battery K)
Anthon Battalion Light Artillery
  20th and 28th Independent Batteries
Anthony Wayne Guards
  135th Infantry (also 6th Heavy Artillery)
Anthony's (George T.) Battery
  17th Independent Battery
Arndt's (Albert) Battery
  1st Independent Battalion Light Artillery
  (Battery A), afterwards known as 29th
  Independent Battery
Arnold's (Joseph S.) Company Sharpshooters
  112th Infantry (Co. L), afterwards 7th
  Company, 1st Independent Battalion
  Sharpshooters
Arnold's (Joseph S.), formerly W. S. Rowland's
  Battalion Sharpshooters
  1st Independent Battalion (6th, 7th, 8th, and
  9th Companies) Sharpshooters
Artillery Company
  15th Militia
Artillery Regiment, 1st, Light Battery A
  2nd Independent Battery

Artizans and Engineers
    1st Engineers
Ashby's (George E.) Battery
    3rd Light Artillery (Battery E)
Ashcroft's (James E.) Batteries
    3rd Light Artillery (Battery C, old, and
    Battery B)
Astor Regiment, 1st
    29th Infantry
Astor Regiment, 2nd
    30th Infantry
Astor Regiment (Charles Rosefield's)
    61st Infantry (Companies I and K)
Astor Rifles
    29th Infantry
Auburn Regiment
    75th Infantry
Auburn Regiment, 2nd
    138th Infantry, afterwards, 9th Artillery
Avery Rifles
    12th Militia, afterwards 102nd Infantry
    (Co. A)

B
Bacon's (Charles Graham) 36th Independent
    Battery
    13th Heavy Artillery (part)
Baden Artillery
    1st Battalion of Artillery
Baker Rifles
    103rd Infantry
Baker's Brigade Battery
    E. D. Baker's Brigade (Light Artillery
    Company A), afterwards 13th Independent
    Battery
Baker's (John T.) Infantry Company
    19th Infantry (Co. A), afterwards 3rd Light
    Artillery (Battery A)
Baker's (William), afterwards Edward B.
    Kinney's, Company Engineers
    6th Militia (three months, 1861 Engineer
    Company)
Bannockburn Battalion
    79th Infantry
Barnes's (Almont)
    1st Light Artillery (Battery C)
Barnes's (J. Warren) Rifle Battery
    26th Independent Battery
Barnes's (James) Battery
    21st Independent Battery
Barnes's (Thomas) Battery

1st Independent Battalion Light Artillery,
    Militia (100 days, Battery A)
Barnes's (William B.) 11th Regiment Heavy
    Artillery, Companies A-D
    4th Heavy Artillery (Companies I-M)
Barney Black Rifles or Hiram Barney Rifles
    54th Infantry
Barry's (General) Rocket Battalion Artillery
    Rocket Battalion Artillery (Companies A and
    B), afterwards 23rd and 24th Independent
    Batteries
Bartlett's Naval Brigade
    99th Infantry
Bates's (Thomas H.) Battery
    1st Light Artillery (Battery A)
Battery A, New York Volunteer Artillery
    2nd Independent Battery
Battery B, New York Volunteer Artillery
    3rd Independent Battery
Battery C, New York Volunteer Artillery
    4th Independent Battery
Battery D, New York Volunteer Artillery
    4th Independent Battery
Baxter Light Guards
    31st Infantry
Beecher's Pets
    67th Infantry (Co. E)
Bell Jefferson Rifles
    94th Infantry
Bemis Heights Regiment
    77th Infantry
Bensen Guard of 125th Regiment
    12th Militia
Bevines's (John), formerly Richard H.
    Richardson's Independent Company Infantry
    80th Infantry (part)
Biligs's (George C. L.) Battery
    1st Independent Battalion Light Artillery
    (Battery C), afterwards 31st Independent
    Battery
Billinghurst Battery
    18th Independent Battery
Billy Wilson's Zouaves
    6th Infantry
Binghamton Regiment
    109th Infantry
Black Horse Artillery
    18th Independent Battery
Black Horse Cavalry, Northern
    7th Cavalry
Black River Artillery, 1st Battalion (4th

Independent Battalion Artillery), Companies
A–D
10th Heavy Artillery (Companies E, D, M,
and B)
Black River Artillery, 2nd Battalion (5th
Independent Battalion Artillery) Companies
A–D
10th Heavy Artillery (Companies A, G, C,
and F)
Black River Artillery, 3rd Battalion (6th
Independent Battalion Artillery), Companies
A, B, C, and D
5th Heavy Artillery (Companies I, K, L, and M)
Black River Artillery, 4th Battalion (7th
Independent Battalion Artillery), Companies
A, B, C, and D
10th Heavy Artillery (Companies H, I, K, and L)
Blair Rifles
178th Infantry (part)
Blenker's Battery
2nd Independent Battery
Blenker's Rifles
8th Infantry
Bliss Cavalry
5th Cavalry (part)
Bock's (Wolfgang) 2nd Independent Battery
15th Heavy Artillery (part)
Bookwood's (Charles) Battery
2nd Independent Battery
Boonville Regiment
97th Infantry
Boyd's (William H.) Company C, Cavalry
Regiment Pennsylvania Volunteers
1st (Lincoln) Cavalry (Co. C)
Bradley's (Thomas S.) Company Sharpshooters
9th Company, 1st Independent Battalion
Sharpshooters
Brady's Light Infantry
11th Infantry (reorganization of 1863)
Brainerd's (Wesley) Regiment Engineers
15th Engineers (new)
Bramhall's (Walter M.) Battery
6th Independent Battery
Breck's (George) Battery
1st Light Artillery (Battery L)
Brickel's (Andrew) Battalion Artillery
1st Independent Battalion Light Artillery
(Batteries A, B, C, and D), afterwards 29th,
30th, 31st, and 32nd Independent Batteries)
British Volunteers, The
36th Infantry (part)

Brooklyn Chasseurs
84th Infantry
Brooklyn Phalanx
67th Infantry
Brooklyn Rifles
87th Infantry (except Companies C and E)
Breun's (Edward) Independent Company
Infantry
143rd Infantry and 169th Infantry (part)
Breun's (John T.) Battery
10th Independent Battery
Buffalo Irish Regiment
164th Infantry
Buffalo Light Artillery
27th Independent Battery
Buffalo Regiment, 1st Regiment
21st Infantry
Buffalo Regiment, 2nd Regiment
49th Infantry
Buffalo Regiment, 3rd Regiment
100th Infantry
Bundy's (Henry) Battery
13th Independent Battery
Bunting's (Thomas B.) Battery
9th Militia (83rd Infantry Co. K old),
afterwards 6th Independent Battery
Burgesses Corps
25th Militia (Co. K)
Burnside Rifles, Companies A and B
178th Infantry (Companies C and B)
Burnside's Escort
Oneida Independent Company Cavalry
Burton's (John E.) Battery
11th Independent Battery
Busteed's (Richard Jr.) Battery (Chicago Light
Artillery)
1st Light Artillery (Batteries B and G, part)
and 4th Independent Battery (part)
Butler's (Benjamin C.) Battalion Sharpshooters
93rd Infantry (Companies A, C, & D)
Butt's (Richard) Company Sappers and Miners
(Engineers)
84th Infantry (14th Militia)

C

Cady's (A. Lester) Battery
24th Independent Battery
Calcium Light Sharpshooters, Robert Grant's
102nd Infantry (Co. E)
California Regiment, 1st
32nd Infantry

Cameron Highlanders, or Highlanders
    79th Infantry
Cameron Legion
    59th Infantry (Co. K)
Cameron Rifle Highlanders (old) 78th Regiment
    Infantry, Samuel McKenzie Elliot's (1861–
    1862), Companies B and C
    102nd Infantry (Companies I and K)
Cameron Rifle Highlanders (new) Samuel
    McKenzie Elliot's (1864–1865)
    79th Infantry (part)
Cameron Rifles
    59th Infantry (part); also 68th Infantry
Campbell Guards
    107th Infantry
Carbine Rangers
    1st Cavalry
Carryl's (James B.) 35th Independent Battery
    16th Heavy Artillery (Co. A)
Carthage Battery
    2nd Artillery (Co. H)
Cattaraugus Regiment
    64th Infantry
Cavalry, 2nd Regiment (Northern Black Horse)
    7th Cavalry
Cavalry, 7th Regiment (Dodge's)
    1st Mounted Rifles, afterwards 4th Provisional
    Cavalry
Cavalry, 7th Regiment United States or New York
    2nd (Harris Light) Cavalry
Cavalry, 12th Regiment
    13th Cavalry
Cavalry, 17th Regiment
    18th Cavalry; also 1st Veteran Cavalry
Cavalry, 19th Regiment
    130th Infantry, afterwards 19th Cavalry,
    afterwards 1st Dragoons
Cayuga and Wayne County Regiment
    138th Infantry, later 9th Artillery
Cayuga County Regiment, 1st
    19th Infantry, later 3rd Artillery
Cayuga County Regiment, 2nd
    75th Infantry
Central New York Battalion
    26th Infantry
Cerro Gordo Legion
    32nd Infantry (part)
Chasseurs a Pied
    84th Infantry
Chautauqua Regiment
    112th Infantry

Cherry Valley Regiment
    76th Infantry (3 companies); also 3rd Artillery
    (part)
Chicago Light Artillery (Richard Busteed's Jr.
    Battery)
    1st Light Artillery (Batteries B and G, part),
    and 4th Independent Battery (part)
Chrysler's (E. S.) Independent Company Infantry
    10th Cavalry (part)
Church's (Benjamin S.) Engineer Corps
    12th Militia (3 months, 1861)
City Guard
    83rd Infantry
Clark's (Charles A.) Battery
    12th Independent Battery
Clark's (John D.) Battery
    3rd Light Artillery (Battery I)
Clark's (Moses P.) Battery
    6th Independent Battery
Clinton Guard, 1st Regiment
    61st Infantry
Clinton Rifles
    57th Infantry (Companies F and G)
Coast Guard
    99th Infantry
Coddington's (Gilbert S.) Battery
    20th Independent Battery
Colgate's (Clinton G.) Regiment Engineers
    15th Engineers (old)
Columbia County Regiment
    91st Infantry
Columbia County Regiment, 2nd
    159th Infantry
Conkling Rifles
    97th Infantry
Connecticut Cavalry, 1st Squadron, Companies A
    and B
    2nd (Harris Light) Cavalry (Companies C
    and D)
Constitution Guards, 1st
    40th Infantry
Continental Guard
    66th Infantry (Co. B, part)
Continental Guard, 1st
    48th Infantry
Continental Guard, 2nd
    87th Infantry (part)
Corbin's (Dewitt C.) Artillery Company
    67th Militia (30 days, 1863)
Corcoran Guard
    164th Infantry

Corcoran Zouaves
  164th Infantry
Corcoran's Brigade or Irish Legion, 1st Regiment
  182nd Infantry
Corcoran's Brigade or Irish Legion, 2nd (formerly
    5th Regiment)
  155th Infantry
Corcoran's Brigade or Irish Legion, 3rd Regiment
  164th Infantry
Corcoran's Brigade or Irish Legion, 4th (formerly
    2nd Regiment)
  170th Infantry
Corcoran's Brigade or Irish Legion, 5th Regiment
  175th Infantry (Companies A, B, and C)
Corning Light Cavalry
  18th Cavalry
Corning Light Infantry
  18th Cavalry
Cornwall Company
  124th Infantry (Co. C)
Corps d'Elite
  103rd Infantry (Co. C, old)
Cortland County Regiment
  76th Infantry; also 185th Infantry
Cortland Regiment
  157th Infantry
Cothran's (George W.) Battery
  1st Light Artillery (Battery M)
Couch's Escort
  6th Cavalry (Companies D and K)
Cowan's (Andrew) Battery
  1st Independent Battery
Cromwellian Regiment
  76th Infantry
Crounse's (Lorenzo) Battery
  1st Light Artillery (Battery K)

D

Davey's (George W.) Battery
  11th Independent Battery
Davies Light Cavalry
  13th Cavalry
Davis's (Henry W.) Battery
  1st Light Artillery (Battery E)
Day's (Samuel C.) Battery
  3rd Light Artillery (Battery F)
DeCamp's Cavalry
  14th Cavalry (part)
Defenders, The
  178th Infantry (part)

De Forest Cavalry
  5th Cavalry
De Kalb Regiment
  41st Infantry
Delaware Battery
  8th Independent Battery
D'Epineuil Zouaves
  53rd Infantry (old)
Devin's Independent Cavalry Company
  Thomas C. Devin's Company A, 1st Militia
  Cavalry
Dickel's Mounted Rifles
  4th Cavalry
Dickinson Guard
  89th Infantry
Dickinson Light Artillery
  16th Independent Battery
Dieckmann's (Julius) Battery
  13th Independent Battery
Diederich's (Otto) Battery
  1st Independent Battalion Light Artillery
  (Battery A) afterwards 29th Independent
  Battery
Die-no-mores
  48th Infantry (Co. D)
Dodge's (Jeremiah P. B.) Engineer Corps
  5th Militia
Dodge's Mounted Rifles
  1st Mounted Rifles
Doubleday (Col. Thomas D.) Heavy Artillery
  4th Heavy Artillery
Dozen, The
  12th Infantry
Dragoons, 1st Regiment
  130th Infantry, afterwards 19th Cavalry,
  afterwards 1st Dragoons
Drew's (Henry Z.) Company, Mechanics
  Rifles
  51st Infantry (Co. C, part)
Duryee's Zouaves, 1st
  5th Infantry
Duryee's Zouaves, 2nd Battalion
  165th Infantry
Dutchess County Regiment or Legion
  150th Infantry
Dutchess County Regiment, 2nd
  159th Infantry

E

Eagle Brigade, or Scroggs's Brigade, 1st Regiment
  78th Infantry

Eagle Brigade, or Scroggs's Brigade, 2nd Regiment
   100th Infantry
Eagle Brigade, or Scroggs's Brigade, 3rd Regiment
   95th Infantry (Companies I and K)
Eagle Brigade, or Scroggs's Brigade, 4th Regiment
   78th Infantry (part)
Eagle Brigade, or Scroggs's Brigade, 5th Regiment
   53rd Infantry (new)
Eaton's (John B.) Battery
   27th Independent Battery
Eighth Ward Rangers
   25th Infantry (Co. D)
Ellis's (William H.) Battery
   12th Independent Battery
Ellsworth's Avengers
   44th Infantry
Ellsworth's Grays
   21st Militia
Ellsworth's Zouaves
   11th Infantry
Empire Battery
   1st Artillery, Battery A
Empire Brigade, or Spinola's Brigade, 1st
   Regiment
   158th Infantry
Empire Brigade, or Spinola's Brigade, 2nd
   Regiment
   132nd Infantry
Empire Brigade, or Spinola's Brigade, 3rd
   Regiment
   163rd Infantry
Empire Brigade, or Spinola's Brigade, 4th
   Regiment
   164th Infantry
Empire City Regiment or Guard
   6th Infantry (Co. D); also 32nd Infantry (Co. K)
Empire Light Cavalry
   2nd Veteran Cavalry
Empire Zouaves
   51st Infantry (part); also 66th Infantry (Co. B)
Enfants Perdus
   Independent Battalion of Infantry
Engineers and Artisans
   1st Engineers; also 2nd Engineers; also 15th
   Engineers (part)
Engineer Corps, Benjamin S. Church's
   12th Militia (3 months, 1861)
Engineer Corps, E. A. Quintard's
   71st Militia (3 months, 1861)
Engineer Corps, Francis Page's
   69th Militia (3 months, 1862)

Engineer Corps, Jeremiah P. B. Dodge's
   5th Militia (3 months, 1861)
Engineer Corps (Sappers and Miners), John
   Maralious's
   13th Militia (3 months, 1861)
Engineers, 2nd Regiment, Henry V. Slosson's
   Company
   15th Engineers (new, Co. D)
Engineers, James Quinlan's Company
   69th Militia (3 months, 1861)
Engineers, Peter McQuade's Company
   69th Militia (30 days, 1863 Co. L)
Engineers (Sappers and Miners), C. D.
   Westbrook's Company
   80th Infantry (20th Militia)
Engineers (Sappers and Miners), Daniel T. Van
   Buren's Company
   20th Militia (3 months, 1861)
Engineers (Sappers and Miners), Richard Butts's
   Company
   84th Infantry (14th Militia)
Engineers, William Baker's, afterwards Edward
   B. Kinney's Company
   6th Militia (3 months, 1861)
Engineers, William M. Walton's Company
   8th Militia (3 months, 1861 Co. K)
Ethan Allen Regiment
   178th Infantry (part)
Excelsior Battery, 1st
   5th Independent Battery
Excelsior Battery, 2nd
   10th Independent Battery
Excelsior Battery, 3rd
   10th Independent Battery (part)
Excelsior Brigade, or Sickles's Brigade, 1st
   Regiment
   70th Infantry
Excelsior Brigade, or Sickles's Brigade, 2nd
   Regiment
   71st Infantry
Excelsior Brigade, or Sickles's Brigade, 3rd
   Regiment
   72nd Infantry
Excelsior Brigade, or Sickles's Brigade, 4th
   Regiment
   73rd Infantry
Excelsior Brigade, or Sickles's Brigade, 5th
   Regiment
   74th Infantry
Excelsior Rifle Blues
   92nd Infantry

Excelsior Rifle Legion, New York
92nd Infantry

F

Faugh-a-ballagh
63rd Infantry

Federal Guard
178th Infantry (part)

Fifth Ward Volunteers
5th Infantry (Co. D)

Fifty-sixth Regiment Battery (Fitch's), 2nd
8th Independent Battery

Fifty-sixth Regiment Battery (Regan's), 1st
7th Independent Battery

Fire Brigade
73rd Infantry

Fire Zouaves, 1st
11th Infantry

Fire Zouaves, 2nd
73rd Infantry

Fisher's Cavalry
14th Cavalry (part)

Fitch's (Butler) Battery
56th Infantry (2nd Light Artillery Company),
afterwards 8th Independent Battery

Fitzhugh's (Robert H.) Battery
1st Light Artillery (Battery K)

Flank Company, 108th Volunteers
6th Company Sharpshooters

Flushing Light Artillery
2nd Artillery (Battery L, old), later 34th
Independent Battery

Foerster's (Hermann) Independent Company
Infantry
8th Infantry (Independent Company,
retained men), afterwards 68th Infantry
(part)

Foreign Rifles, 1st
39th Infantry

Fort Plain Battery
1st Artillery (Battery K)

Foster's Heavy Artillery
16th Heavy Artillery (part)

Fox's (George W.) Battery
26th Independent Battery

Franklin's Body Guard
14th Cavalry (Co. B)

Franklin's Own
98th Infantry

Frank's (John D.) Battery
1st Light Artillery (Battery G)

Fredendall Regiment
Failed to organize; 91st Infantry (part)

Fremont Regiment
46th Infantry

Fremont Rifles, Palmer's Company
49th Infantry (Co. C)

French Regiment
55th Infantry

Friends' Rifle Guards
70th Infantry (Co. E)

Frontier Cavalry, 1st
26th Cavalry

G

Gallatin Rifles
58th Infantry (part)

Garde Lafayette
55th Infantry; also 55th Militia

Garabaldi Guard
39th Infantry

Garrad's (Jeptha) Cavalry Company (6th
Independent Company Ohio Cavalry)
3rd Cavalry (Co. L)

Garrard's Tigers
146th Infantry

Gavigan's (Owen) Battery
3rd Light Artillery (Battery D)

Geneseo Regiment
104th Infantry

German Battalion Artillery, 1st
1st Independent Battalion Light Artillery
(Batteries A, B, C, and D), afterwards
29th, 30th, 31st, and 32nd Independent
Batteries

German Cavalry, 1st
4th Cavalry (Co. H, new and part of Co. I)

German Heavy Artillery, Adam Senges's
Battalion, Companies A-E
3rd Independent Battalion Artillery
(Companies A-E), afterwards 15th Heavy
Artillery (Companies A-E)

German Infantry, 1st Regiment
29th Infantry

German Legion
Enfants Perdus (part)

German Rangers
52nd Infantry

German Regiment
29th Infantry

German Rifles, 1st
8th Infantry

German Rifles, 2nd
68th Infantry
German Rifles, 3rd
103rd Infantry (part)
German Rifles, 5th
45th Infantry
Glens Falls Company (Milo E. Washburn's)
175th Infantry (part) and 186th Infantry (Co. K, part)
Goodwin's (William F.) Battery, 11th Regiment Heavy Artillery
4th Heavy Artillery (part)
Goshen Company
124th Infantry (Co. B)
Governor Morgan's United States Light Artillery, 2nd Regiment
2nd Heavy Artillery
Governor's Guard
2nd Mounted Rifles
Governor's Guard
6th Militia
Governor's Guard
66th Infantry
Grant's (Robert) Calcium Light Sharpshooters
102nd Infantry (Co. E)
Gray's (Abijah C.) Company Sharpshooters
108th Infantry (Flank Company), afterwards 6th Company, 1st Independent Battalion Sharpshooters
Grenadier Regiment, 1st
65th Infantry
Grenadiers
103rd Infantry (Co. A)
Grimm's (Edward) Battery
1st Independent Battalion Light Artillery (Battery D), afterwards 32nd Independent Battery
Grinnell Light Artillery
3rd Artillery (part Co. H)
Griswold Light Cavalry
21st Cavalry
Grow's (John A.) Battery
25th Independent Battery
Guards of Liberty and Union
Mohawk Rangers

H
Halleck Guard
13th Cavalry (Co. H)
Halleck Guard, Company A
119th Infantry (Co. A)

Halleck Infantry
146th Infantry
Hall's (James F.) Regiment Engineers
1st Engineers
Halstead's (William) 2nd Regiment New Jersey Cavalry, Van Reypen's Company
Cornelius G. Van Reypen's Unattached Co. A, New Jersey Cavalry, afterwards 3rd New York Cavalry (Co. M, old), afterwards 1st New Jersey Cavalry (part)
Hamilton Light Artillery
Thomas L. Robinson's Company, Hamilton Light Artillery, afterwards 2nd Heavy Artillery (Co. L, old), afterwards 34th Independent Battery
Hancock Guards
90th Infantry (part)
Hancock Regiment
101st Infantry (part)
Hannum's (Josiah C.) Battery
28th Independent Battery
Harlan's (Josiah) Cavalry Regiment, Abram H. Krom's Company
5th Cavalry (Co. G)
Harn's (William A.) Battery
3rd Independent Battery
Harris Light Cavalry
2nd (Harris Light) Cavalry
Hart's (Patrick) Batteries
15th and 32nd Independent Batteries
Havelock Battery
11th Independent Battery
Hawkins's Zouaves, 1st
9th Infantry
Hawkins's Zouaves, 2nd
178th Infantry (part)
Hazelton's (James B.) Battery
1st Light Artillery (Battery D)
Heavy Artillery, 1st Regiment
2nd Heavy Artillery (Co. B); also 4th Heavy Artillery
Heavy Artillery, Jackson, 2nd Regiment
5th Heavy Artillery
Heavy Artillery
4th Militia; also 13th Militia
Heintzelman's Escort
5th Cavalry (Co. I)
Herkimer Regiment
34th Infantry; also 121st Infantry
Highlanders, or Cameron Highlanders
79th Infantry

Highlanders, 78th
78th Infantry
Highland Guard
79th Infantry
Hiller's (Frederick L. Battery)
16th Independent Battery
Hillhouse Light Infantry
132nd Infantry
Hiram Barney Rifles, or Barney Black Rifles
54th Infantry
Hobart's (Elijah) Company, 2nd Regiment United
States Sharpshooters
93rd Infantry (Co. B)
Hogan's (William H.) Battery
5th Artillery, Irish Brigade (Co. A), afterwards
2nd Independent Battalion Light Artillery
(Battery A), afterwards 14th Independent
Battery
Honved Regiment
45th Infantry (part); also 52nd Infantry
(part)
Hooker's Escort
2nd (Harris Light) Cavalry (Companies A, B, I,
and K)
Horatio Seymour Cavalry, 1st Regiment,
Companies A and B
13th Cavalry (Companies E and F)
Horse Artillery, United States Volunteers, 1st
Regiment
2nd Heavy Artillery (Companies A, B, and I)
Houck's (Phillip) Artillery Company
65th Militia (30 days, 1863)
Howard Artillery
1st Marine Artillery
Howell's (John H.) Battery
3rd Light Artillery (Battery M)
Howe's Rifles
45th Infantry
Humbold Yaegers
58th Infantry (part)
Hungarian Regiment
39th Infantry (part)
Hussars
George W. Sauer's Company C, 3rd Militia
Cavalry
Hyde's (W. B.) Cavalry
14th Cavalry (part)

I
Imperial Zouaves
47th Infantry (part)

Independence Guard
12th Militia
Independence Guard
12th Infantry
Independence Guard
12th Militia (Co. A), later 102nd Infantry
(Co. A)
Independent Battalion Artillery, 3rd (Companies
A-E)
15th Heavy Artillery (Companies A-E)
Independent Battalion Artillery, 4th (1st Battalion
Black River Artillery), Companies A, B, C,
and D
10th Heavy Artillery (Companies E, D, M,
and B)
Independent Battalion Artillery, 5th (2nd
Battalion Black River Artillery), Companies A,
B, C, and D
10th Heavy Artillery (Companies A, G, C,
and F)
Independent Battalion Artillery, 6th (3rd
Battalion Black River Artillery), Companies A,
B, C, and D
5th Heavy Artillery (Companies I, K, L, and M)
Independent Battalion Artillery, 7th (4th
Battalion Black River Artillery), Companies A,
B, C, and D
10th Heavy Artillery (Companies H, I, K, and L)
Independent Battalion Light Artillery, 1st,
Batteries A, B, C, and D
29th, 30th, 31st, and 32nd Independent
Batteries
Independent Battalion, Light Artillery, 2nd,
Batteries A and B
14th and 15th Independent Batteries
Independent Battery, Flying Artillery
11th Independent Battery
Independent Battery, 2nd (reorganizing)
Wolfgang Bock's
15th Heavy Artillery (part)
Independent Battery, 10th, Edwin S. Jenney's
3rd Light Artillery (Battery F)
Independent Battery, 34th, Hermann Jahn's
15th Heavy Artillery (part)
Independent Battery, 35th, James B. Caryl's
16th Heavy Artillery (Co. A)
Independent Battery, 36th, Charles Graham
Bacon's
13th Heavy Artillery (part)
Independent Battery B, or 2nd
3rd Independent Battery

Independent Company
  8th Infantry; also 29th Infantry; also 35th
  Infantry; also 45th Infantry
Independent Company Infantry, 9th
  194th Infantry (Co. D)
Independent Company Infantry, 12th (part)
  194th Infantry (Co. H, part)
Independent Company Infantry, 17th
  194th Infantry (Co. I)
Independent Company Infantry, 21st
  194th Infantry (Co. F)
Independent Company Infantry, 31st
  75th Infantry (Co. F, new)
Independent Company Infantry, 49th
  194th Infantry (Co. G)
Independent Company of Infantry (Edw. Breen's)
  143rd Infantry (part); also 169th Infantry (part)
Independent Company of Infantry (Amos Soper's)
  189th Infantry (Co. K)
Independent Corps New York Light Infantry
  Enfants Perdus
Independent Engineers
  50th Engineers
Independent Irish Regiment
  63rd Infantry
Independent Rifles
  151st Infantry
Independent Tompkins Blues
  12th Militia
Independent Volunteers
  50th Engineers
Infantry, 19th Regiment
  3rd Light Artillery
Infantry, 113th Regiment
  7th Heavy Artillery
Infantry, 129th Regiment
  8th Heavy Artillery
Infantry, 130th Regiment
  19th Cavalry, afterwards 1st Dragoons
Infantry, 135th Regiment
  6th Heavy Artillery
Infantry, 138th Regiment
  9th Heavy Artillery
Ira Harris Guard, 1st
  5th Cavalry
Ira Harris Guard, 2nd
  6th Cavalry
Ira Harris Guard, 3rd
  12th Cavalry
Irish Brigade, Meagher's (2nd Brigade, 1st
  Division, 2nd Corps)

28th Massachusetts, 63rd, 69th, and 88th New
  York, and 116th Pennsylvania)
Irish Brigade, Meagher's, 1st Regiment
  69th Infantry
Irish Brigade, Meagher's, 3rd Regiment
  63rd Infantry
Irish Brigade, Meagher's, 5th Regiment, formerly
  4th Regiment
  88th Infantry
Irish Brigade, Meagher's, 5th Regiment Artillery
  2nd Independent Battalion Light Artillery
  (Batteries A and B), afterwards 14th and 15th
  Independent Batteries
Irish Legion, Corcoran's, 1st Regiment
  182nd Infantry
Irish Legion, Corcoran's, 2nd Regiment (formerly
  5th Regiment)
  155th Infantry
Irish Legion, Corcoran's, 3rd Regiment
  164th Infantry
Irish Legion, Corcoran's, 4th Regiment (formerly
  2nd Regiment)
  170th Infantry
Irish Legion, Corcoran's, 5th Regiment
  175th Infantry
Irish Regiment, 3rd
  63rd Infantry
Irish Regiment
  105th Infantry
Irish Regiment, Buffalo
  164th Infantry
Irish Rifles
  37th Infantry
Ironclads
  136th Infantry
Ironhearted
  115th Infantry
Ironsides
  176th Infantry
Italian Guard
  12th Militia
Italian Legion
  39th Infantry (part)
Ithaca Volunteers
  32nd Infantry (Co. A)

J
Jackson Artillery
  5th Artillery (part)
Jackson Guards
  42nd Infantry

Jackson Heavy Artillery, 2nd Regiment
  5th Heavy Artillery
Jackson Horse Guard
    Thomas C. Devin's Company A, 1st Militia
    Cavalry
Jackson Regiment, Excelsior Brigade or Jackson
    Light Infantry
    71st Infantry
Jahn's (Hermann) Battery
    2nd Independent Battery
Jahn's (Hermann) 34th Independent Battery
    15th Heavy Artillery (part)
Jefferson County Regiment
    35th Infantry; also 10th Artillery
Jefferson Greys
    35th Infantry (Co. B)
Jefferson Guard
    5th Militia
Jenney's (Edwin S.) 10th Independent Battery
    3rd Light Artillery (Battery F)
Jersey Company
    48th Infantry (Co. D)
Jones's (Enoch) Battery
    3rd Light Artillery (Battery H)

K

Keith's (Robert) Independent Company Infantry
    102nd Infantry (part), and 124th Infantry (Co.
    E, part)
Kelsey's (William A.) Battery
    3rd Light Artillery (Battery G)
Kenka Rifles
    33rd Infantry (Co. I)
Kennedy's (Terrance J.) Battery
    1st Independent Battery
Kennedy's (Terrance J.) Infantry Company
    19th Infantry (Co. B), afterwards 3rd Light
    Artillery (part)
Kerrigan Rangers
    25th Infantry
Keuka Rifles
    33rd Infantry (Co. I)
Kings County Volunteers, Company A
    63rd Infantry (Co. C, new)
Kinney's (Edw. B.), afterwards William Baker's
    Company Engineers
    6th Militia (3 months, 1861)
Kirby's (William M.) Battery
    3rd Light Artillery (Battery I)
Kittenger's (Samuel) Battery
    23rd Independent Battery

Knieriem's (John) Battery
    1st Independent Battalion Light Artillery
    (Battery C), afterwards 31st Independent
    Battery
Kossuth Rifles
    59th Infantry (part)
Krom's (Abram H.) Company, Josiah Harlan's
    Cavalry Regiment
    5th Cavalry (Co. G)
Kusserow's (Charles) Battery
    1st Independent Battalion Light Artillery
    (Battery D), afterwards 32nd Independent
    Battery

L

LaFayette's Fusiliers
    12th Militia
LaFayette Guard
    55th Infantry
Langner's (Robert) Battery
    1st Independent Battalion Light Artillery
    (Battery C), afterwards 31st Independent
    Battery
Latson's (John W.) Regiment Light Artillery,
    Companies B and C
    2nd Heavy Artillery (Companies A and I)
Lee's (Jay E.) Battery
    Rocket Battalion Artillery (Co. B), afterwards
    24th Independent Battery
Lee's (Richard H.) Battery
    16th Independent Battery
LeRoy Regiment
    105th Infantry
Les Enfants Perdus
    Independent Corps, Light Infantry
Leslie Guards
    66th Infantry (part)
Lewis's (George W.) Company G, 13th Regiment
    Infantry (3 months)
    3rd Cavalry (Co. K)
Lewis's (William M.) Battalion Artillery
    1st Independent Battalion Light Artillery,
    Militia
Lewis County Battalion
    3rd Battalion Artillery
Light Artillery, 3rd Regiment, Company L
    1st Independent Battery Light Artillery
Light Artillery, Governor Morgan's United States
    2nd Regiment
    2nd Heavy Artillery

Light Battery A, 1st Regiment
  2nd Independent Battery
Light Guard, 106th Regiment
  12th Militia
Lincoln Cavalry
  1st Cavalry
Lincoln Divers
  99th Infantry
Lincoln Greens
  4th Cavalry
Lincoln Regiment of Independent Volunteers,
  Anson N. Norton's Michigan Company
  1st Cavalry (Co. K)
Lindsey Blues
  102nd Militia (Co. A)
Lion's (Thomas William) Battalion Artillery
  Rocket Battalion Artillery (Companies A and
  B), afterwards 23rd and 24th Independent
  Batteries
Little Zouaves
  9th Infantry
Livingston County Regiment
  104th Infantry
Locke's (Milo W.) Battery
  16th Independent Battery
Lochiel Cameron Highlanders
  78th Infantry (old), Elliot's Organization
Long Island Volunteers, 1st
  67th Infantry
Lost Children
  Les Enfants Perdus
Lyons Regiment
  98th Infantry

M

McChesney's (Waters W.) Zouaves
  10th Infantry
McClellan Cavalry
  20th Cavalry
McClellan Chausseurs
  90th Infantry (Companies F and K)
McClellan Infantry, Company C
  87th Infantry (Co. E)
McClellan Infantry
  54th Infantry (part); also 102nd Infantry (one
  company)
McClellan Rifles
  90th Infantry (Companies A to E)
McClellan's Escort
  Oneida Independent Cavalry Company

McClellan's (Samuel A.) Battery
  1st Light Artillery (Battery G)
McKnight's (George F.) Battery
  12th Independent Battery
McMahon's (Henry J.) Battery
  5th New York State Artillery Volunteers, Irish
  Brigade (Co. B), afterwards 2nd Independent
  Battalion Light Artillery (Battery B),
  afterwards 15th Independent Battery
McQuade's (Peter) Company Engineers
  69th Militia (Engineer Co. L, 30 days, 1863)
Mack's (Albert G.) Battery
  108th Infantry (Rifle Battery), afterwards 18th
  Independent Battery
Macomb Regiment
  96th Infantry
Madison and Cortland Regiment
  157th Infantry
Malone's (Robert A.) Independent Company
  Infantry
  124th Infantry (part)
Malone Regiment
  98th Infantry
Manhattan Rifles
  57th Infantry (part); also 43rd Infantry (Co. G,
  old)
Mann's (Daniel P.) Cavalry Company
  Oneida Independent Cavalry Company
Maralious's (John) Engineer Corps (Sappers and
  Miners)
  13th Militia (Engineer Corps Company, 3
  months, 1861)
Marine Artillery Regiment (Naval Brigade)
  1st Marine Artillery
Martin's (Joseph W.) Battery
  6th Independent Battery
Massachusetts Battalion Cavalry, Frontier
  Service
  26th Cavalry (Companies A-E)
Matthewson's (Angel) Battery
  1st Light Artillery (Battery E)
Meade's Escort
  2nd (Harris Light) Cavalry (Companies A, B, I,
  and K)
Meagher's Irish Brigade
  See Irish Brigade
Meagher's Own
  88th Infantry
Mechanic's Rifles, Henry Z. Drew's Company
  51st Infantry (Co. C part)

Mechanics Rifles (part)
66th Infantry (part)
Mercer's (William E.) Battery
3rd Light Artillery (Battery C, new)
Merchant's Brigade, 3rd Regiment
178th Infantry (part)
Merriam's (G. F.) Battalion Artillery
6th Independent Battalion Artillery
(Companies A, B, C, and D), afterwards
5th Heavy Artillery (Companies I, K, L,
and M)
Mersereau's (Thomas J.) Battery
3rd Light Artillery (Battery B)
Metropolitan Cavalry
14th Cavalry
Metropolitan Guard, 1st Regiment
131st Infantry
Metropolitan Guard, 2nd Regiment
133rd Infantry
Metropolitan Guard, 3rd Regiment
162nd Infantry
Metropolitan Guard, 4th Regiment
173rd Infantry
Metropolitan Guard, 5th Regiment
174th Infantry
Michigan Company (Anson N. Norton's)
1st (Lincoln) Cavalry (Co. K)
Middleton's (S.) Battalion Artillery
7th Independent Battalion Artillery
(Companies A, B, C, and D), afterwards 10th
Regiment Heavy Artillery (Companies H, I, K,
and L)
Militia Cavalry, Company A
Thomas C. Devin's Company A, 1st Militia
Cavalry (3 months, 1861)
Militia Cavalry, Company C
George W. Sauer's Company C, 3rd Militia
Cavalry (Hussars, 3 months, 1861)
Militia, 1st Battalion Light Artillery (Rochester
Union Grays)
1st Light Artillery (Battery L, part)
Militia, 2nd Regiment
82nd Infantry
Militia, 2nd Regiment (82nd Infantry), Company
D (old)
3rd Independent Battery
Militia, 4th Regiment Heavy Artillery
4th Militia Artillery (30 days, 1863)
Militia, 6th Regiment
66th Infantry

Militia, 9th Regiment
83rd Infantry
Militia, 9th Regiment (83rd Infantry), Company
K (old)
6th Independent Battery
Militia, 10th Regiment
177th Infantry
Militia, 12th Regiment (Henry A. Weeks's)
12th Infantry (Companies B, C, D, E, and F)
Militia, 12th Regiment (Henry A. Weeks's),
Company A
102nd Infantry (Co. A)
Militia, 13th Regiment
87th Infantry (part)
Militia, 13th Regiment Heavy Artillery
13th Militia Artillery (3 months, 1861)
Militia, 14th Regiment
84th Infantry
Militia, 18th Regiment (part)
74th Infantry (part)
Militia, 19th Regiment
168th Infantry
Militia, 20th Regiment
80th Infantry
Militia, 38th Regiment
34th Infantry (part)
Militia, 50th Regiment, Companies A and B)
58th Militia (Companies L and M)
Militia, 52nd Regiment
176th Infantry
Militia, 55th Regiment
55th Infantry
Militia, 64th Regiment
64th Infantry
Militia, 65th Regiment
1st Light Artillery (Battery I, part)
Militia, 65th Regiment
21st Infantry (part)
Militia, 65th Regiment
49th Infantry (part)
Militia, 65th Regiment
187th Infantry
Militia, 69th Regiment
182nd Infantry
Militia, 70th Regiment
5th Heavy Artillery
Militia, 74th Regiment
21st Infantry
Militia, 79th Regiment
79th Infantry

Millard's (Cyprian H.) Battery
    28th Independent Battery
Ming's Own
    59th Infantry (part)
Mink's (Charles E.) Battery
    1st Light Artillery (Battery H)
Mitchell's (Michael) Battery
    5th New York State Artillery Volunteers, Irish
    Brigade (Co. C), afterwards 2nd Independent
    Battalion Light Artillery (Battery B, part)
Mix's Cavalry Regiment
    3rd Cavalry
Mix's New Cavalry, or Mix's Battalion Cavalry
    23rd Battalion Cavalry
Mohawk Rifles
    81st Infantry (part)
Monitors
    176th Infantry
Monroe County Regiment
    140th Infantry
Montezuma Battalion
    31st Infantry
Mooer's Company
    124th Infantry (Co. E, part)
Morgan Artillery
    2nd Artillery (part)
Morgan Cavalry
    10th Cavalry (part)
Morgan Guards
    104th Infantry (Companies H, I, and K)
Morgan Light Artillery
    1st Light Artillery; also 2nd Light Artillery
    (part)
Morgan Rifles
    93rd Infantry
Morgan Rifles, 1st
    58th Infantry (Companies A to F)
Morgan's (Governor) United States Light
    Artillery, 2nd Regiment
    2nd Heavy Artillery
Morgan State Zouaves
    10th Infantry (Co. F)
Morris's (Richard H.) Battery
    9th Infantry (retained men), afterwards 3rd
    Infantry (part)
Morrison's (Joseph J.) Battery
    3rd Regiment Light Artillery (Battery B)
Morton's (Peter) Battery
    8th Independent Battery
Mott's (Thaddeus P.) Battery

2nd Militia (82nd Infantry Co. D, old),
    afterwards 3rd Independent Battery
Mountain Legion
    156th Infantry
Mounted Infantry, 75th Regiment (temporarily)
    75th Infantry
Mounted Rifles, 1st Regiment
    1st Mounted Rifles, afterwards 4th Provisional
    Cavalry
Mounted Rifles, 2nd Regiment
    2nd Mounted Rifles
Mounted Rifles, Dickel's
    4th Cavalry
Mower's (Lewis H.) Battery
    3rd Light Artillery (Battery L)
Mozart Regiment
    40th Infantry
Murphy's (John McLeod) Regiment Engineers
    15th Engineers (old)

N
Nail Factory Company
    169th Infantry (Co. I)
National Cadets
    69th Militia
National Grays
    13th Militia Artillery
National Guard
    see Militia
National Guard
    1st Infantry
National Guard
    7th Militia
National Guard, 4th Regiment
    173rd Infantry
National Guard, 5th Regiment
    174th Infantry
National Guard, 1st Battalion Light Artillery
    1st Independent Battalion Light Artillery,
    Militia (100 days)
National Guard, 4th Regiment Heavy Artillery
    4th Militia Artillery (30 days)
National Guard Artillery
    18th Militia (30 days, 1863)
National Guard Artillery
    69th Militia
National Guard Artillery, 69th Regiment
    182nd Infantry
National Guard Rifles
    57th Infantry (part)

National Guard Zouaves
    10th Infantry (Co. A)
National Union Rangers
    2nd Artillery (part)
National Volunteers
    127th Infantry
National Zouaves
    5th Infantry; also 10th Infantry
Naval Brigade
    99th Infantry
Naval Brigade (Marine Artillery Regiment)
    1st Marine Artillery
Netherland Legion
    39th Infantry (part)
Newburg Guard
    168th Infantry (Co. F)
New Jersey Cavalry, Halstead's (William) 2nd
    Regiment, Van Reypen's Company
    Cornelius G. Van Reypen's Unattached
    Company A, New Jersey Cavalry, afterwards
    3rd New York Cavalry (Co. M, old), afterwards
    1st New Jersey Cavalry (part)
New Paltz Volunteers
    156th Infantry (part)
New York and Virginia Coast Guard
    99th Infantry
New York Battery; part of Baker's Rifles
    103rd Infantry
New York Cavalry, Battalion, Frontier Service
    26th Cavalry (Companies G, H, I, K,
    and L)
New York Cavalry, 7th Regiment
    2nd Cavalry
New York City Artillery, 1st
    12th Heavy Artillery, afterwards 15th Heavy
    Artillery (part)
New York Excelsior Rifle Legion
    92nd Infantry
New York Fire Zouaves, 2nd
    73rd Infantry
New York Light Infantry
    15th Engineers (Co. G)
New York Riflemen
    93rd Infantry (Companies A to D)
New York Rifles
    51st Infantry
New York Sappers and Miners
    15th Engineers
New York Sharpshooters, 5th Company
    56th Infantry

New York State Light Infantry, 2nd
    Regiment
    82nd Infantry
New York State Rifles
    18th Infantry
New York Union Volunteers, 1st
    31st Infantry
New York, or United States Cavalry, 7th
    Regiment
    2nd (Harris Light) Cavalry
New York Volunteers Corps of Engineers
    1st Engineers
New York Zouaves
    9th Infantry
New York Zouaves, 1st Regiment
    11th Infantry
New York's Own
    59th Infantry (Co. I)
Niagara Rifles
    28th Infantry
Normal School Company
    44th Infantry (Co. E, new)
Northern Black Horse Cavalry
    7th Cavalry
Northern New York Regiment, 1st
    16th Infantry
Northern New York Regiment, 2nd
    22nd Infantry
Northern Sharpshooters
    93rd Infantry (part)
Northern Tier Regiment
    22nd Infantry
Norton's (Anson N.) Michigan Company
    1st (Lincoln) Cavalry (Co. K)
Numan's (John D.) Battery
    22nd Independent Battery
Nyack Volunteers
    17th Infantry (part)

O
O'Donohue's (William) Battery
    10th Regiment, 5th Irish Brigade (4th Battery,
    D), afterwards 2nd Independent Battalion
    Light Artillery (Battery A, part)
Ogdensburgh Regiment
    60th Infantry
Ohio Cavalry, 6th Independent Company
    3rd Cavalry (Co. L)
One Hundred and Eighth New York Volunteers
    6th Co. Sharpshooters

One Hundred and Twelfth New York Volunteers,
Co. L
7th Co. Sharpshooters
Oneida County Regiment, 1st
14th Infantry
Oneida County Regiment, 2nd
26th Infantry
Oneida County Regiment, 3rd
97th Infantry
Oneida County Regiment, 4th
117th Infantry
Oneida County Regiment, 5th
146th Infantry
Oneida Independent Cavalry Company
Oneida Cavalry Company
O'Neil's (Thomas) Battalion Artillery
2nd Independent Battalion Light Artillery
(Batteries A and B), afterwards 14th and 15th
Independent Batteries
Onondaga and Cortland County Regiment
185th Infantry
Onondaga Cavalry
3rd Cavalry (part)
Onondaga County Regiment
12th Infantry
Onondaga County Regiment, 2nd, Co. F
101st Infantry (Co. K)
Onondaga County Regiment, 3rd
122nd Infantry
Onondaga County Regiment, 4th
149th Infantry
Onondaga County Regiment, 6th
185th Infantry
Onondagas
122nd Infantry
Ontario County Regiment
33rd Infantry
Orange and Sullivan Regiment
56th Infantry
Orange Blossoms
124th Infantry
Oregon Rifles
1st Infantry
Orleans Battery
17th Independent Battery
Osborn's (T. W.) Battalion Artillery
5th Independent Battalion Artillery
(Companies A, B, C, and D), afterwards 10th
Heavy Artillery (Companies A, G, C, and F)
Osborn's (Thomas Ward) Battery
1st Light Artillery (Battery D)

Oswego County Regiment, 1st
24th Infantry
Oswego County Regiment, 2nd
81st Infantry (seven companies)
Oswego County Regiment, 3rd
110th Infantry
Oswego County Regiment, 4th
147th Infantry
Otsego County Regiment
76th Infantry

P
Page's (Francis) Engineer Corps
69th Militia (Engineer Corps Company, 3
months, 1862)
Palmer's Artillery
2nd Artillery
Palmer's Company, Fremont Rifles
49th Infantry (Co. C)
Parmenter Riflemen
71st Militia (Howitzer Co. I), originally 19th
Militia (Co. L)
Parrott Battery
4th Independent Battery
Paw Paw (Michigan) Company
70th Infantry (Co. C)
Peirce's (Milton P.) Company Sharpshooters
8th Company, 1st Independent Battalion
Sharpshooters (part)
Pennsylvania Volunteers, Cavalry Regiment,
William H. Boyd's Company C
1st (Lincoln) Cavalry (Co. C)
People's Ellsworth Regiment
44th Infantry
Perkin's Rifles
171st Infantry
Perry's Saints
48th Infantry
Pettes's (William H.) Regiment Engineers
50th Engineers
Pettit's (Rufus D.) Battery
1st Light Artillery (Battery B)
Phoenix Regiment
164th Infantry (part)
Pierrepont Cavalry
14th Cavalry (part)
Pierrepont Rifles
14th Cavalry (part)
Plattsburg Regiment
96th Infantry
Polish Legion

39th Infantry (part); also 58th Infantry
(part)
Porter Guard
10th Cavalry
Potsdam Regiment
92nd Infantry
Poughkeepsie Drill Guards
21st Militia
Poughkeepsie Guards
21st Militia
Pratt Guard
178th Infantry (part)
President's Life Guard (Company A)
59th Infantry (Co. A)
Provisional Cavalry, 1st–4th Regiments
1st–4th Provisional Cavalry
Putnam Rifles
66th Infantry

Q

Quinlan's (James) Company Engineers
69th Militia (Engineer Company, 3 months,
1861)
Quinn's (Michael R.) Battery
1st Independent Battalion Light Artillery,
Militia (100 days, Battery B)
Quintard's (E. A.) Engineer Corps
71st Militia (Engineer Company, 3 months,
1861)

R

Railway Brigade
109th Infantry
Raines's Artillery
15th Artillery (part)
Ramsey's (Albert C.) United States Voltigeurs, or
Rangers, Company A
51st Infantry (Co. D)
Ramsey's (Albert C.) United States Voltigeurs, or
Rangers, Companies B and C
57th Infantry (Companies I and K)
Raney's (James A.) Battery
80th Infantry (part)
Ransom's (Alfred) Battery
Rocket Battalion Artillery (Co. A), afterwards
7th Independent Battery
Regan's (Peter C.) Battery
56th Infantry (1st Light Artillery Company),
afterwards 7th Independent Battery
Remington Guard
81st Infantry (part)

Reynolds's (Gilbert H.) Battery
1st Light Artillery (Battery L)
Reynolds's (John A.) Battery
1st Light Artillery (Battery L)
Richardson's (Henry) Independent Company
Infantry
35th Independent Company Infantry
Richardson's (Richard H.), afterwards John
Bevines's, Independent Company Infantry
80th Infantry (part)
Richmond Guards
33rd Infantry (Co. G)
Rifle Battery
26th Independent Battery
Rifle Battery, 108 Volunteers (Mack's)
18th Independent Battery
Riflemen
18th Infantry
Rifle Regiment
13th Infantry
Rifles
28th Regiment Militia
Rifles, 75th
37th Infantry
Riggs' (William J.) Battery
3rd Light Artillery (Battery H)
Ritchie's (David F.) Battery
1st Light Artillery (Battery C)
Robinson's Battery
Thomas L. Robinson's Company, Hamilton
Light Artillery, afterwards 2nd Heavy
Artillery (Co. L, old), afterwards 34th
Independent Battery
Robinson's (Edward G.) Company Sharpshooters
8th Company 1st Independent Battalion
Sharpshooters
Rochester Cavalry Regiment
8th Cavalry; also 22nd Cavalry
Rochester Infantry Regiments
13th Infantry; also 105th Infantry; also 108th
Infantry
Rochester Racehorses
140th Infantry
Rochester Union Grays
1st Independent Battalion Light Artillery,
Militia (part, 100 days)
Rochester Union Greys (1st Battalion Light
Artillery Militia)
1st Light Artillery (Battery L part)
Rocket Battalion Artillery, Companies A and B
23rd and 24th Independent Batteries

Roemer's (Jacob) Battery
  2nd Heavy Artillery (Co. L, old), afterwards
  34th Independent Battery
Rogers's (Edward W.) Battery
  19th Independent Battery
Rogers's (Robert E.) Battery
  1st Light Artillery (Battery B)
Rorty's (James McKay) Battery
  14th Independent Battery
Rowland's (W. S.), afterwards Joseph S. Arnold's,
  Battalion Sharpshooters
  1st Independent Battalion (6th, 7th, 8th, and
  9th Companies) Sharpshooters
Russell's (Samuel P.) Battery
  3rd Light Artillery (Battery A)
Ryer's (B. Franklin) Battery
  20th Independent Battery

S
Sabre Regiment
  1st Cavalry
Sackett's Harbor Regiment
  94th Infantry
Sahm's (Nicholas) Battery
  1st Light Artillery (Battery I)
Saint Lawrence County Regiment
  16th Infantry
Saint Lawrence County Regiment, 1st
  60th Infantry
Saint Lawrence County Regiment, 2nd
  92nd Infantry
Saint Lawrence County Regiment, 3rd
  106th Infantry
Saint Lawrence County Regiment, 4th
  142nd Infantry
Salt Rangers
  149th Infantry
Sappers and Miners (Engineer Corps), John
  Maralious's
  13th Militia (Engineer Corps Company, 3
  months, 1861)
Sappers and Miners (Engineers), C. D.
  Westbrook's Company
  80th Infantry (20th Militia, Engineer
  Company)
Sappers and Miners (Engineers) Daniel T. Van
  Burens's Company
  20th Militia (Sappers and Miners Company, 3
  months, 1861)

Sappers and Miners (Engineers), Richard Butt's
  Company
  84th Infantry (14th Militia, Sappers and
  Miners or Engineer Company)
Sappers and Miners, New York
  15th Engineers
Saratoga Regiment
  77th Infantry
Sarsfield Rifles
  59th Infantry (part)
Sauer's Cavalry Company
  George W. Sauer's Company C, 3rd Militia
  Cavalry (Hussars, 3 months)
Scandinavian Volunteers
  1st Infantry (Co. I)
Schenck's (Theodore H.) Battery
  3rd Light Artillery (Battery E)
Schirmer's (Louis) Battery
  2nd Independent Battery
Schoeninger's (Joseph A.) Independent Company
  Infantry
  29th Infantry (Independent Company, retained
  men), afterwards 68th Infantry (part)
Schubert's (Emil) Battery
  9th Independent Battery
Schwarze Jager
  54th Infantry
Scott Life Guard
  28th Infantry
Scott Life Guard, 1st Regiment
  4th Infantry
Scott Life Guard, 2nd Regiment
  38th Infantry
Scott Rifles
  51st Infantry (part)
Scott's Nine Hundred
  11th Cavalry
Scroggs Brigade, or Eagle Brigade, 1st Regiment
  78th Infantry
Scroggs Brigade, or Eagle Brigade, 2nd Regiment
  100th Infantry
Scroggs Brigade, or Eagle Brigade, 3rd Regiment
  95th Infantry (Companies I and K)
Scroggs Brigade, or Eagle Brigade, 4th Regiment
  78th Infantry (part)
Scroggs Brigade, or Eagle Brigade, 5th Regiment
  53rd Infantry (new)
Senges's (Adam) Battalion German Heavy
  Artillery, Companies A-E
  3rd Independent Battalion Artillery

(Companies A-E), afterwards 15th Heavy
Artillery (Companies A-E)
Serrell's Artillery
4th Independent Battery
Serrell's (Edward W.) Regiment Engineers
1st Engineers
Seventy-Fifth Rifles
37th Infantry
Seward Artillery
3rd Light Artillery
Seward Infantry
19th Infantry; also 103rd Infantry
Seymour Cavalry, Horatio, 1st Regiment,
(Companies A and B)
13th Cavalry (Companies E and F)
Seymour Guard
7th Artillery
Seymour Light Cavalry
13th Cavalry
Seymour Light Infantry
178th Infantry (part)
Sharpshooters, 5th Company, Tenth Legion
56th Infantry (Co. L)
Sharpshooters, 6th, 7th, 8th, and 9th Companies
1st Independent Battalion Sharpshooters
Sharpshooters, Benjamin C. Butler's Battalion
93rd Infantry (Companies A-D)
Sharpshooters, Milton P. Pierce's Company
8th Company, Battalion Sharpshooters
(part)
Sharpshooters, Robert Grant's Calcium Light
102nd Infantry (Co. E)
Sharpshooters, Sigel's
119th Infantry (part)
Sharpshooters, United States, 2nd Regiment,
Elijah Hobart's Company
93rd Infantry (Co. B)
Sheldon's (Albert S.) Battery
1st Light Artillery (Battery B)
Shepard Rifles
51st Infantry
Sickles's Brigade, or Excelsior Brigade, 1st
Regiment
70th Infantry
Sickles's Brigade, or Excelsior Brigade, 2nd
Regiment
71st Infantry
Sickles's Brigade, or Excelsior Brigade, 3rd
Regiment
72nd Infantry

Sickles's Brigade, or Excelsior Brigade,
4th Regiment
73rd Infantry
Sickles's Brigade, or Excelsior Brigade,
5th Regiment
74th Infantry
Sickles Cavalry
25th Cavalry
Sidway's Buffalo Regiment
151st Infantry (part)
Sigel Life Guard, Company A
119th Infantry (Co. D)
Sigel Rifles
52nd Infantry
Smith's (James E.) Battery
1st Engineers (Artillery Co. L), afterwards
4th Independent Battery
Smith's (William F.) Escort
10th Cavalry (Co. L), and 6th
Pennsylvania Cavalry (Companies I
and K)
Smith's Zouaves
165th Infantry
Soper's (Amos) Independent Company Infantry
189th Infantry (Co. K)
Southern Tier Regiment
23rd Infantry
Southworth's (Irving D.) Battery
25th Independent Battery
Special Regiment New York Volunteers
Enfants Perdus
Spinola's Brigade, or Empire Brigade,
1st Regiment
158th Infantry
Spinola's Brigade, or Empire Brigade,
2nd Regiment
132nd Infantry
Spinola's Brigade, or Empire Brigade,
3rd Regiment
163rd Infantry
Spinola's Brigade, or Empire Brigade,
4th Regiment
164th Infantry
Sprague Light Cavalry
16th Cavalry
Spratt's (Joseph) Battalion Artillery
4th Independent Battalion Artillery
(Companies A, B, C, and D), afterwards
10th Heavy Artillery (Companies E, D, M,
and B)

Spratt's (Joseph) Battery
    1st Light Artillery (Battery H)
Stahl's (William H.) Battery
    19th Independent Battery
Stanton Legion
    145th Infantry
State Rifles, New York
    18th Infantry
Steuben Rangers, or Rifles, or 1st Steuben
    Regiment
    7th Infantry
Steuben Rangers, 2nd
    86th Infantry
Steven's Sharpshooters
    Enfants Perdus (Co. C)
Stewart's (Charles H.) Infantry Company
    19th Infantry (Co. G), afterwards 3rd Light
    Artillery (Battery G)
Stocking's (Solon W.) Battery
    1st Light Artillery (Battery K)
Stocum's (John) Battery
    1st Light Artillery (Battery E)
Stoneman Cavalry Regiment
    9th Cavalry
Stoneman's Body Guard
    Oneida Independent Company Cavalry
Stuart's (Charles B.) Regiment Engineers
    50th Engineers
Stuart's (William) Battery
    3rd Independent Battery
Sturmfels' (Emil) Battery
    E. D. Baker's Brigade (Light Artillery Company
    A), afterwards 13th Independent Battery
Sullivan County Regiment
    56th Infantry; also 143rd Infantry
Sumner's Escort
    6th Cavalry (Companies D and K)
Swain's Cavalry Regiment
    11th Cavalry
Syracuse Regiment
    101st Infantry (part)
Syracuse Zouaves
    3rd Infantry (Co. D)

T
Taft's (Elijah D.) Battery
    5th Independent Battery
Tamblin's (John W.) Battery
    1st Light Artillery (Battery C)
Tammany Jackson Guards or Regiment
    42nd Infantry

Taylor's (David A.) Battery
    3rd Light Artillery (Battery F)
Tenth Legion
    56th Infantry
Tenth Legion Artillery
    56th Infantry (1st and 2nd Light Artillery
    Companies), afterwards 7th and 8th
    Independent Batteries
Tenth Legion Cavalry
    56th Infantry (1st and 2nd Cavalry
    Companies), afterwards 1st Mounted Rifles
    (Companies D and C)
Tenth Legion Sharpshooters (5th Company
    Sharpshooters)
    56th Infantry (Co. L)
Tenth National Guard
    177th Infantry
Tenth Ward Rangers
    25th Infantry (Co. A)
Ticonderoga Cavalry Company
    2nd (Harris Light) Cavalry (Co. E, new)
Tompkins's Blues
    12th Militia
Tompkins Cavalry, 1st Regiment
    13th Cavalry (Companies B and C)
Troy Regiment, 1st
    2nd Infantry
Troy Regiment, 2nd
    22nd Infantry
Turner Rifles
    20th Infantry

U
Ulster Guard
    20th Militia (80th Infantry)
Ulster Regiment
    120th Infantry
Underhill's (Edward H.) Battery
    1st Light Artillery (Battery M)
Union Brigade, 1st Regiment
    101st Infantry
Union Coast Guard
    99th Infantry
Union Grays or Greys
    22nd Militia
Union Grenadiers, Company A
    103rd Infantry (Co. E)
Union Guards
    59th Infantry
Union Rangers
    25th Infantry

Union Regiment
    27th Infantry
Union Rifles
    51st Infantry (part)
Union Sharpshooters
    17th Infantry (3 years, part)
Union Volunteers
    6th Infantry
United States Chasseurs, 1st
    65th Infantry
United States Constitution Guard
    40th Infantry
United States Lancers
    9th Cavalry (Co. M, part); also 4th Artillery
    (Companies A and B, part)
United States Light Artillery, 2nd Regiment,
    Governor Morgan's
    2nd Heavy Artillery
United States National Guards
    11th Infantry
United States, or New York Cavalry, 7th Regiment
    2nd (Harris Light) Cavalry
United States Rifles, or Rangers
    58th Infantry
United States Sharpshooters, 2nd Regiment,
    Elijah Hobart's Company
    93rd Infantry (Co. B)
United States Van Guard, or Union Guard, or Van
    Guard Regiment
    59th Infantry
United States Voltigeurs or Rangers, Co. A
    51st Infantry (Co. D)
United States Voltigeurs, Companies B and C
    57th Infantry (Companies I and K)
United States Volunteer Cavalry, 1st Regiment
    1st Cavalry; also 11th Cavalry
United States Volunteers, 1st Regiment Horse
    Artillery
    2nd Heavy Artillery (Companies A, B, and I)
United States Volunteers
    43rd Infantry (Captain Chatfield's Co.); also
    57th Infantry (part); also 59th Infantry
    (part)
United States Zouave Cadets, Co. B
    74th Infantry (John P. Glass, Co. A)
United Turner Rifles
    20th Infantry
Utica Citizen Corps
    14th Infantry (Co. A)
Utica Regiment
    26th Infantry

V
Van Alen Cavalry
    3rd Cavalry
Van Buren Light Infantry
    102nd Infantry
Van Buren's (Daniel T.) Company Sappers and
    Miners
    20th Militia (Sappers and Miners Company,
    3 months, 1861)
Van Guard Regiment
    59th Infantry
Van Hensen's (Stephen) Battery
    3rd Light Artillery (Battery D)
Van Reypen's Company
    Cornelius G. Van Reypen's Unattached
    Company A, New Jersey Cavalry, afterwards
    3rd New York Cavalry (Co. M, old), afterwards
    1st New Jersey Cavalry (part)
Varian's (Joshua M.) Battery
    8th Militia (Artillery Co. I, 3 months, 1861)
Vermont Battalion Cavalry
    26th Cavalry (Companies M and F)
Vinton Rifles
    43rd Infantry
Virginia Coast Guard
    99th Infantry
Voegelee's (Adolph) Battery
    1st Independent Battalion Light Artillery
    (Battery B), afterwards 30th Independent
    Battery
Volunteer State Zouaves
    10th Infantry (Co. C)
Von Beck Canal Rangers or Rifles, 1st Regiment
    102nd Infantry (Companies B and G)
Von Blucher's (Gustav) Battery
    31st Independent Battery
Von Kleiser's (Alfred) Battery
    30th Independent Battery
Von Morozowiis (Adalbert) Battery
    41st Infantry (Co. F, old), afterwards 9th
    Independent Battery
Von Puttkammer's (Albert A.) Battery
    11th Independent Battery
Vosburgh Chasseurs
    71st Militia; also 53rd Infantry (new)

W
Wadsworth Guards
    104th Infantry
Walkill Guards
    18th Infantry (Co. D)

Wall's (John) Battery
    3rd Light Artillery (Battery G)
Walton's (William M.) Company Engineers
    8th Militia (Company K, 3 months, 1861)
Warren Rifles
    95th Infantry
Washburn's (Milo E.) Independent Company
    Infantry
    175th Infantry (part), and 186th Infantry (Co.
    K, part)
Washington Continentals
    10th Militia (Co. B); also 168th Infantry (Co.
    D); also 177th Infantry (Co. B)
Washington County Regiment
    93rd Infantry; also 123rd Infantry
Washington Grays
    8th Militia
Washington Grays, 1st Regiment
    47th Infantry
Washington Grays, 1st Troop
    8th Militia, Artillery Company Washington
    Grays, 1st Troop
    1st Engineers (Artillery Co. L), afterwards 4th
    Independent Battery (part)
Washington Guards
    120th Infantry
Washington Light Cavalry, Companies A and B
    16th Cavalry (Companies L and M)
Washington Rifles
    11th Militia
Washington Volunteers
    36th Infantry
Washington Zouaves
    57th Infantry (part); also 87th Infantry (part)
Waterloo Wright Guards
    33rd Infantry (Co. C)
Wayne County Regiment
    98th Infantry (part); also 138th Infantry (part)
Wayne Guards, Anthony
    135th Infantry, afterwards 6th Heavy Artillery
Westbrook's (C. D.) Company Sappers and Miners
    80th Infantry, Engineer Company (also 20th
    Militia)
Westchester Chasseurs
    17th Infantry (2 years)
Westchester Light Infantry
    178th Infantry (part)
Western Irish Regiment
    105th Infantry (Companies G, H, and I)
Westfield Cavalry
    9th Cavalry

Wever's (Bernhard) Battery
    29th Independent Battery
Wheeler's (Algar M.) Battery
    33rd Independent Battery
Wheeler's (Charles C.) Battery
    1st Light Artillery (Battery E)
Wheeler's (William) Battery
    13th Independent Battery
Whitehall Light Guards
    22nd Infantry (Co. G)
White's (Charles) Battery
    3rd Light Artillery (Battery A)
White's (James V.) Battery
    76th Infantry (Co. I, old) afterwards 3rd Light
    Artillery (Co. M)
Wickham's (Benjamin) Independent Company
    Infantry
    142nd Infantry (part)
Wiecker's (Arthur) Battery
    20th Independent Battery
Wiedrich's (Michael) Battery
    1st Light Artillery (Battery I)
Willard's (F. W.) Battalion Artillery (Anthon
    Battalion Light Artillery)
    20th and 28th Independent Batteries
Wilcox's Escort
    6th Cavalry (Companies B and C)
Williamsburg Volunteers
    3rd Infantry (Co. A)
Wilson's (William R.) Battery
    1st Light Artillery (Battery F)
Wilson's Zouaves
    6th Infantry
Winegar's (Charles E.) Battery
    1st Light Artillery (Battery I)
Winslow's (George B.) Battery
    1st Light Artillery (Battery D)
Winslow's (Hiram A.) Independent Company
    Infantry
    142nd Infantry (part)
Woodbury's (John D.) Battery
    1st Light Artillery (Battery M)
Wool's Body Guard
    1st Mounted Rifles (1st Battalion)

Y
Yager Regiment, 2nd
    41st Infantry
Yates's Rifles
    43rd Infantry (two companies); also 51st
    Infantry (part)

Yonkers Regiment
    172nd Infantry, afterwards 6th Heavy
    Artillery (Companies L and M, and parts of
    Companies B, D, I, and K)

Z
Zook's Voltigeurs
    57th Infantry
Zoo-Zoos
    9th Infantry
Zouaves, 2nd
    A transient organization of men who joined the
    40th Infantry

Appendix K
Selected Bibliography

Below is a brief, annotated list of publications and repositories that are frequently utilized in researching an individual's military service record or the history of a particular military unit. These publications, and the records held by research repositories such as the National Archives, frequently supplement the information contained in military service records available from the New York State Archives. Many of the publications listed in this appendix are available from most major research institutions throughout the country.

GENERAL BIBLIOGRAPHY

Aimone, Alan C. and Barbara. *A User's Guide to the Official Records of the American Civil War* (Shippensburg, Pa.: White Mane, 1993). This guide provides potential users of the massive and complex *Official Records* cited below with valuable information concerning the historical background, editorial policy, purpose, and organization of the "ORs." The Aimones also provide information concerning available finding aids that researchers can employ to locate and analyze material contained within these valuable volumes. Researchers unfamiliar with the *Official Records*, and wishing to gain an understanding of its strengths and limitations, are strongly encouraged to refer to this inexpensive publication.

Dornbusch, Charles E. *Military Bibliography of the Civil War*. 4 vols. (Vols. 1–3: New York: The New York Public Library, 1961–1972); (Vol. 4: Dayton: Morningside House, 1987). Commonly referred to as "Dornbusch," this reference work is an indispensable guide to identifying publications concerning regiments that participated in the Civil War. Dornbusch is also useful for locating other publications that are non-regimental in their orientation.

Dyer, Frederick Henry. *A Compendium of the War of the Rebellion*. 3 vols. (New York: Thomas Yoseloff, 1959). Originally published in 1908 in one volume, this publication, commonly referred to as "Dyer's" or "Dyer's Compendium," provides extensive summary information concerning all Union units and their role during the Civil War. Like Phisterer's *New York in the War of the Rebellion* (see below), Dyer's *Compendium* is excellent for obtaining summary information about specific New York State regiments and their role during the war.

Groene, Bertram H. *Tracing Your Civil War Ancestor*. (Winston-Salem, N.C.: John F. Blair, 1987). This inexpensive book (also available in paperback) is the best work on the subject. Groene provides straightforward advice on how to conduct basic and detailed research about Civil War veterans. The book contains a good bibliography of publications useful in conducting Civil War research as well as a list of the names and addresses of state archives in the United States. This book is highly recommended not only for the useful information it contains, but also because it will prevent novice researchers from making time-consuming false starts.

National Historical Publications Records Commission. *Directory of Archives and Manuscript Repositories in the United States*. 2nd ed. (Phoenix: The Oryx Press, 1988). This directory provides the address, phone number, and collection strengths of those institutions holding historical papers and records which may be of use to a researcher. This publication is available at most major research libraries.

National Union Catalog of Manuscripts Collections, 1959–1993. (Washington: Library of Congress, 1962–1994). Commonly referred to as "NUCMC," this catalog is by far the most comprehensive listing of personal papers contained in repositories throughout the United States. NUCMC is particularly useful in trying to locate the papers of officers who commanded military units during the Civil War. NUCMC is normally available at most major research libraries or manuscript repositories.

Index to Personnel Names in the National Union Catalog of Manuscript Collections, 1959–1984. 2 vols (Alexandria, Va.: Chadwyck-Healy, 1988). These volumes serve as the name index to the above volumes.

New York State Adjutant General. *Registers of New York Volunteer Regiments in the War of the Rebellion.* 43 vols. (Albany: various publishers, 1894–1906). These are commonly referred to as "The Adjutant General Reports" or "Annual Reports." The Adjutant General Reports are available in hard copy and on microfiche from the State Library's Manuscripts and Special Collections Unit. The published reports normally contain the following information: name of soldier, date and place of enlistment, date mustered in, in what grade, term of enlistment, date and place mustered out, and remarks (e.g., promotions, desertions, wounds received, death, battles, etc.). These reports are also available through *Civil War Unit Histories: Regimental Histories and Personal Narratives* (see below). This publication is available in microfiche format through the New York State Library's Microform Section (7th Floor, Cultural Education Center at Albany). The fiche numbers for these reports are #138 through #680. For a list of units contained within each volume, see Appendix G of this guide.

Phisterer, Frederick, comp. *New York in the War of the Rebellion, 1861–1865.* 3rd. ed. 6 vols. (Albany: J. B. Lyon, 1912). This work provides detailed information on various aspects concerning New York State's role during the Civil War. Among the topics covered are New York State's political role during the war; statistical data concerning the thousands of battles, actions, engagements, etc. in which New York State troops participated; biographical data on officers; and numerous other subjects. However, the most valuable section, particularly for researchers interested in specific regiments and their role during the war, is that which contains the regimental

histories compiled by Phisterer. Detailed information is provided as to when and where a regiment was recruited; officers; battles in which the regiment participated; and casualties suffered. Difficult to find today in good condition, *New York in the War of the Rebellion* is also available on microfiche as part of the *Civil War Unit Histories* microfiche publication described in more detail below.

Sellers, John R., comp. *Civil War Manuscripts: A Guide to Collections in the Manuscripts Division of the Library of Congress.* (Washington, D.C.: Library of Congress, 1986). The Library of Congress maintains one of the most important and extensive collections of Civil War-related materials in the country. The library's manuscripts collection consists mainly of the personal papers of prominent Americans, as opposed to the official government records maintained by the National Archives. *Civil War Manuscripts* is particularly useful in trying to locate the papers of officers who commanded military units during the Civil War or collections dealing with particular units. Entries in Sellers's guide are arranged alphabetically by collection title. Each collection is then described in terms of its nature (e.g., person or family papers, letters, diaries, etc.), inclusive dates, size, and subject matter. The guide also provides information on the availability of finding aids, indices, and (if applicable), availability on microfilm.

Szucs, Loretto Dennis and Sandra Hargreaves Luebking. *The Source: A Guidebook of American Genealogy: Revised Edition.* (Salt Lake City: Ancestry Incorporated, 1997). This work is a genealogical "how to" that covers all aspects of genealogical research. Chapter 9, "Research in Military Records" contains a very useful discussion on what military records are, how they can be used, and what information they contain.

U.S. War Department. *Bibliography of State Participation in the Civil War, 1861–1866.* 3d ed. Document #432 (Washington, D.C.: U.S. Government Printing Office, 1913). Although largely superseded by Dornbusch, this publication is nevertheless still useful since it provides many more obscure references not found in Dornbusch.

U.S. War Department. *Official Army Register of the Volunteer Force of the United States Army: For the Years 1861, '62, '63, '64, '65*. 8 vols. (Washington, D.C.: U.S. Government Printing Office, 1865). This extremely valuable work lists all officers who served in volunteer regiments and battalions of the U.S. Army during the Civil War. Information provided includes ranks and dates of appointment and dates of muster-out. The work also provides information on officers who resigned, were discharged, mustered out on expiration of term of service, were promoted, or died. There is also summary information available concerning each unit's prominent battles. Volume Two contains the lists of officers who served from New York State.

U.S. War Department. *War of the Rebellion: A Compilation of the Official Records of the Union and Confederate Armies*. 70 vols. in 128 serials, index, and atlas. (Washington, D.C.: U.S. Government Printing Office, 1880–1901). An absolutely indispensable resource for conducting any type of Civil War research. A complete set of the "ORs" is available for use in the reading room shared by the New York State Archives and the State Library's Manuscripts and Special Collections on the 11th floor of the Cultural Education Center at Albany. Researchers interested in the naval aspect of the war should consult the *Official Records of the Union and Confederate Navies in the War of the Rebellion*. The "ORN" is also available for use in the 11th-floor reading room. The ORs and ORN are also available in many public and college libraries.

Welcher, Frank J. *The Union Army, 1861–1865. Organization and Operations* 2 vols., consisting of vol. 1, "The Eastern Theater" [1989] and vol. 2, "The Western Theater" [1992] (Bloomington: Indiana University Press, 1989). Totaling 2,073 pages and based largely on the *War of the Rebellion: A Compilation of the Official Records of the Union and Confederate Armies*, this reference work provides a complete and continuous account of the organization of all Union military divisions, departments, armies, army corps, brigades, and the numerous special commands that were in existence during the Civil War. Data is provided for each unit's creation, composition, changes in organization and command, and date discontinued. Welcher also provides details about every military department of the army, along with its dates, geographical boundaries, districts, organization of troops, military operations, and commanders. Other sections describe the command of the armies of the United States, miscellaneous organizations, and battles and campaigns. Despite its flaws, this is a valuable reference tool because it collates much information that would require laborious searching by those interested in the structure, command, and activities of Union units.

REPOSITORY BIBLIOGRAPHY

New York State Library Manuscripts and Special Collections

The Manuscripts and Special Collections Unit of the New York State Library is located on the same floor as the New York State Archives. In fact, the two repositories share the same reference room and working hours. Telephone inquiries concerning Manuscripts and Special Collections' holdings can be made by dialing (518) 474–6282.

The records relating to the Civil War held by the Manuscripts and Special Collections Unit consist of a wide and rich body of materials that are much too numerous to list here. For the most part, this material consists of the private papers of families, soldiers' diaries and letters, public newspapers, broadsides, engravings, lithographs, photographs, imprints, and some state government documents. These materials often contain significant information about individual soldiers and the units in which they served. The collection is described and can be accessed electronically via the online public access catalog called "Excelsior" (http://www.nysl.nysed.gov).

In addition to the holdings of the New York State Library's Manuscripts and Special Collections Unit, the New York State Library's Microform Section also maintains a large collection of materials. The most complete collection is embodied in the micro-publication *Civil War Unit Histories: Regimental Histories and Personal Narratives*. Published by University Publications of America, this collection consists of annual reports from the states' various military administrative bodies, publications subsequently published after the war by the states, published regimental histories, general reference works such as Dyer's *Compendium* (see above), and other publications issued by post-war organizations such as the Grand Army of the Republic. Many of these works are difficult or almost impossible to find in their original format. The State Library presently maintains microfiche for the following states: Connecticut, Maine, Massachusetts, New Hampshire, New Jersey, New York, Pennsylvania, Rhode Island, and Vermont.

New York State Museum

Although not as extensive as the New York State Library, the New York State Museum contains many rare and historically significant Civil War–related items. These include some exquisite artifacts, such as the sword presented to General Gouverneur K. Warren by the citizens of Cold Spring in recognition of his faithful service during the war, as well as various small arms, uniforms, and accoutrements. The State Museum also holds many unique broadsides, engravings, lithographs, and other printed matter pertaining to the war. Information concerning the extent and availability of the State Museum's Civil War holdings may be obtained by contacting the museum at (518) 474–5353. Additional information regarding the State Museum is available through its Web site (http://www.nysm.nysed.gov).

New York State Division of Military and Naval Affairs

The Division of Military and Naval Affairs maintains one of the largest collection of Civil War artifacts in New York State. Many of these artifacts pertain to specific individuals or regiments from New York State. Included among these artifacts are more than 900 flags borne by the state's regiments throughout the war, as well as a significant number of photographs of New York men who served during the war. The images consist of *cartes-des-visites*, albumens, tintypes, ferrotypes, and daguerreotypes. In addition, the division maintains a significant collection of recruiting broadsides, newspaper clippings, Confederate newspapers, soldiers' letters and diaries, officers' commissions, muster rolls,

military manuals, unit histories, scrapbooks, and approximately 10,000 cards that record the burial locations of New York State residents who fought in the Civil War. Information about the collection can be obtained by contacting the division at:

Division of Military and Naval Affairs
New York State Military Museum
Watervliet Arsenal, Building 124
Worth Road
Watervliet, NY 12189
(518) 786–4371

or

330 Old Niskayuna Road
Latham, NY 12110–2224
http://www.dmna.state.ny.us

Researchers should be aware that an agreement may be reached between the Division of Military and Naval Affairs and the New York State Archives that will provide for the physical transfer of the paper files (including the photographic images) to the State Archives. The Division will retain custody of the artifacts (e.g., flags, arms, uniforms, etc.), but the non-artifactual material will be transferred to the State Archives, thereby reuniting a substantial portion of the holdings originally compiled by the Bureau of Military Statistics.

After the records have been transferred to the custody of the State Archives, they will not be available for research until they have been arranged, described, rehoused, and catalogued according to basic archival principles. Information concerning the availability of these records can be obtained by calling (518) 474–8955.

The National Archives and Records Aministration

The National Archives contains by far the largest collection of Civil War-related records in the country. No serious research can be considered complete without referring to the vast and important records held by this institution. National Archives staff will conduct research for those interested in obtaining the service records of individuals who fought in the Civil War. However, their search is restricted to basic military service and pension records. Nevertheless, these records will frequently contain a wealth of information on Civil War veterans. In order to utilize these records you must first obtain copies of NATF-80, "Order For Copies of Veterans Records." This can be done either by phone (202 501–5430) or by writing to:

> Reference Services Branch (NNIR)
> National Archives & Records Administration
> 7th and Pennsylvania Ave. NW
> Washington, DC 20408
> http://www.nara.gov/genealogy/civilwar.html

Do not send any money with the request. National Archives staff will inform you of any costs after they have researched your request. Separate NATF-80s must be filled out for each file of which you request a search. For those interested in conducting their own research at the National Archives, it is strongly recommended that the following works be examined:

Munden, Kenneth W. and Henry P. Beers, *The Union: A Guide to the Federal Archives Relating to the Civil War*. (Washington, D.C.: National Archives Trust Fund Board, 1986). This guide describes in great detail the voluminous records relating to the Civil War that are maintained not only by the National Archives but also by federal records centers and agencies. The guide is an invaluable tool for researchers seeking information on the National Archives' Civil War holdings. In addition to describing the records pertaining to the conduct of the war itself, the guide also describes records relating to the war that were created after 1865. The guide also contains lengthy administrative histories of federal agencies that prosecuted the Union's war efforts, which greatly add to an overall understanding of the records these agencies created.

Beers, Henry P. *The Confederacy: A Guide to the Archives of the Government of the Confederate States of America*. (Washington, D.C.: National Archives Trust Fund Board, 1986). This is the companion volume to the guide described above and describes in detail records pertaining exclusively to the Confederacy. Although the bulk of the guide pertains to materials held by the National Archives, Confederate records maintained in other institutions are included.

Guide to Genealogical Research in the National Archives. (Washington, D.C.: National Archives Trust Fund Board, 1983). Chapter 5, "Service Records of Volunteers," deals specifically with military service and related records documenting the Civil War. The guide contains an excellent discussion of why these records were created, how they are arranged, how they can be used, and what information one can expect to find. The guide also provides additional facts about the availability of microfilm, finding aids, and research strategies. For those planning to utilize the holdings of the National Archives for genealogical purposes, this book is invaluable.

Military Service Records: A Select Catalog of National Archives Microfilm Publications (Washington, D.C.: National Archives Trust Fund Board, 1985). This catalog describes all military service records microfilmed by the National Archives. Many of these records pertain to personnel who served during the Civil War. The catalog is organized by type of record (compiled military service records, records relating to service in the regular U.S. Army or Navy, claims for bounty land and pensions; and miscellaneous records relating to military service). Brief descriptions of the records are followed by roll listings of the contents. The catalog also provides information on the National Archives' microfilm pricing policy, availability, and specifications.

United States Army Military History Institute

Researchers who are interested in possibly obtaining a photograph of a particular soldier or seaman who served during the Civil War should first contact the United States Army Military History Institute. Located at Carlisle Barracks, Pennsylvania, the Institute contains the nation's largest collection of identified images of men who served during the Civil War. Information concerning the extent and availability of the photographic collection may be obtained by contacting the Institute at:

> United States Army Military History Institute
> 22 Ashburn Drive
> Carlisle Barracks, PA 17013-5008
> (717) 245–3434
> http://carlisle-www.army.mil/usamhi

Index

Quartermaster General's Office, 46–50, 77, 99
    annual reports of, 112–13
    correspondence, 48
Queens County, 133
Questionnaires
    for local officials, 57–58, 60
    for soldiers, 17–18, 21

Record series
    by creating office, 98–103
    on microfilm, 109
    by series number, 104–108
Regimental flags, 21, 56, 165
Regiment, definition of, 24
Rensselaer County, 121, 133
Republican party, 1, 3–5, 7, 9–10
Resignations, records of, 34, 39
Richmond County, 121, 133
Rockefeller, Nelson, 85–86
Rockland County, 121, 133
Rutgers University, 86

St. Lawrence County, 121, 133–34
Salaries, expenditures for, abstracts of, 35
Saratoga County, 121–22, 134
Schenectady County, 122, 134
Schofield, John M., 11
Schoharie County, 122, 134
    enrollment lists for, 62
Schuyler County, 122, 134
    Board of Supervisors proceedings for, 64
Schuyler, Hartley, and Graham, 79
Scott, Winfield, 5, 11
Seneca County, 122, 135
Seward, William H., 4, 7
Seymour, Horatio, 7–11, 17, 76
Seymour, John F., 47–48
Sharpshooters, muster roll abstracts for, 65–66, 93
Sheridan, Philip, 11
Sherman, William T., 9
Shrine for the Emancipation Proclamation, 85–86
    papers pertaining to, 87
Sickles, Daniel E., 83
Sketches, of soldiers, 17, 21, 165
Slavery, New York and, 1
Slocum, Henry W., 11
Soldiers' Depot, 32, 47–48, 59, 75
    Board of Managers
        annual reports of, 111

proceedings and reports of, 48–49
    records of, 49
    surgeon general and, 54
Sprague, John T., 37
Squad, definition of, 24
Stanton, Edwin M., 61, 94n
Steuben County, 122, 135
    Surgeon's report on examination of exemption
        applicants from, 63
Stock certificates, 80
Stoneman, George, 11
Strong, George Templeton, 3
Substitutes, unassigned to any unit, muster roll
        abstracts for, 67–68
Suffolk County, 122
Sullivan County, 122, 135–36
Surgeon General's Office, 54–55, 100
    annual reports of, 113
    correspondence, 54–55
    telegrams received, 55
Sweeney, Peter B., 11
Swetland, S. H., 47

Tammany Hall, 11
Thanksgiving proclamations, 62
Tioga County, 122, 136
Tolman, Mason, 86
Tompkins, Daniel, 75
Tompkins County, 122, 136
Tonawanda, Registers of Enrollment of Persons
        Liable to Military Duty, 34
Towns and cities
    registers
        of men furnished, 57, 60, 93–94, 119–22
        of monies raised and expended, 60, 94
    units recruited from, 123–38
Townsend, Edward D., 90n
Turner Rifles, 15
Tweed, William M., 11

Ulster County, 122, 136
Ulysses S. Grant Association, 86–87
Unassigned men, muster roll abstracts for, 67–68
Union party, 9–10
United States Army Military History Institute,
        166
United States Constitution
    Fifteenth Amendment, 11
    Thirteenth Amendment, 10
United States Military Academy, West Point, 5